I0866342

Tolkien, Enchantment, and Loss

Tolkien, Enchantment, and Loss

Steps on the Developmental Journey

JOHN ROSEGRANT

The Kent State University Press
KENT, OHIO

© 2022 by The Kent State University Press, Kent, Ohio 44242
All rights reserved

ISBN 978-1-60635-435-3
Manufactured in the United States of America

No part of this book may be used or reproduced, in any manner whatsoever, without written permission from the Publisher, except in the case of short quotations in critical reviews or articles.

Cataloging information for this title is available at the Library of Congress.

26 25 24 23 22   5 4 3 2 1

For my wife Donna, always a loving companion and support whether I am writing a book or not, and for our son Joseph, who understands the worth of fantasy in the arts. Also for my parents, who are no longer here to see it but started me on the road to this book by giving my siblings and me *The Hobbit* when I was six years old.

Investigations of this kind are not intended to explain an author's genius, but they show what motive forces aroused it and what material was offered to him by destiny.

—Sigmund Freud

The theme of the ring leaves one once again with the impression of how hard it is for the psychoanalyst to discover anything new that has not been known before by some creative writer.

—Sigmund Freud, reflecting on spouses ambivalently attached to their wedding rings

"Yet," said Eriol, "tell me, Rúmil, I beg, some of what you know even of the first beginnings, that I may begin to understand those things that are told me in this isle."

—J. R. R. Tolkien

Contents

Acknowledgments xi

Introduction 1

1 Tolkien's Dialogue between Enchantment and Loss 15

2 My Mother She Killed Me, My Father He Ate Me 32

3 Bilbo Baggins, the Master of Laketown, and the Fate of Enchantment 44

4 In Deep with *The Hobbit* 54

5 Mother Music 68

6 The Man-Maiden and the Spider with Horns 85

7 Seeing the Self in the Mirror of Galadriel 98

8 From the Ineluctable Wave to the Realization of Imagined Wonder 112

9 Something Has Gone Crack 129

10 The One Ring and Tom Bombadil 150

11 Late Life Loss of Transitionality 164

Epilogue 173

Notes 176

Bibliography 194

Index 203

Acknowledgments

I wrote this book at the convergence of two fields that fascinate me: Tolkien Studies and Psychoanalysis. From the area of Tolkien Studies I want to thank first of all the numerous attendees at Mythcons who have listened and responded to earlier versions of some of my chapters. Specific people to whom I am grateful for clarifying various questions about Tolkien include David Bratman, Janet Brennan Croft, Jason Fisher, Carl Hostetter, and Kris Swank. And I thank Verlyn Flieger for encouraging me to put my thinking about Tolkien into a book.

From the psychoanalytic area I want to express my appreciation for the following mentors and colleagues who have been especially helpful to me over the years: Sheldon Bach, Donna Bender, Tom Cummings, Steve Ellman, Marsha Levy-Warren, Martin Nass, and Irving Steingart. Thanks also to my patients, supervisees, and students for all you have taught me.

I also want to acknowledge the reviewers of my manuscript for many helpful suggestions.

Portions of the following chapters have appeared in previous publications, and are reprinted with permission:

CHAPTER I

"Tolkien's Dialogue between Enchantment and Loss." *Mythlore* 33 (2015): 27–138.

"The Interplay between Loss and Enchantment in the Works of J. R. R. Tolkien." *Psychoanalytic Psychology* 33 (2016): 610–20.

CHAPTER 3

"Bilbo Baggins, Harry Potter, and the Fate of Enchantment." In *Critical Insights:* The Hobbit, edited by Stephen Potts, 68–82. Amenia, NY: Grey House, 2016.

CHAPTER 5

"Mother Music." *Tolkien Studies* 16 (2019): 111–31.

CHAPTER 8

"From the Ineluctable Wave to the Realization of Imagined Wonder: Tolkien's Transformation of Psychic Pain into Art." *Mythlore* 35 (2017): 133–51.

CHAPTER 9

"Fault Lines Beneath the Crack." In *Something Has Gone Crack—New Perspectives on J. R. R. Tolkien in the Great War,* edited by Janet Croft and Annika Rottinger, 95–120. Zurich, Walking Tree, 2019.

CHAPTER 10

"J. R. R. Tolkien and Creativity II: Symbols of Transitionality and the Fetish in The Lord of the Rings." *American Imago* 76 (2019): 165–82.

CHAPTER 11

"J. R. R. Tolkien and Creativity I: Transitionality and the Creative Process." *American Imago* 76 (2019): 145–64.

Introduction

Stepping onto the Road

In Crickhollow, between fleeing from Black Riders and plunging into the Old Forest, Frodo has a "vague" dream: "he seemed to be looking out of a high window over a dark sea of tangled trees. Down below among the roots there was the sound of creatures crawling and snuffling. He felt sure they would smell him out sooner or later.

"Then he heard a noise in the distance. At first he thought it was a great wind coming over the leaves of the forest. Then he knew that it was not leaves, but the sound of the Sea far-off; a sound he had never heard in waking life, though it had often troubled his dreams. Suddenly he found he was out in the open. There were no trees after all. He was on a dark heath, and there was a strange salt smell in the air. Looking up he saw before him a tall white tower, standing alone on a high ridge. A great desire came over him to climb the tower and see the Sea. He started to struggle up the ridge towards the tower: but suddenly a light came in the sky and there was a noise of thunder."[1]

Frodo's dream provides a fitting gateway for this book's journey into a forest of meanings because it is rooted in three intertwined topics that I will explore. At a basic level, it vividly presents one of the major themes of Tolkien's legendarium: the tension between enchantment and disenchantment. It also alludes to Tolkien's understanding of creativity as a search for enchantment. And behind this, it is built on what Tolkien himself described as a fundamental psychological "complex": the fear of being overwhelmed by a wave that we can recognize as a signifier of loss and related emotions.

Let us begin unpacking the dream by interrogating the surprising "vague" that begins this passage. What makes this dream "vague"? The images themselves are no less clearly depicted than is typical in dreams. But it is replete with a sense of something *more,* something that cannot be fully understood, whether in a practical sense—what is that snuffling down among the roots? (Surely the Black Riders are the day residue that partly inspired this dream image, but what are the Black Riders?) How can Frodo reach the tower?—and in the sense that the tower and the sea are imbued with mysterious meaning. The dreamer is reaching for something beyond the edges of his experience in a way that touches on etymological connections of *vague* with *vagabond* and *vagrant,* all deriving from Latin for *wander.*"[2]

In the dream Frodo wanderingly approaches but never reaches a greatly desired but also dangerous mystery. Images transform from "a dark sea of tangled trees" to "wind coming over the leaves" to "not leaves, but the sound of the [actual] Sea" to a "dark heath" with a "strange salt smell" to "a great desire to climb the tower and see the Sea"—a desire finally thwarted by light and thunder. This is a depiction of a tension that is at the heart of Tolkien's legendarium: the longing for something beyond the quotidian that can never quite be grasped or, if grasped, is threatened with loss.

This tension is Tolkien's response to the phenomenon of modernization that Weber famously named "the disenchantment of the world." Weber stated that in traditional society "the world remain[s] a great enchanted garden" imbued with meaning and mysterious spiritual powers.[3] The process of rationalization that defines modernity, on the other hand, "means that in principle, then, we are not ruled by mysterious, unpredictable forces, but that, on the contrary, we can in principle control everything by means of calculation. That in turn means the disenchantment of the world."[4] Tolkien did not accept that the world was irremediably disenchanted, but neither did he lodge himself in premodern magic.[5] For Tolkien, enchantment remains always in sight but always threatened.

I do not think it is an accident that the tower overlooking the sea toward which Frodo struggles recapitulates an image Tolkien had already used in his well-known allegory about *Beowulf* studies:

> A man inherited a field in which was an accumulation of old stone, part of an older hall. Of the old stone some had already been used in building the house in which he actually lived, not far from the old house of his fathers. Of the rest he took some and built a tower. But his friends coming perceived at once (without troubling to climb the steps) that these stones had formerly

> belonged to a more ancient building. So they pushed the tower over, with no little labor, in order to look for hidden carvings and inscriptions, or to discover whence the man's distant forefathers had obtained their building material. Some suspecting a deposit of coal under the soil began to dig for it, and forgot even the stones. They all said: "This tower is most interesting." But they also said (after pushing it over): "What a muddle it is in!" And even the man's own descendants, who might have been expected to consider what he had been about, were heard to murmur: "He is such an odd fellow! Imagine his using these old stones just to build a nonsensical tower! Why did he not restore the old house? He had no sense of proportion." But from the top of that tower the man had been able to look out upon the sea.[6]

This allegory leads us toward a picture of the creative process as a means of engaging with the tension Tolkien felt between enchantment and disenchantment. The tower is the *Beowulf* poem, and the builder of the tower is the *Beowulf* poet. The people who push over the tower to study its stones and the soil beneath are the scholars who have only thought the poem worthwhile for what it told about factual history. Tolkien is saying that a certain kind of experience was most important to the *Beowulf* poet. And note that the experience does not produce something like "understanding" or "measuring" the sea, which would fit with the disenchanting perspective that "in principle, everything can be explained"—it is "looking out upon it."

But this enchanted view is imbued with potential and actual loss. Not only is the tower vulnerable to being knocked over, but the view from its top is itself full of loss. For Tolkien thought that the *Beowulf* poet was looking back at the enchanted pagan world of monsters, heroes, and magic from a Christianity that was new enough that the pagan world still carried meaning but could not be dwelt in unquestioningly.[7] (For Tolkien, of course, the Christian world carried its own enchantment that modernity does not, but this does not diminish the sense of longing for pagan enchantments that are fading.)

So Frodo in his dream and the *Beowulf* poet were after the same thing, but Frodo could not quite reach it, whereas the *Beowulf* poet was able to view it only to see it fading, and then his vantage point crumbled.

And I think we are justified in inferring that Tolkien's description of the *Beowulf* poet's creative process was also a description of his own creativity. Tolkien seems to have identified with the *Beowulf* poet, as we see in his playfully beginning classes on the poem by shouting the opening line like an Anglo-Saxon bard, in his translating *Beowulf*, and in his writing "Sellic Spell," a fairy tale that he imagined the *Beowulf* poet basing his work upon.[8] Furthermore, Tolkien described the esthetic experience of fairy stories with a metaphor very similar to the allegory of the *Beowulf* tower in "On Fairy-Stories," an essay that is widely accepted as a description of his own process creating *The Lord of the Rings:* "with regard to fairy stories, I feel that it is more interesting, and also in its way more difficult, to consider what they are, what they have become for us, and what values the long alchemic processes of time have produced in them. In Dasent's words I would say: 'We must be satisfied with the soup that is set before us, and not desire to see the bones of the ox out of which it has been boiled.' . . . By 'the soup' I mean the story as it is served up by its author or teller, and by 'the bones' its sources or material."[9]

Like valuing the view from a tower more than the blocks from which it was built, Tolkien values the taste of the soup more than knowledge of its ingredients. Soup is much less grand than a tower, but I believe that it is in the spirit of Tolkien's concept of *recovery*—freeing things from the "drab blur of triteness or familiarity"—to recognize the full enjoyment of soup as a minor, everyday sort of enchantment.[10] The hobbits certainly seemed to feel that way about the soup that Barliman Butterbur served them in Bree. And although Tolkien doesn't directly touch on disenchantment in this metaphor—the soup does not get spilled the way the tower is knocked down—the concept of recovery that I just touched upon, as well as *consolation* and *escape* as basic values of fairy stories, all show fairy-tale creativity as a way to combat disenchantment.

Tolkien's own use of the word *enchantment* also shows an affinity between Frodo's dream and the experience of creativity. "If you are present at a Faërian drama you yourself are, or think that you are, bodily inside its Secondary World. The experience may be very similar to Dreaming and has (it would seem) sometimes (by men) been confounded with it. . . . We need a word for this Elvish craft . . . I will, for lack of a less debatable word, call [it] Enchantment. Enchantment produces a Secondary World into which both designer and spectator can enter, to the satisfaction of their senses while they are inside."[11] And in the same passage Tolkien shows enchantment to be both related to and contrasted with a form of disenchantment that he calls "magic": "in its purity [Enchantment] is artistic in desire and purpose. Magic produces, or pretends to produce, an alteration in the Primary World . . . it is not an art but a technique; its desire is *power* in this world, domination of things and wills."

Thus we see that Tolkien depicted his creation Frodo (among other characters I will discuss in later chapters) and the creative process itself as engaged in tension between enchantment and disenchantment. In this book I will explore the idea that this tension was so important in Tolkien's creativity because it grew out of a psychological strain that he himself struggled with throughout his life. The sea lay readily to Tolkien's mind to use as a metaphor in Frodo's dream and the allegory of the Beowulf tower because the sea was an important image of this personal complex. Tolkien had a recurring dream of being overwhelmed by an enormous wave, a dream that "always ends by surrender, and I awake gasping out of deep water."[12] (I discuss this dream in more detail in chapter 8.) And this dream gives us an intimation of why Frodo and the *Beowulf* poet wished to engage the sea from the top of a tower rather than by wading in it: from the top of a tower one is safer from inundation. After all, as Aragorn says about Lothlórien, enchantment is perilous as well as fair.[13]

Of course, in my project of exploring how Tolkien's psychology contributed to his works, I am myself looking at the architectural building blocks, at the ingredients of the soup. I could give a weak defense of thus going against Tolkien's professed view by saying that I am only doing what many Tolkien scholars have already done: although publications on Tolkien's psychology are rare, publications on his sources are voluminous. But I think we should question what Tolkien really meant by his statements that favored the finished product over its elements. As is well known, he liked to build fictional historical foundations for his writings: *The Hobbit, The Lord of the Rings,* and *The Adventures of Tom Bombadil* came from the *Red Book of Westmarch,* and *The Lost Tales* were stories that Eriol/Aelfwine heard from the Elves; although the published *Silmarillion* is presented without any such edifice, Christopher Tolkien later regretted that he had not attributed them to the readily available "books of Elvish lore" transcribed by Bilbo in Rivendell.[14] The appendices to *The Lord of the Rings* are full of information about how "actual" languages and dating systems in Middle-earth were translated for the published work. The Silmarillion itself is the historical foundation for *The Hobbit* and *The Lord of the Rings.* All of these are looks at the building blocks rather than the tower, and although Tolkien was concerned that he risked detracting from the view of the sea—he stated that readers who were uninterested in the Appendices could ignore them,[15] and he worried that reading *The Silmarillion* might remove the enchanting sense of mysterious depth given by allusions to ancient history in *The Lord of the Rings*[16]—it is clear that Tolkien himself felt that these historical foundations enhanced rather than destroyed the later works. After all, a central part of his professional philological studies was to enrich current understanding of words by exploring their history and variants to determine what earlier forms served as their bones.

I think the best way to understand all this is that in casting a dim eye on building blocks and soup bones, Tolkien was repudiating a particular atomizing attitude toward understanding where literature comes from, rather than condemning such understanding in general. It all depends on how you look at the building blocks and bones. Tolkien was rightly concerned with the kind of thinking that reduces the product to what it is made of—for the *Beowulf* scholars, only the building blocks were important. But many people experience a richer enjoyment of the final product if they also reflect on how it was made. I think the wonder of Stonehenge is enhanced when we realize that the bluestones were quarried and transported from Wales, 140 miles distant,[17] and the delight in a flavorful soup is increased with the knowledge that, say, the potatoes in it were first cultivated in the Peruvian Andes and the curry spices in India.

Three psychoanalysts will be the primary guides for my psychological exploration. The first is Sigmund Freud. He has been little used heretofore in Tolkien studies, and my impression is that this is because Tolkienists think of Freud on the one hand as being simplistically blunt, and on the other hand as a disenchanter, as one of those scholars who considers towers uninteresting and knocks them over to study the stones. The simplistically blunt version is seen, for example, when Randel Helms writes that Bag End is a womb and that Bilbo's growing maturity is shown by him obtaining a phallic sword from the troll's cave hidden by bushes (you can almost see Helms winking as he emphasizes "hidden by bushes"),[18] etc.; or when Thomas Honegger writes "'In a hole in the ground there lived a somewhat retarded, orally fixated pre-adolescent who was almost pathological in his refusal to interact in a socially responsible way with the outer world. This is the story of how he overcame, with a little help from his psychologist, some of his neurotic complexes.'"[19] But such simplistic symbolic equations have little to do with Freud's work or that of contemporary psychoanalysts. At least Helms and Honegger acknowledge that they are writing parodies.

C. S. Lewis, with his caricature of Freud as "Sigismund Enlightenment," who reduces beliefs to misunderstood wishes,[20] provides a good example of pigeonholing Freud as a disenchanter.[21] And it is true that Freud was like that at times, for example, in his critique of religious beliefs in "The Future of an Illusion."[22] But Freud took many positions throughout his long career and never fully unified them, so there are many versions of Freud. Interestingly, W. H. Auden, a staunch supporter of Tolkien, also valued Freud, and

I think that he recognized an aspect of Freud that would be sympathetic to Tolkien in his elegy upon Freud's death, "In Memory of Sigmund Freud"[23]:

For about him till the very end were still
those he had studied, the fauna of the night,
and shades that still waited to enter
the bright circle of his recognition

turned elsewhere with their disappointment as he
was taken away from his life interest
. . .

Only Hate was happy, hoping to augment
his practice now, and his dingy clientele
who think they can be cured by killing
and covering the garden with ashes
. . .

he went his way
down among the lost people like Dante, down
to the stinking fosse where the injured
lead the ugly life of the rejected,

and showed us what evil is, not, as we thought,
deeds that must be punished, but our lack of faith,
our dishonest mood of denial,
the concupiscence of the oppressor
. . .

but he would have us remember most of all
to be enthusiastic over the night,
not only for the sense of wonder
it alone has to offer, but also

because it needs our love. With large sad eyes
its delectable creatures look up and beg
us dumbly to ask them to follow:
they are exiles who long for the future
. . .

What Auden is poetically describing is a basic Freudian approach to understanding the mind that has great value even if one is not wedded to all the specific mental contents that Freud believed he had discovered: Everything about the mind, even those parts that seem trivial or shameful, has meaning. Important parts of the mind are not available to consciousness, either because they would be very upsetting and so are kept unconscious, or because they were formed under traumatic conditions that prevented their ever being organized into conscious form. Nevertheless, it is possible by following emotional and cognitive associations to integrate unconscious and conscious parts of the mind, to "make friends with [one's] own repressed complexes"[24] and "live in harmony with them" (letter from Freud to Ferenczi).[25]

Freud's thinking about creativity focused mainly on the building blocks and soup ingredients; he theorized that creative writers access unconscious material through their daydreams, and then shape this material into forms that are appealing to an audience. But he hinted at a theory of the creative process when he compared daydreaming to childhood play and stated, "The opposite of play is not what is serious but what is real. In spite of all the emotion with which he cathects his world of play, the child distinguishes it quite well from reality."[26] The incipient idea here is that creativity takes place in a particular state of mind, separate from mundane reality but quite serious.

This idea was developed much further by the second psychoanalyst whose thinking influences my approach, D. W. Winnicott. To my knowledge, his ideas have not been used by other Tolkienists, but I find his perspective particularly resonant with Tolkien's project. Winnicott was a British psychoanalyst who was roughly contemporary with Tolkien. He originally trained as a pediatrician and continued working as a pediatrician concurrently with his analytic career, a practice that kept him focused on play, interpersonal attachment, and the interactions between imagination and the environment. He was a great theorist of what facilitates or challenges creativity, both in the specific sense and in the general sense of living creatively.

The third psychoanalyst who makes a major contribution to my approach is Julia Kristeva. Coming from a different (Lacanian) tradition than Freud and Winnicott, her darker view complements Winnicott's cheerier one in a way that is helpful in reflecting Tolkien's mixture of darkness and light.

I have already used the word *enchantment* to mean things ranging all the way from towers to soup, so before briefly describing the rest of the book, I want to clarify what I mean by *enchantment*. The *Oxford English Dictionary Online* defines it as: "1 The action or process of enchanting, or of employing magic or sorcery; 2 Alluring or overpowering charm; enraptured condition; (delusive) appearance of beauty." But this definition only makes a stab at what Weber was talking about and what is most important in Tolkien, and in fact hints at complexities that it does not pursue: enchantment can be "delusive," and definitions 1 and 2 can be in contradiction, since it is not necessarily charming to be under a magic spell—just ask the hobbits about Old Man Willow. Much of Frodo's dream discussed above is no less enchanting for being dangerous. As I mentioned previously, enchantment for Tolkien is both perilous and fair.

My earlier quote from Weber indicates three crucial aspects of the enchanted worldview: everything is connected (like a great garden), the world is affected by mysterious forces, and not everything can be explained rationally. Tolkien's contrasting enchantment with magic is consistent with this definition, but it is his description of the realm of Faërie as a whole that best fits with Weber's thought and points to his own deeper project: "The realm of fairy-story is wide and deep and high and filled with many things: all manner of beasts and birds are found there; shoreless seas and stars uncounted; beauty that is an enchantment, and an ever-present peril; both joy and sorrow as sharp as swords."[27] I think that what lies at the core of these ideas is *a sense of wonder, meaningfulness, and connection to an Other*. But neither the quote from Weber nor the quote from Tolkien gives a precise definition of enchantment, and perhaps that is because too much precision would approach the calculations of disenchantment; the vagueness that Tolkien built into his description of Frodo's dream is part of the concept.

Because for Tolkien enchantment and disenchantment are always in tension, never resolved, the wandering without reaching a final destination that Tolkien built into the dream is also part of the concept. Bilbo's walking songs together with Frodo's modifications of them are imbued with this quality. (My understanding of the implications of Frodo's word changes to these songs is indebted to Shippey's lengthier discussion.[28]) The cheerful song that the hobbits sing before their first encounter with a Black Rider is quite direct about the idea that wandering is enchanting:

> Upon the hearth the fire is red,
> Beneath the roof there is a bed;
> But not yet weary are our feet,
> Still round the corner we may meet
> A sudden tree or standing stone
> That none have seen but we alone . . .
> Still round the corner there may wait

A new road or a secret gate,
And though we pass them by today,
Tomorrow we may come this way
And take the hidden paths that run
Towards the Moon or to the Sun

Enchantment, yes, but no sign of disenchantment here. The same is true of Bilbo's shorter walking song:

The Road goes ever on and on
Down from the door where it began.
Now far ahead the Road has gone,
And I must follow, if I can,
Pursuing it with eager feet,
Until it joins some larger way
Where many paths and errands meet.
And whither then? I cannot say.

It is Frodo's alterations of these songs that ties disenchantment into the enchantment. By substituting one word he changes the mood of the simple walking song from one of wonder and freedom to one of labor and oppression:

The Road goes ever on and on
Down from the door where it began.
Now far ahead the Road has gone,
And I must follow, if I can,
Pursuing it with *weary* feet,
Until it joins some larger way,
Where many paths and errands meet.
And whither then? I cannot say. [italics added]

Frodo also revises the first cheerful walking song as he joins the Elves on the way to the Grey Havens at the end of *The Lord of the Rings*. By themselves, the words he chooses emphasize enchantment even more than the original version because they show certainty that he will take the hidden paths, and because for the reader they allude to the title of a familiar fairy tale:

Still round the corner there may wait
A new road or a secret gate;

> And though I oft have passed them by,
> A day will come at last when I
> Shall take the hidden paths that run
> West of the Moon, East of the Sun.

But disenchantment is found here in the context. Frodo has lost the Ring, he has lost his health, and he is about to lose Sam and the Shire.

So we can say that a central topic in Tolkien's work is enchantment in tension with disenchantment, and at the same time it is about the struggle to live creatively. His Elves embody this duality of enchantment and creativity. As defining dwellers in Faërie they represent enchantment, and at the same time "the Elves are there (in my tales) to demonstrate the difference [between Elvish and other kinds of magic]. Their 'magic' is Art, delivered from many of its human limitations: more effortless, more quick, more complete (product, and vision in unflawed correspondence). And its object is Art not Power."[29] Therefore, "It [his legendarium] is, I suppose, fundamentally concerned with the problem of the relation of art (and sub-creation) and Primary Reality."[30] Shippey has cogently made the case that Tolkien wrote in the fantasy genre because realism was inadequate to capture the horrors of the Great War.[31] I think another reason that he wrote fantasies, fairy stories, is because therein he found a perfect match between form and content. In fact, in this special way of form and content expressing each other (and I say this in full expectation that Tolkien in his persona as a hobbit would blush to be called an Elf), Tolkien's product and vision are in unflawed correspondence.[32]

In the following chapters I explore how Tolkien created his enchanting legendarium about enchantment and disenchantment. Three themes will intertwine throughout: the tension between enchantment and disenchantment; creativity as a particular source of enchantment; and Tolkien's personal experience of enchantment and loss.

The first two chapters explain Winnicott's and Kristeva's psychological concepts as they relate to enchantment and disenchantment in Tolkien's work and life. In chapter 1, I use Winnicott's ideas to explore how Tolkien creates a dialogue between enchantment and loss, primarily focusing on *The Lord of the Rings*. Enchantment, found in the fairy tale and mythological content as well as in Tolkien's language, is countered by the consistent threat of fading and loss, and Tolkien never resolves whether enchantment or loss "wins." I argue that this ambiguity resonates with tension in general psychological development when old forms of enchantment must be given up and new forms found, a tension that is especially strong during adolescence, a time when many readers first fall in love with Tolkien's works. I then explore how Tolkien's own life experience of enchantment and loss equipped him to write so deeply on this subject.

In chapter 2, I examine Tolkien's appreciation of "The Juniper Tree," a particularly gruesome fairy tale. Tolkien believed that the cannibalism in this fairy tale was essential to its creation of a door into "Other Time." By exploring Kristeva's concept of the abject, and psychological and anthropological understandings of cannibalism, I develop the idea that Tolkien's appreciation of this fairy tale stemmed from his experience of enchantment tangling at its edges with horror and the uncanny.

Chapters 3 and 4 apply these understandings to *The Hobbit.* In chapter 3, I contrast the developmental paths of Bilbo Baggins and the Master of Laketown. Both begin in the mundane world and then receive invitations to join a wider, enchanted world. Bilbo resists but then accepts the invitation, experiences increasing enchantment only to lose much of it in conflict with adult realities, and ends up discovering just how much enchantment he can hold onto. The Master refuses the invitation and stagnates in mundane reality until he is struck by a disastrous enchantment. This contrast endorses psychological development toward a form of maturity that intermingles rational thought with creative fantasy.

By contrasting Bilbo's comfortable hole with nasty, wormy holes and dry sandy holes in the opening lines of *The Hobbit,* Tolkien shows us two perils that Bilbo avoids. In chapter 4 I explore the implications of these contrasting perils. Gollum's nasty hole and Smaug the Worm's hole represent primal fears of the uncontrolled body that Bilbo must overcome. There are no dry sandy holes in *The Hobbit,* but the word *dry* is used to describe the comforts of home. I link this to close examination of Tolkien's paintings *Undertenishness* and *Grownupishness* to make the case that the dry sandy hole represents the danger of adulthood made bleak by overcontrolling one's impulses and too strongly avoiding adventure. Tolkien was confronted by this aspect of adulthood as he graded boring exam papers, and repudiated it by writing the opening line of *The Hobbit* and thus going on an adventure.

Chapters 5 through 7 examine early childhood experience, mothering, and parental loss in Tolkien's work and life.[33] Our first experiences of enchantment and loss are as infants and small children with our mothers. Although little is known about Tolkien's early relationship with his mother, we can sense the quality of this relationship in many of his songs and poems. In chapter 5 I explore one group of songs that expresses relational disruption and repair, and another group that depicts women singing to seduce listeners into or out of states of nonverbal bliss. Tolkien appears to have been particularly sensitive both to relational enchantment with his mother, and to its disruption and repair. I explore whether this is better understood as a response to being orphaned, or to a mixture of painful and pleasurable experience when he was younger.

Galadriel and Shelob are linked in the plot of *The Lord of the Rings* by the Phial containing the light of Eärendil that Galadriel gives to Frodo, which Frodo later uses to drive Shelob back. In chapter 6 I explore how this plot linkage points to a psychological linkage: Galadriel and Shelob are two of the most powerful females in Tolkien's writings, the one a paragon of good and the other of evil. Visible behind their obvious femininity are masculine qualities; for example, Galadriel's Elvish name meant Man-Maiden, and Shelob had phallic organs—horns and a stinger—not found on real spiders. This blending of male and female is also found in the poem "Shadow Bride." Splitting evil qualities from good qualities is a way to preserve the image of goodness in a loved one in the face of painful experiences with him or her. I argue that behind the images of Galadriel and Shelob are Tolkien's pain at the loss of his mother and father.

Psychologists have learned that an important building block of the self is how we are mirrored in the gaze of others: when we look at someone looking at us, what we see in her eyes is related to what she is seeing in us. In chapter 7 I explore how these psychological processes play out in the scene of Galadriel's Mirror. When Frodo and Sam look into Galadriel's Mirror, they see alternate views of themselves between which they must choose. This scene occurs soon after Gandalf's seeming death, when Frodo and Sam feel fragile and in need of emotional bolstering. Since Galadriel's Mirror is a basin filled with water, and stars are given prominence both as reflections in the Mirror and in the way that Eärendil's star bounds the scene, I trace Tolkien's images of stars and water in *The Lord of the Rings* and elsewhere. These images form another complex where he balances deep feelings of enchantment and loss.

Chapters 8 through 11 explore the impact on Tolkien's work of traumas he experienced. In chapter 8 I deepen my discussion of how Tolkien's sensitive treatment of the dialogue between enchantment and loss grew out of his personal experience with this issue. Beginning in early childhood Tolkien was troubled by a recurring dream of being overwhelmed by an enormous wave. During the writing of *The Lord of the Rings* Tolkien was blocked for over a year until he had put this wave into his legendarium as the destruction of Númenor. I examine the destruction of Númenor to make the case that Tolkien's dream was formed out of anxiety about hubris toward his dead father, and that it was only when he was able to transform this anxiety in his creation that he was freed to continue writing *The Lord of the Rings.*

It is well known that Tolkien was strongly affected by World War I, but the war's effect cannot be understood in isolation from his earlier life. In chapter 9 I discuss how Tolkien entered the war with vulnerabilities to interpersonal loss and to expressing psychic pain through somatic symptoms. I investigate Tolkien's letters to the Tea Club and Barrovian Society[34] and his medical withdrawal from combat to show that he experienced the war as a trauma shaped by these earlier vulnerabilities. He continued to experience these vulnerabilities for the rest of his life, and they contributed to his depiction of responses to war by Frodo, Faramir, Éowyn, Kullervo/Túrin, Gorlim, Maeglin, and Beren and Lúthien.

In chapter 10 I explore how the struggle to maintain creativity rather than falling into constriction is manifested in *The Lord of the Rings.* The One Ring is a symbol of constricted thinking dedicated to controlling people seen only as objects, countered by Tom Bombadil as an opposite symbol of flexibility, creativity, and love.

In chapter 11 I return to Tolkien's own struggle against constriction, which he overcame in the episode described in chapter 8. This struggle recurred in later life when Tolkien began to think he had to give up his imaginative "flat-earth" cosmos for a realistic round world, when he conceived of the whole world as Morgoth's Ring, and when he wrote a poem in which even Tom Bombadil is losing his powers.

I close with a brief epilogue that summarizes Tolkien's developmental journey.

CHAPTER I

Tolkien's Dialogue between Enchantment and Loss

At the center of Tolkien's enchanted edifice in *The Lord of the Rings* is the idea that the enchantment out of which this edifice is built must crumble. Or as Saruman gloats to the Elves: "you pulled down your own house when you destroyed mine."[1] This simultaneous creation and demolition of enchantment creates a deep psychological impact that I shall explore in this chapter: *Tolkien reinstates enchantment to create feelings of wonder and relatedness, but simultaneously alerts the reader that this enchantment is at risk for loss.* Tolkien never establishes that either enchantment or loss is "victorious," instead leaving them in a conversation that maintains this fundamental uncertainty. As Verlyn Flieger has pointed out, it is in balancing tensions between opposites rather than resolving them that Tolkien's greatness lies.[2]

I agree with previous writers who have recognized that loss is a primary content theme of *The Lord of the Rings* and Tolkien's other writings, but I think this idea must be further contextualized. Senior described "the sustained and grieved sense of loss, of which death is but one form, that floods through the history of Middle-earth."[3] Hannon stated that "the many quick-moving scenes . . . are secondary to the sense the book conveys of things slipping into—or already become part of—an irrecoverable past."[4] Parker is close to my approach when he states, "Tolkien's whole marvelous, intricate structure has been reared to be destroyed, that we may regret it."[5] But I am adding to these readings the idea that loss in *The Lord of the Rings* and Tolkien's other works can only be understood by considering the way that it interacts with enchanting features: loss and enchantment intertwine in such a way that each undoes the other. Tolkien gave us enchanting works about disenchantment.

I use the term *enchantment* rather than related words such as *magic* or *fantasy* to align my analysis with Weber's concept of the disenchantment of the world, described in the introduction. Patrick Curry discussed how Tolkien's works create a reenchanted premodern universe saturated with meaning based on valuing communion and the natural world.[6] I follow Curry in using Tolkien's own words to define enchantment (although Tolkien did not specifically use the word *enchantment* in this context): "the primal desire at the heart of Faerie [is] the realization, independent of the conceiving mind, of imagined wonder."[7] Related to this is Tolkien's definition of *recovery*, by which he meant "We should meet the centaur and the dragon, and then perhaps suddenly behold, like the ancient shepherds, sheep and dogs, and horses—and wolves . . . recovery . . . is a regaining—regaining of a clear view."[8] And also related is Tolkien's discussion of *consolation*, the highest consolation being that which gives "a fleeting glimpse of Joy, Joy beyond the walls of the world, poignant as grief."[9] This description of consolation highlights my thesis by showing loss inherent even in what Tolkien describes as a deeply enchanting experience.

The dialogue between enchantment and loss in *The Lord of the Rings* is found both in its content, working within and extending the traditional fairy-tale genre and its magical idealized beings, and its style, using composition and word choice to heighten this dialogue. To begin with content, the perilous relationship between enchantment and loss is situated at the very heart of *The Lord of the Rings* in the immutable linkage between the One Ring of Power created by Sauron and the Three Rings created by the Elves. Frodo's quest to destroy the One Ring is the common fairy tale and fantasy quest to destroy dark powers. What Tolkien uniquely and crucially adds is the twist that destroying the dark enchantment will also inevitably destroy good enchantment as well.

The reason Sauron created the One Ring was to control by sympathetic magic all rings of power, especially the three rings of the Elves. The Elves wish to preserve beautiful timeless enchantments and sublime natural environments, but they have invested much of their power in the three rings, and if the One Ring is destroyed, the three rings will lose their power and the Elves must depart or fade. In the frequent longing allusions in *The Lord of the Rings* to ancient days when Elves were stronger and fought in alliance with heroic men, and in the mournful scenes describing Elves passing over the Sea never to return, the reader is simultaneously confronted with enchantment and its loss. Are readers witnessing the power of enchantment? Or the power of loss?

The loss of Elvish enchantment that must ensue if the Ring is destroyed is mirrored by other losses threatening other enchantments in Tolkien's writings. Frodo's many torments as he strives to destroy the Ring have been thoroughly described by Anna Smol;[10] these include his losing touch with ordinary experiences of enchantment, such as feelings of friendship, safety, and pleasure in food and nature.

Loss in the form of death always threatens in *The Lord of the Rings,* and even in the supposed children's book *The Hobbit* in which three favorite characters are killed in war. Tolkien referred in his correspondence to "the oldest and deepest desire, the Great Escape: the Escape from Death,"[11] and stated that death and immortality are the main theme of *The Lord of the Rings;*[12] this statement should not be taken as definitive about what he considered the main theme, but it does indicate the importance of death to him. Tolkien wants readers to feel the loss, to grieve, when important characters die. Although there are many hopeful moments in the book, Tolkien often represents the importance of fighting to the death in a hopeless cause. And in addition to the grief and loss we feel about what we might call a normal death, Tolkien weaves in death as a direct challenge to enchantment in the tales of love between Elves and humans: When an Elf weds a human, the Elf must surrender her immortality; this is a shift toward ordinary life, as opposed to shifting toward enchantment if the human were to become immortal.

The Lord of the Rings is also pervaded by the loss or diminution of a comforting and beautiful natural world. Whether looking at fairy-tale nature—Bombadil's shrinking domain, the fading of Lórien, the last march of the Ents—or more "ordinarily enchanted" nature such as the Shire under Sharkey's men, the natural world is increasingly threatened with disenchantment.

Now I will turn from the central plot entanglement of enchantment and loss to explore how Tolkien mingled enchantment and loss stylistically. Verlyn Flieger has discussed the ways that Tolkien's language usage reflects his belief that language and mythology are coeval; in using language this way, he creates an experience of otherness and imagined wonder.[13] Tolkien imbued the already magical fairy-tale genre with a deeper sense of enchantment by employing various unusual forms—chanting, singing, Elvish language, archaic language and word order, and unconventional capitalization—even as he described events that demonstrate the world inevitably evolving toward the disenchanted Age of Men.

For a first example, discussed by Shippey, here is a brief conversation between Treebeard the Ent and Galadriel and her husband Celeborn speaking about the end of their time together in archaic English, which also includes a phrase of Elvish:[14]

> Then Treebeard said farewell to each of them in turn, and he bowed three times slowly and with great reverence to Celeborn and Galadriel. "It is long, long since we met by stock or by stone, *A vanimar, vanimálion nostari!*" he said. "It is sad that we should meet only thus at the ending. For the world is changing: I feel it in the water, I feel it in the earth, and I smell it in the air. I do not think we shall meet again."
>
> And Celeborn said, "I do not know, eldest." But Galadriel said: "Not in Middle-earth, nor until the lands that lie under the wave are lifted up again. Then in the willow-meads of Tasarinan we may meet again. Farewell!"[15]

In Shippey's discussion he responds to a harsh critic of Tolkien who complained (among other things) about the cadence and pitch of this passage. Shippey notes that the critic may have been irritated by "the boldly untranslated fragment of Quenya, or the triple repetition of 'feel . . . feel . . . smell,' or the sudden change to less plain language in Galadriel's speech" but decides that the main offense must have come from "by stock or by stone." The *Oxford English Dictionary Online* tells us that Treebeard's use of *stock* to mean *stump* is archaic or obsolete, and Shippey shows that Tolkien in using this phrase was deliberately echoing the medieval *Pearl* manuscript that Tolkien translated. Shippey concludes that "Tolkien was trying continually to extend the frontiers of style beyond the barbed wire of modern opinion." I want to emphasize that all the extensions of style that Shippey identified—cadence, pitch, repetition, shifts between levels of formality of English and between English and Elvish—create an air of enchantment by taking the reader away from mundane expectable rhythms of life.

Cadence plays a similar role in this example from *The Lord of the Rings* as Sam expresses his grief about the departure of the Elves: "it was an old tradition that away over there stood the Grey Havens, from which at times elven-ships set sail, never to return. 'They are sailing, sailing, sailing over the Sea, they are going into the West and leaving us,' said Sam half chanting the words, shaking his head sadly and solemnly."[16] The reader experiences Sam as half chanting not only because of direct authorial comment but because the three repetitions of "sailing" emphasize the drawn-out cadence of the word, and the capital *W* suggests that West is spoken with extra emphasis. The enchanting nature of this passage is emphasized by its contrast with Ted Sandyman's cynical response composed of short staccato syllables: "I don't see what it matters to me or you. Let them sail!"

As a final example, here is the Elven Lady Galadriel lamenting in song both the fading of Lórien and her uncertainty whether she will be able to sail away:

> O Lórien! The Winter comes, the bare and leafless Day;
> The leaves are falling in the stream, the River flows away.
> O Lórien! Too long I have dwelt upon this Hither Shore
> And in a fading crown have twined the golden elanor.
> But if of ships I now should sing, what ship would come to me,
> What ship would bear me ever back across so wide a Sea? (373)

The common nouns *Winter, Day, River, Hither Shore,* and *Sea* in this song are promoted to proper nouns, so to speak, by unusual capitalization. This capitalization creates an enchanted feeling in two ways: the words in question all have to do with the natural world and so emphasize a separation from ordinary humanness; and these aspects of the natural world for reasons that are mysterious carry special import. The Winter and Day that are coming stand outside the ordinary cycle of time; the River, Hither Shore, and Sea stand outside ordinary landscapes and traversing them would not be ordinary travel.

I will now shift from examining the dialogue between enchantment and loss in Tolkien's work to exploring how this dialogue expresses an internal psychological struggle that is common in the modern Western world: the need to find new forms of enchantment in the face of the disenchantment identified by Weber. Let's begin by taking a closer look at the experience of enchantment.

As I indicated in the introduction, enchantment is not easy to define, but drawing on Weber and Tolkien I approached its definition as a sense of wonder, meaningfulness, and connection to an Other, with the lack of precise boundaries to this definition in fact being intrinsic to the concept. All these qualities are best experienced in a state of mind that is situated intermediate between reality and unreality. Tolkien invoked this state of mind in the quote that I used earlier as his definition of enchantment ("the primal desire at the heart of Faërie [is] the realization, independent of the conceiving mind, of imagined wonder"): the denizens of Faërie and the realm of Faërie itself are experienced both as having independent existence and as in a sense existing because of ("imagined" by) the believer.

This state of mind has been explicated by D. W. Winnicott as transitionality. *Transitional space, transitional objects,* and *transitional phenomena* are concepts that I will use frequently in this book to understand Tolkien's literary and personal experiences of enchantment. Winnicott stated that in addition to the internal world and the external world, "the third part of the life of a human being . . . is an intermediate world of *experiencing,* to which inner reality and external life both contribute. It is an area that is not challenged, because no claim is made on its behalf except that it shall exist as a resting-place for the individual engaged in the perpetual human task of keeping inner and outer reality separate and yet interrelated."[17] In describing the developmental origin of the transitional object in infancy, Winnicott stated, "It comes from without from our point of view, but not so from the point of view of the baby. Neither does it come from within; it is not a hallucination."[18] And Winnicott clarifies that he is "studying the substance of *illusion,* that which is allowed to the infant, and which in adult life is inherent in art and religion."[19]

By "transitional" experience Winnicott means experience that is transitional between the experience of Me and the experience of Not-Me. His thesis is that it is psychologically important to have the capacity for experience that is neither entirely located in external, objective reality (the Not-me), nor entirely located in internal, private reality (Me), but instead integrates or blends the Not-me and the Me. The capacity for such transitional experience is important both in early development and later life because it helps to manage the anxiety of being a unitary individual in a multitudinous world, and because it helps create a rich and interesting life.

By formulating the elements of the magical worldview in this way—wonder, connectedness, and transitionality—it can be recognized as a way of being in the world that many people experience and value, at least at times. People who would scoff at the idea of magic as something that actually physically affects the material world may nevertheless find much of what is of value in life to be metaphorically enchanted. Patrick Curry gave as potential sources of such metaphorical or ordinary enchantments nature, love, ritual, art, sports, food, and learning.[20] People never find the loss of magic fully satisfying because much of the richness in life derives from interplay between aspects of magical thinking and realistic thinking. Winnicott noted that play and then broader cultural phenomena like art and religion are crucial for a fulfilling life.[21] Loewald maintained that true maturity does not derive from relying only upon advanced forms of thought, but from being able to shift flexibly between advanced and early symbiotic forms.[22] Rationality untempered by wonder, and wonder untempered by rationality, are both problematic.

Tolkien in "On Fairy-Stories" defended fairy tales from charges of escapism by declaring that they deliver appropriate and necessary escape as though from prison. This is another way of describing the process of reenchantment. But Tolkien is actually doing something much more psychologically powerful than simply providing reenchantment: he is providing reenchantment while calling it into question; he is providing escape routes from prison while at the same time saying that they may all be closed. This is not escapism in the sense of indulging in wild imagination to divert one's attention from the real issues. Rather, it is a direct engagement with the real issue: the dialogue between enchantment and disillusionment that is part of life.

Since people's experience of enchantment typically changes across the life span, this psychological struggle is best understood from a developmental perspective. It is generally accepted in Western thought that the magical worldview is more prominent among children than adults, and that disenchantment of the world is a normal part of maturing. It is therefore a crucial developmental task throughout life to attain a partial disenchantment of the world while retaining a sense of enchantment by finding it in more mature forms.

Freud described the gradual and ambivalent developmental transformation away from a pleasure ego to a reality ego, a transformation that is never complete and leaves areas where magical thinking can still prevail, such as fantasy, art, and sexuality.[23] This parallels the Winnicottian idea that in the process of maturation, childhood forms of transitionality must be given up and new forms of transitionality found. Winnicott proposed that transitional experience becomes important in early development at the point when the infant begins to realize that he or she is a separate individual in a larger world. At birth, the infant does not clearly differentiate himself or herself from the caretaking environment. With good-enough mothering (which nowadays we would call good-enough parenting since the father can fulfill this role as well), the child's needs for nurturance are met in a sufficiently timely fashion that the child does not have to confront the idea that he or she is a dependent being who cannot survive without the efforts of someone external to him or her. Over time, with cognitive maturation and experience of small enough disappointments, the infant begins to recognize the difference between inner and outer realities. To tolerate and manage this difference, the child begins to create illusory experience that we can think of as neither internal nor external, or as both internal and external at the same time.

The most familiar example of such infantile illusory experience is the transitional object, such as a beloved teddy bear or Linus van Pelt's security blanket.[24] Such an object is transitional between the Not-me and the Me because it is both a thing in objective reality and a creation of the baby, who has imbued it with meaning and importance. Any parent of a child with, say, a security blanket knows that while it is definitely a blanket, it is not "just a blanket." The transitional object assumes great importance for the baby because by being both their creation and separate from them at the same time, it shows that it is possible to securely integrate these realities that have been newly recognized as separate.

Typically, children lose interest in their transitional objects over time, either forgetting them completely or remembering them fondly but no longer needing them in order to feel secure. But transitional experience remains important throughout the life span because people of all ages confront the task of both developing as separate individuals and integrating themselves into a world much larger than themselves. Winnicott thought that older children enter transitional space when they play, and that religion, art, and culture more broadly take place in adult transitional space.[25] (Notice that religion, art, and culture are consonant with Curry's examples of ordinary enchantment given on page 20.) People who are unable to find transitional space as they mature live relatively concrete and sterile lives.

Although I see no evidence that Tolkien had it consciously in mind as he wrote *The Hobbit* and *The Lord of the Rings,* he showed at the beginning and end of his career that he recognized the developmental arc of enchantment and disenchantment. In the earliest form of the legendarium that appears in the *Lost Tales,* children have a special access to enchantment: Eriol heard the tales of the Elves in the Cottage of Lost Play and learned of the Olórë Mallë, the Path of Dreams by which children of men traveled to Valinor. Tolkien's early poem "You and Me in the Cottage of Lost Play" depicts the speaker and a loved partner as children in Faërie. It is true that Tolkien later repudiated the similar cuteness of his poem "Goblin Feet,"[26] and in "On Fairy-Stories" exploded the idea that fairy tales are especially for children, but this effort was intended to open adult minds to enchantment rather than to deny its importance for children. And as part of this effort, Tolkien recognized that children engage seriously with fairy tales, even though they are aware that the tales do not represent factual reality. Using his own child self as an example, he wrote "at no time can I remember that the enjoyment of a story was dependent on belief that such things could happen, or had happened, in 'real life.' Fairy stories were plainly not primarily concerned with possibility, but with desirability. If they awakened *desire,* satisfying it while often whetting it unbearably, they succeeded."[27] This attitude is very much in accord with the comment of Freud's, which I quoted in the introduction: "The opposite of play is not what is serious but what is real."

In the last work published in his lifetime, *Smith of Wootton Major,* Tolkien again depicted children as more connected to Faërie than are adults, with rare exceptions. The star that is a token of entrance to Faërie is baked into a Great Cake that is served at the Feast of Good Children, and the child who will receive the star is chosen in advance by the King of Faërie (although at the end he would have acceded to Smith if Smith had chosen a different child to be his successor). And when Smith has to give up the star so that another child may find it, we see the developmental need to surrender childhood enchantments and accept the quieter enchantments that can be found in adulthood.

In *The Hobbit* and *The Lord of the Rings,* Tolkien illustrated the developmental relevance of the dialogue between enchantment and loss by deepening a common fairy tale framing device in a way that emphasizes the developmental trajectory of his central characters. Fairy tales frequently have a structure in which a child or adolescent encounters Faërie, a world of wonder and peril, and then returns to the ordinary mortal world with a more mature status; familiar examples include Cinderella, Snow White, and Jack the Giant-Killer, all of whom have magical adventures that culminate in them marrying royalty. Many classic modern fantasies show the same structure at least in part; for example, Dorothy is blown to magical Oz by a tornado and after her adventures returns with the wisdom that there is no place like home; and Christopher Robin's tale ends when he sadly leaves Pooh behind for the adult world. One reason why this motif of an ordinary mortal entering a magical world engages us is that it symbolizes the reinstatement or strengthening of the enchantments that have been lost or threatened during the normal course of development. But in traditional fairy tales and many classic fantasies, this transition to and from the magical world is accomplished very quickly or presented as a minor framing device (for example, Dorothy was dreaming in the movie version of *The Wizard of Oz,* as was Alice in *Alice in Wonderland*).

Tolkien had a low opinion of these brief transitions, stating, "It is at any rate essential to a genuine fairy-story, as distinct from the employment of this form for lesser or debased purposes, that it should be presented as 'true' . . . since the fairy-story deals with 'marvels,' it cannot tolerate any frame or machinery suggesting that the whole story in which they occur is a figment or illusion."[28] Tolkien elaborated this point novelistically in his posthumously published "Notion Club Papers," when he had characters dismiss such devices and assert the importance of a convincing frame that matches the depth of the story. Dolbear, the character who is interested in psychoanalysis, sums up a conversation in which several members have criticized Ramer for the framing device in the story he just told them as follows: "Your real story is *wholly* out of keeping with what you call the frame. . . . I've never felt such a jar before, not in any of your work. . . . I find it hard to believe that the [framing] machine and the tale were made by the same man. . . . You wrote the first chapter, the space voyage, and also the homecoming (rather slipshod that, and my attention wandered): you *made it up*, as they say. . . . But I don't think you wrote the story inside."[29] And then Ramer acknowledges that he actually experienced what is in the body of the story, thus explaining how it has truthfulness not found in the framing device.

Tolkien paid attention to Dolbear's critique, so to speak. In *The Hobbit* and especially in *The Lord of the Rings* Tolkien expanded the fairy-tale transition motif greatly and made its truthfulness commensurate with the body of his stories. By doing so, he demonstrated the importance of Winnicottian transitional space for negotiating the emotional tension between quotidian life and the enchanted world, and between childhood and adulthood.

In *The Hobbit*, written for children, much of the transition to the enchanted world is played humorously, but Tolkien nevertheless extended it compared to traditional tales, spending all of "An Unexpected Party" on the transition. The chapter begins with Bilbo fully ensconced in mundane life trying to shoo away the enchanter Gandalf; increasing impingement from the enchanted world is demonstrated by the serial arrival of the dwarves; Bilbo responds to their presence and conversation with ebbing and flowing excitement until, chivvied the next morning by Gandalf, he finally gives in to the call to adventure and runs off to join the dwarves, although, "To the end of his days Bilbo could never remember how."[30] In *The Lord of the Rings* Tolkien elaborated the transition to the enchanted world, together with its tensions, a great deal further. "The Shadow of the Past" with Gandalf's description of the meaning and history of the Ring, is at the center of this, but all of book I and the first two chapters of book 2 provide a gradual enlightenment for Frodo, his companions, and the reader that a deeper and richer world is out there. Buckland, the Old Forest, Tom Bombadil and Goldberry, and the Barrow-Downs are progressively more unusual and magical compared to Hobbiton. The chapters set in the Shire and Bree also show other hobbits and rustic men reacting with caution to envoys from this wider world, such as Rangers and travelers from the south. It is not until the

Council of Elrond that enchanting history, geography, and peoples are assembled and explained so that together with Frodo we find ourselves fully situated in Faërie.

Hobbits are effective in manifesting these tensions because they symbolize both childhood and the ordinary, nonmagical world. Their childlike qualities include their diminutive size—even though often plump, they are typically only two to four feet tall—and their custom of going barefoot since the soles of their feet were leathery and tough. In addition, hobbits are unsophisticated, carefree, and happily oral: "And laugh they did, and eat and drink, often and heartily, being fond of simple jests at all times, and of six meals a day."[31] They are so orally oriented that they even invented smoking tobacco. At the same time, hobbits are shown by their character and attitude to fundamentally represent ordinary denizens of a preindustrial, agricultural England. This can be seen in their appreciation of order, in their expectation that everyone, including themselves, will behave decently, in their practical common sense, in their garments, and in the varieties of food and drink they enjoy.

That the hobbits represent childhood and conventionality is another feature that Tolkien represented not only in content but also stylistically. Tom Shippey described how Tolkien's uses of more everyday style for the hobbits and higher, romantic style for figures such as Elves and wizards enhances the content depictions of their differences.[32] Here is one among many possible examples: Elrond, describing the task of destroying the Ring, says,

> "The road must be trod, but it will be very hard. And neither strength nor wisdom will carry us far upon it. . . . Yet such is oft the course of deeds that move the wheels of the world: small hands do them because they must, while the eyes of the great are elsewhere." And Bilbo the hobbit replies: "Say no more! It is plain enough what you are pointing at. Bilbo the silly hobbit started this affair, and Bilbo had better finish it, or himself. I was very comfortable here."[33]

Here Elrond sounds both enchanted and paternal, and Bilbo sounds both ordinary and small.

This pair of tensions signified by the way that the hobbits gradually increase their engagement with the enchanted world—the tension between childhood and adulthood, and the tension between enchantment and the ordinary—can be understood as two facets of the developmental need to surrender and transform childhood enchantments. This is the psychological experience that Tolkien's use of enchantment amplifies for the reader: by reinstating enchantment while simultaneously putting it at risk, he provides a powerful exemplar of the developmental task of integrating enchantment with rational life.

This developmental understanding can also help us understand why Tolkien's fiction seems to have a special appeal for teens. Tolkien intended *The Lord of the Rings* for adults, and certainly many adults esteem it greatly, but my sense is that many of them originally fell for it as teenagers. Its appeal for teens became very apparent when the first American paperback edition of *The Lord of the Rings* was published in the late 1960s and sales took off among the college counterculture with the result that a bemused Tolkien had to endure midnight phone calls from inquisitive Americans—so much so that after he retired and moved with his wife to Bournemouth, they kept their address and phone number secret.[34]

The content of fantasy adventure and war with idealized fairy-tale figures is an obvious surface reason that the books have immense appeal for adolescents, but on a deeper level *The Lord of the Rings* engages the primary adolescent developmental issue of maintaining a sense of meaning in the face of disillusionment: Adolescence is the developmental phase when the biggest step from childish magic to an adult form of relating to reality is optimally taken. It is during this phase that formal operational thought provides the cognitive capacity to more accurately comprehend reality,[35] and when youths develop their identities with recognizable, more or less stable positions in the social system and the larger world.[36] This is when one begins to relativize the family of origin, understanding that it provides only one way to be in the world rather than taking it for granted as the center of the way things are and should be. Many adolescents, and adults who retain access to adolescent experience, may love *The Lord of the Rings* because it expresses their age-expectable struggle with disenchantment.

Now let us turn to take a look at how Tolkien's own life experience equipped him to write so knowingly about the tension between enchantment and loss. Tolkien deeply experienced this tension in his own life, and his creativity appears to have served him (as it serves many readers) as an avenue to engage loss with enchantment. This can be seen in microcosm in the way Tolkien shaped a recurring dream that he associated with the Atlantis myth: "the dreadful dream of the ineluctable Wave, either coming out of the quiet sea, or coming in towering over the green inlands. It still occurs occasionally, though now exorcized by writing about it. It always ends by surrender, and I awake gasping out of deep water."[37] In this passage Tolkien is indicating that he mastered this signifier of destruction and loss by integrating it into his enchanted world: the exorcism by writing was performed as Tolkien composed the tale of Númenor being sunk beneath an enormous wave. (I discuss this dream and Tolkien's response to it in much more detail in chapter 8.) And yet Tolkien continued both to be enchanted by the sea and to experience it as having mournful qualities, as we know from his biography and his poetry.[38] Enchantment and loss intertwined for him in the seductive call of the waves.

Tolkien experienced a litany of deep and painful losses. He was born in 1892 in South Africa, where his English parents had emigrated for his father's work. With his mother and younger brother Hilary, he returned to England for an extended vacation when he was three. His father intended to join them there but died of rheumatic fever while still in South Africa when Tolkien was four. When Tolkien was eight years old, his mother converted to Catholicism from Baptist, and her disapproving family withdrew the financial support that they had relied on. Tolkien's mother died of diabetes when he was twelve, and he and Hilary became wards of Father Francis Morgan, a Catholic priest who had already been aiding the family. Tolkien's emotional pain resonates in brief comments he made about his childhood: Upon his mother's death he wrote in a letter about "vainly waving my hand at the sky and saying, 'It is so empty and cold.'"[39] In a passing look back as an adult, Tolkien referred to childhood as "that (I nearly wrote 'happy' or 'golden,' it was really a sad and troublous) time."[40] After his wife died, the eighty-year-old Tolkien wrote to his son Christopher, referring to "the dreadful sufferings of our childhoods, from which we rescued one another, but could not wholly heal the wounds that later often proved disabling."[41]

At the age of twenty-four Tolkien was deployed to France to serve in World War I. Many years later he recalled his feelings when it was time for him to go to the front: "Junior officers were being killed off, a dozen a minute. Parting from my wife then . . . it was like a death."[42] He took part in the Battle of the Somme, where two of his three best friends were killed. Tolkien developed trench fever, a bacterial disease transmitted by lice, and was sent back to England to recuperate. Trench fever typically lasts three months or less, but Tolkien went through a series of partial recoveries and relapses that lasted for the duration of the war and therefore never had to return to battle. Tolkien appears to have been vulnerable to various ailments, some of them only vaguely defined, throughout his life: his sickliness during his early years was one of the reasons that his mother wanted to leave South Africa, and during adulthood his sufferings included bronchitis, influenza, bad teeth, lumbago, joint pains, and physical exhaustion. At times these illnesses interrupted his work and doctors ordered him to rest. This pattern suggests that Tolkien sometimes expressed emotional distress via somatic suffering, so it is likely that his trench fever was partly a post-traumatic stress reaction. (I go into this question in depth in chapter 9.)

Tolkien also agonized over the diminution of the bucolic English countryside. He longingly remembered the quiet Midlands village and environs where he lived from the ages of four to eight, and bemoaned its industrialization. He stated that he was inspired to write his tale "Leaf by Niggle" when a neighbor chopped down a big, beautiful tree for no good reason. He quit driving in his later years to protest the destruction of the landscape wrought by automobiles and roads.

So it is clear that throughout his life Tolkien endured a barrage of losses. In parallel with this, fantasy and creating art about fantasy served as enchantments of utmost importance to him. Tolkien remembered enchanting otherness as already being very important to him in childhood: "The dragon had the trademark *Of Faërie* written plain upon him. In whatever world he had his being, it was an Other-world. Fantasy, the making or glimpsing of Other-worlds, was the heart of the desire of Faërie. I desired dragons with a profound desire."[43]

Tolkien's first effort to write his own story (about a dragon) came at age seven. Beginning in adolescence, writing was central to his experience of himself. Throughout his life Tolkien's closest friendships were with men who shared and critiqued each other's writings, whether during adolescence within the informal club called the TCBS, or with the Inklings during adulthood. The TCBS hoped for their writings to change not only literature but society as a whole by reimbuing it with their values. Part of the grief they felt about World War I and the death of two of their members was that this mission would not be completed. Maturity tempered Tolkien's wishes that he could change the world, but he remained as passionate as ever about his writing. He described the Elves, whose story is central to his enchanted world, as representing the artistic and poetic part of human nature. And upon finishing *The Lord of the Rings,* Tolkien wrote, "It is written in my lifeblood, such as that is, thick or thin; and I can no other."[44]

Furthermore, Tolkien overtly related aspects of his own life to characters and events in his created world. Sometimes he did this lightly: he considered himself to be a hobbit and described cruel and destructive people as orcs.[45] More poignantly, he experienced the love that he shared with his wife Edith through the lens of his enchanted world, and vice versa: During a period of their courtship while Edith lived in Warwick, Tolkien wrote a poem inspired by Warwick ("Kortirion among the Leaves"), depicting it as a town where Elves still lived, and he later developed Kortirion as an important Elvish town in the prehistory behind *The Lord of the Rings.*

The tale of Lúthien and Beren is, of course, one of the pillars of Tolkien's legendarium, and upon Edith's death, Tolkien had the name "Lúthien" inscribed on the tombstone; after his own death, his children had "Beren" added to the tombstone.[46] The tale of Lúthien and Beren was inspired when Tolkien watched Edith dancing, and Curry considered this moment to be one of the clearest examples of Tolkien himself experiencing enchantment.[47] Here is Tolkien's description of Beren's first encounter with Lúthien from *The Silmarillion:* "he came upon Lúthien . . . at a time of evening under moonrise, as she danced upon the unfading grass in the glades. . . . As the light upon the leaves of trees, as the voice of clear waters, as the stars above the mists of the world, such was her glory and her loveliness; and in her face was a shining light."[48] Compare this with Tolkien's description of Edith after her death. Tolkien wrote to one of his sons about how she had inspired the myth of Lúthien early in their courtship: "I never called Edith Lúthien—but she was the source of the story that in time became the chief part of the *Silmarillion.* It was first conceived in a small woodland glade filled with hemlocks. . . . In those days her hair was raven, her skin clear, her eyes brighter than you have seen them, and she could sing—and *dance.*"[49]

Tolkien also used his enchanted world and his writing to transform his World War I experiences. He himself only acknowledged this in regard to the stricken Middle-earth landscape of the Dead Marshes, which Tolkien said were inspired by the wartime landscape of the Somme.[50] But several scholars have elucidated how aspects of the battle scenes, plot, relationships, and mood of *The Lord of the Rings* are linked to Tolkien's war experience.[51] It was during the war that Tolkien began his legendarium, and he wrote about the Fall of Gondolin, the first extended war story set in his enchanted world, while in hospital recuperating from trench fever.

In light of all this, Tolkien's fantasy and writings may be seen as an expression of his struggle to maintain enchantment in the face of the many losses he experienced, ranging from his becoming an orphan to the horrors of World War I. Shippey has pointed out that many writers who lived through this war turned to fantasy fiction to express their experience because the ordinary cultural forms of expression had failed.[52] I think we can make the even stronger statement that by using fantasy, Tolkien was in fact able to write more directly about the effects of war than would have been possible with realism. Although on the surface fantasy is far different from the real world, it directly represents the sense of wonder and connectedness that was threatened by the war.

In closing this chapter, let us look at how the fairy-tale motif of a youngster engaging with an enchanted world comes to a close: Even in simple fairy tales, enchantment is often lost when the ordinary mortal who entered Faërie completes his or her journey and returns to ordinary life. Just as he did with the transition into the enchanted world, Tolkien elaborated upon the return from the enchanted world to emphasize the tensions between enchantment and loss. Although Tolkien stayed close to the traditional ending in *The Hobbit,* highlighting the motif with the subtitle "There and Back Again," even in this simpler book, two pages describing Gandalf and Balin's visit from the wider enchanted world, coming after the statement that Bilbo would live very happily to the end of his days, show that the transition was not yet complete.

In *The Lord of the Rings,* Tolkien complicated the hobbits' return from the enchanted world by including several losses and partial recoveries. If *The Lord of the Rings* were a normal fairy tale, Tolkien would have wrapped up the story soon after the destruction of the Ring and had the protagonists live happily ever after. But such simple optimism would have been untrue for him, so he greatly expanded the experience of disenchantment at the end just as he had greatly expanded the experience of becoming enchanted at the beginning,

Upon returning to the Shire, the hobbits find it pillaged, corrupted, and dehumanized by the debased Saruman and his men. Frodo's companions lead a successful rebellion, although Frodo's ambivalence about the necessary violence limits any feelings of glory. Despite Frodo's attempt to protect Saruman, he is slain by his former servant Wormtongue; Saruman's diminishment from Maia to thug, and his subsequent death, provides another example of disenchantment. The Shire is restored to its former peace and fecundity, but its vulnerability to loss has been clearly demonstrated.

Even in the restored Shire there is no peaceful Happily Ever After for Frodo. His loss of the Ring, after it had so much control of his mind and soul, has left him bereft and wounded beyond cure in this world. In honor of his enormous service, and to give him a chance of healing before he dies, Frodo is allowed a grace forbidden to most mortals: to accompany one of the last ships of the Elves as they sail to Elvenhome.

Is Frodo's sailing with the Elves a reenchantment? Or is it a deepening loss, as he separates irrevocably from his beloved hobbits? Of course it is both, and Tolkien lets his readers feel both.

At the very end, Frodo's companion Sam returns to his loving wife and family and says, "Well, I'm back." Flieger pointed out that it is not clear from the written text if this is meant to be pronounced "Well, I'm *back*," or "Well, *I'm* back"; Flieger discussed how the latter pronunciation implicates all the people *not* back from war, both in Tolkien's works and in his life.[53] The contrasting readings also differ in their implications for the dialogue between enchantment and loss. "Well, I'm *back*" is more weighted in the direction of the ordinary Back Again experience with the loss of enchantment: Sam is back to normal life from the enchanted world. "Well, *I'm* back" is more weighted in the direction of enchantment because it emphasizes that unlike Sam, others are *not* back from the enchantment (although in this reading, too, there is loss of enchantment—the ordinary enchantment of friendship). This subtle ambiguity continues to engage the reader in the dialogue between enchantment and loss.

My impression is that the more common reading (now reinforced by Peter Jackson's planting it in viewers' minds) is "Well, I'm *back*." This reading gives us reason to believe that, surrounded by the ordinary enchantments of family love, Sam will live happily ever after. Yet here as well Tolkien weaves in further enchantment and loss: we learn in an appendix to *The Lord of the Rings* that since Sam was briefly a Ringbearer, he, too, eventually passes over the Sea to Elvenhome. To the last, Tolkien engages us in the struggle to balance the experience of loss with a sense of enchantment, connectedness, and meaning.

CHAPTER 2

My Mother She Killed Me, My Father He Ate Me

In "On Fairy-Stories," Tolkien singled out for particular appreciation the Brothers Grimm's fairy tale "The Juniper Tree," and briefly described what it was about this tale's construction that created its effect on him. This is notable because Tolkien otherwise wrote about fairy tales in only a general way, with passing mention of specific ones by name. (He did state that he had enjoyed a tale called "Puss-Cat-Mew," but he tells us no more about it.[1]) It is also notable because "The Juniper Tree" is particularly gruesome; Maria Tatar has called it "the most shocking of all fairy tales,"[2] and as we see from Tolkien's description, the horror was for him a crucial part of its effect:

> The beauty and horror of *The Juniper Tree* . . . with its exquisite and tragic beginning, the abominable cannibal stew, the gruesome bones, the gay and vengeful bird-spirit coming out of a mist that rose from the tree, has remained with me since childhood; and yet always the chief flavor of that tale lingering in the memory was not beauty or horror, but distance and a great abyss of time. . . . Without the stew and the bones—which children are now too often spared in mollified versions of Grimm—that vision would largely have been lost. I do not think I was harmed by the horror *in the fairy-tale setting,* out of whatever dark beliefs and practices of the past it may have come. Such stories have now a mythical or total (unanalyzable) effect, an effect quite independent of the findings of Comparative Folklore, and one which it cannot spoil or explain; they open a door on Other Time, and if we pass through, though only for a moment, we stand outside our own time, outside Time itself, maybe.[3]

Even if its total effect is unanalyzable, there are important things we can learn about Tolkien's understanding of enchantment by exploring his singular appreciation of this most gruesome of fairy tales. This exploration will also introduce the concepts of the *uncanny* and *abjection,* which play a role in Tolkien's legendarium that I will develop in chapters 4 and 10. But first, we need a summary of the Brothers Grimm's *The Juniper Tree* to orient us.

"The Juniper Tree," like all fairy tales, exists in many variants. Folklorists have rightly criticized efforts to understand the psychology behind fairy tales by examining only single variants like those in the Brothers Grimm, rather than taking multiple variants into consideration. However, Tolkien is clear that he was responding to the Brothers Grimm variant, so that is the variant that matters here. I use the version in Maria Tatar's *Annotated Grimm:*

At least two thousand years ago, a rich man and his beautiful wife were happily married except that they had no children. One winter the wife, while peeling an apple beneath the juniper tree in their courtyard, cut her finger and bled into the snow. She wished for a child as red as blood and as white as snow, and nine months later gave birth to a son but died in childbirth. The grieving father buried her beneath the juniper tree, and eventually remarried and had a daughter by his second wife.

The second wife loved her daughter but hated her stepson because she feared he would stand in the way of her daughter's inheritance. One day the daughter asked for an apple, which her mother gladly gave her, but when she requested one for her brother, her mother became angry and threw the apple in a chest. When the brother came home, the step/mother offered the apple, but when he looked inside the chest, she slammed the lid, cutting off his head.[4] She tied his head back on with a scarf and set him in a chair. When the little girl complained that her brother would not speak, the step/mother told her to slap him, which caused his head to fly off. The woman then cut up her stepson and cooked him into a stew, which she served to the father, who found it so delicious that he ate it all himself.

The girl buried her brother's bones beneath the juniper tree, and then the tree began to sway and gave off a mist out of which flew a beautiful bird. The girl went happily into the house to eat. The bird flew off and three times sang this song:

My mother, she killed me,
My father, he ate me,
My sister Marlene,
Gathered all my bones,

Tied them in a silken scarf,
Laid them beneath the juniper tree,
Tweet, tweet, what a beautiful bird am I.

First, he sang to a goldsmith, who gave him a golden chain; then he sang to a shoemaker, who gave him red shoes, and finally he sang to a miller, who gave him a millstone. He then flew back and sang at home. The father thought he smelled cinnamon, came out, and was given the golden chain. The daughter came out and was given the shoes. The step/mother came out and the bird dropped the millstone on her head, killing her. He turned back into a boy, took the hands of his father and sister, and they all walked back inside and ate happily.

"Horror" indeed! And yet Tolkien (as quoted above) describes his response as being not horror (or beauty) but a "vision" of "distance and a great abyss of time"; "a door on Other Time, and if we pass through, though only for a moment, we stand outside our own time, outside Time itself, maybe"—a description of enchantment. But deep time alone is not enough to create the enchantment; Tolkien also says that "without the stew and the bones—which children are now too often spared in mollified versions of Grimm—that vision would largely have been lost." What is it about embedding the stew and bones in distant time that creates a feeling of enchantment? Surely part of the answer is that distancing these horrors in time makes them less threatening, similar to Tolkien's suggestion that if a child asks if dragons are real, it is helpful to answer, "There is certainly no dragon in England today."[5] But not everything old is enchanting; if deep time makes cannibal stew and bones safe, cannibal stew and bones do something to make deep time "Other Time."

To see what this is, we need to consider what Tolkien leaves out of his memory of what was special in this fairy tale: "The beauty and horror of *The Juniper Tree* . . . with its exquisite and tragic beginning, the abominable cannibal stew, the gruesome bones, the gay and vengeful bird-spirit coming out of a mist that rose from the tree . . ." Where is the step/mother's murder of the little boy? This element is also horrible and just as prominent in the story as is the stew, and more so than the bones and the bird that Tolkien does recall. Its prominence is even highlighted by the Aarne-Thompson-Uther name for this tale-type: My Mother Killed Me, My Father Ate Me.[6] (The Aarne-Thompson-Uther system provides a classification of variants of tales by their primary shared features.) But Tolkien did not name it as contributing in a primary way to the tale's enchantment. It seems he was less moved by the murder, and I think that this is because of the different ways that the tale handles the cannibalism and the murder.

Considering cannibalism first, we see that in "The Juniper Tree" it is handled in a way that appears quite peculiar to the modern Western rational mind. The father greatly enjoys the stew, so much that he eats every bit himself; neither step/mother nor daughter becomes a cannibal. The father never puts two and two together to figure out that he was eating his son, even though this meaty stew is served at the same time that his son disappears, and the bones that the sister later buries would obviously have been human. The father never shows any guilt and is depicted throughout as blameless, deserving of happiness, and unmarked by his action. He isn't even given the excuse of starvation, which is in the background of other fairy tales with cannibalistic themes like "Hansel and Gretel" and "Jack and the Beanstalk."

Compare this to the fear and condemnation evoked by cannibalism in other tales from Western mythology and folklore. Intentional cannibals are depicted as villainous: Cronus devours his children until Zeus, who had been hidden at birth, forces Cronus to disgorge his siblings and then kills him. The huge cyclops Polyphemus devours Odysseus's shipmates one by one until Odysseus manages to deceive him and escape. Jack's giant and Hansel and Gretel's witch are also cannibals who are escaped from by guile. In tales where a cannibal stew is served to unsuspecting diners, the diners, unlike in *The Juniper Tree,* do not react blandly and blamelessly: when Tantalus cooked his son and served him to the gods, the gods were horrified and refused to eat; only Persephone, distraught about her daughter's kidnapping, distractedly took a bite. When Procne cooked and fed their son to her husband Tereus in revenge for his rape and mutilation of her sister, Tereus became enraged and attempted to murder the women.

Real-world cannibalism similarly stirs up horror and fascination, not only in grotesque examples such as serial killers like Jeffrey Dahmer, but even in disasters in which it is required for survival, such as when the Donner party was snowbound in the mountains in 1846–47. In 2010, newspapers carried stories casting doubt on whether the Donner party actually committed cannibalism.[7] It is most likely that cannibalism did take place, but more important for my purposes than whether it did or not is to note that the fascination and discomfort are strong enough to make this otherwise obscure pioneer event newsworthy more than 160 years after it occurred.

The strange way that "The Juniper Tree" handles cannibalism becomes comprehensible in the wider context of food and eating in the story. The son is conceived in the form of his mother's wish when she is peeling an apple. He is later murdered over desire for an apple. When the little girl sees the magical bird arise from the juniper tree, she is happy and goes inside to eat. The bones left over from the meal become a magical bird when they are joined with the mother in her burial place. When the father hears the bird singing that his father ate him, rather than feeling guilty, he is joyous and even imagines the scent of cinnamon in the air. The millstone used to establish justice by slaying the murderous step/mother would ordinarily be used to grind grain. And when father, son, and daughter are reunited at the end, they seal their happiness with a meal. In all these ways "The Juniper Tree" references eating that symbolizes togetherness and communion, and the father eating his son may be considered an ultimate form of communion: the father actually joining the substance of his son to himself. (Tolkien may have been responding to this theme when he referred to "the chief *flavor* of that tale" [italics added].)

Although it is difficult for the modern Western mind to get past horror at cannibalism to recognize its potential as a form of communion, this potential is well attested in folk tales and anthropology. The sexual communion in "Little Red Riding Hood" that Angela Carter made most blatantly apparent is not far below the surface of even the familiar versions.[8] (Perhaps the wolf in the Brothers Grimm and Perrault versions of Little Red Riding Hood that are most familiar is far enough removed from human that his eating Grandma does not count as cannibalism, but in other variants of Little Red Riding Hood, the girl herself unwittingly eats bits of her.[9]) The sexual undertones of the vampire's bite are widely recognized, and in the novels of Anne Rice and Stephanie Meyers, or in the television/graphic novel universe of *Buffy the Vampire Slayer,* vampires sometimes bite specifically to create an immortal companion.

One motivation for actual cannibalism has been to join the eaten with the eater in order to enhance connections between these loved ones, much as we see in *The Juniper Tree.* Thus, filial piety has sometimes been expressed in China by children offering pieces of their bodies to be eaten by their parents, and part of the pre-Westernized funeral rites of the South American Warí and the New Guinea Fore was to eat the deceased to maintain affiliation and show respect for them. (The complex specifics of the meanings of cannibalism differ in these cultures and are beyond the scope of this book.)[10] Lest we think that such cannibalism is confined to "primitives" and foreigners, Europeans until surprisingly recently consumed blood and body parts for health reasons ("corpse medicine"), and some Americans have recently turned to devouring their newborns' placentas. (Bill Schutt lightheartedly surveys these and other examples of cannibalism.) And during Holy Communion, Catholics ingest the body and blood of Christ in the form of transubstantiated bread and wine, thus joining with him and with the community of believers, as Tolkien of course experienced personally and valued greatly: "I find it for myself difficult to believe that anyone who has ever been to Communion, even once, with at least right intention, can ever again reject Him without grave blame. . . . The only cure for sagging of fainting faith is Communion."[11] (Tatar recognizes a sacramental quality of the meal at the end of "The Juniper Tree."[12])

All of these experiences have antecedents in early childhood. Freud's concept that orality is a primary way that infants relate to the world is well known. Although we recognize that infants also engage with caretakers through many other modalities, especially touch, voice, and gaze, it remains true that the mouth on the nipple, actually imbibing substance from the mother's body, is a fundamental way that babies experience attachment—and aggression, as bitten mothers know. The folklorist Alan Dundes has discussed infantile oral fantasies expressed in cannibalism found in traditional variants of "Red Riding Hood."[13] During toddlerhood, cannibalistic fantasies contribute to common play scenes when parents say they love their toddlers so much that they will gobble them up, or playfully snort and chomp at the tummy of the squealing little one. Cannibalistic fairy-tale giants and witches are signifiers of parental attention gone bad.[14] Childhood fears and phobias commonly take the form of animals like dogs, lions, and bears that might bite or eat the child, or ravenous monsters in the closet or under the bed. Sendak knew what he was talking about in his popular *Where the Wild Things Are* when Max leaves the wild things and the monsters roar, "Oh please don't go—we'll eat you up—we love you so!"[15]

This way of "The Juniper Tree" presenting the horror of cannibalism combined with the undertone of love gives it a strange, creepy feeling that takes it into the realm of the uncanny, and this uncanny quality provides a first step toward a feeling of enchantment. This can be clarified by the contrast between how "The Juniper Tree" handles cannibalism and how it handles the part that Tolkien didn't specifically mention, the step/mother murdering the boy.

The murderer is handled in the story in as realistic a way as can be expected in a fairy tale. She is completely reprehensible, but the murder does not exceed what can be read about from time to time in modern newspapers: she prefers her blood daughter and kills the rival for her inheritance.

She commits the act without working any magic or experiencing any intervention from magical creatures. It is true that in her murderous anger she is described as being overcome by the Devil, but this comes across as a superficial rationalization, especially since there is no recourse to the Devil to explain her tricking her daughter into knocking off the head, and then cooking the stew. (The Grimms' version of the story was lightly Christianized, as can also be seen in it being set at least two thousand years ago, but other traditional versions do not share this feature.) At the end the step/mother receives her well-deserved (at least by talion law) death.

Compare the step/mother murdering and being murdered with "the exquisite and tragic beginning," which is also about death, this time of the biological mother, but death that is linked to, even caused by, the mother's love and desire to have a baby, only to die in childbirth. Maria Tatar pointed out a binary that clarifies how the step/mother is a realistic figure: whereas the mother is mystically merged with nature in her communion with the juniper tree, the step/mother is the most differentiated character in the story.[16] She makes cognitive distinctions the others do not make by anticipating the future, planning and trying to cover up a murder, and so on; and she brutally enacts separations by killing and then chopping up the boy.

All these aspects of the step/mother and the murder she commits suggest a reason that her role in the fairy tale moved Tolkien less than the images he mentioned in his memory: The step/mother is an unambiguous symbol of separation and loss—first killing, then being killed—without any seasoning of the uncanny or of enchantment.

The cannibalism and not the murder creates the uneasy, creepy feeling of the uncanny because the cannibalism is an encounter with something that is simultaneously familiar and unfamiliar. Freud defined the uncanny as "that class of the frightening which leads back to what is known of old and long familiar."[17] At the manifest level, "The Juniper Tree" gives us this melding of familiar with unfamiliar in the unquestioned good father who is also a cannibal, and in the delicious family meal that is also the body of the son. Sheldon Bach's understanding that uncanny emotions are evoked when something that promises to be familiar, responsive, or animate turns out to be unfamiliar, unresponsive, or inanimate gives a more precise view of the effect of the cannibalism in "The Juniper Tree": the father's lack of concern about devouring his own son is profoundly unresponsive to usual feelings.[18] Freud thought that uncanny effects could also derive from reexperiencing something that had been familiar in childhood but subsequently repressed or left behind, and to the extent that cannibalism in "The Juniper Tree" expresses communing and joining with the loved one, as discussed above, it is uncanny in this way as well.

Freud and Bach both give, as iconic examples of the uncanny, beings or images that seem to be familiarly human but at the same time are not: doubles, shadowy figures, near-human automatons, and so on. The seated boy who refuses to answer questions, and then turns out to be a corpse whose head flies off when the sister strikes him, is such a figure, and this adds to the uncanny effect of "The Juniper Tree." Tatar describes the uncanny effect perfectly in her caption to an illustration showing this scene just before the girl strikes her dead brother: "The scarf around the boy's neck conceals the fact that he has been decapitated by his stepmother. His sister is perplexed and frightened but unable to determine his condition."[19]

Tolkien believed that he was not harmed by the horror of the cannibalism because it was "*in the fairy-tale setting,*" but did not mention needing the horror of the murder toned down. What the fairy-tale setting toned down for him, I think, is not simply the horror but the uncanny quality of the horror being merged with normal family life. As Freud stated, "Wish-fulfillments, secret powers, omnipotence of thoughts, animation of inanimate objects, all the elements so common in fairy stories, can exert no uncanny influence here; for . . . that feeling cannot arise unless there is a conflict of judgment as to whether things which . . . are regarded as incredible may not, after all, be possible; and this problem is eliminated from the outset by the postulates of the world of fairy tales."[20]

But while Freud's statement that "that feeling [the uncanny] cannot arise" in fairy tales is true for examples such as one he gives—Snow-White being reanimated by a kiss—it is an exaggeration regarding "The Juniper Tree," which retains some of its uncanniness. That is because the particular form of the uncanny in "The Juniper Tree" lies in the realm of what Julia Kristeva calls the *abject,* which both disgusts and attracts. Kristeva described the abject as that which must be expelled from the self in order to maintain a bounded sense of self, that which must be disavowed and repudiated so that one can constitute oneself as a coherent member of society: "what is abject . . . is radically excluded and draws me toward the place where meaning collapses"; and abjection is caused by "what disturbs identity, system, order. . . . The in-between, the ambiguous, the composite."[21] Kristeva sees abjection as arising in very early life when the child must differentiate himself or herself from the mother and her body that he or she was originally connected to. This means that although the abject has been expelled, one may still be drawn to relate to it or even own and identify with it since it was once part of the self; it may even be experienced as fascinating.

Although at first glance Kristeva's concept of abjection appears very different from Winnicott's concept of transitional phenomena, which I introduced in chapter 1, both are approaches to understanding the vicissitudes of maintaining a coherent sense of self while engaged in the process of relating with other people and the larger world. Both of them are talking about processes that begin in very early life as the infant separates from the matrix of maternal connection, and continue to be important throughout life as the person negotiates degrees of closeness with other people and the environment. The difference is that Winnicott focuses more on benign and comforting aspects of this process, and Kristeva focuses more on frightening and disorienting aspects. Both are important to understanding Tolkien with his mixture of light and dark, and I will continue to use both concepts in later chapters.

Specimens of the abject mentioned by Kristeva include "the criminal with a good conscience, the shameless rapist, the killer who claims he is a savior."[22] To return to "The Juniper Tree," a blameless cannibal fits easily into this series.

So the fairy-tale setting of "The Juniper Tree" contextualizes the cannibalism as in the service of enchantment for the reader, but the abject quality of the cannibalism is severe enough that it is still felt as uncanny. All this suggests that the cannibalism in "The Juniper Tree" is an example of what Tzvetan Todorov called "the fantastic." (Todorov's terminology was idiosyncratic: what most people would think of as fantastic literature he classified in the "marvelous," only using the term *fantastic* in the special sense I am about to describe.) Todorov situated the fantastic between the uncanny and what he called the marvelous. An encounter with the uncanny produces creepiness or fear. An encounter with the marvelous would be an encounter with enchantment as Tolkien described it in "On Fairy-Stories." The fantastic, according to Todorov, is a moment of balance or hesitation between whether something is uncanny or marvelous:

> In a world which is indeed our world, the one we know . . . there occurs an event that cannot be explained by the laws of this same familiar world. The person who experiences the event must opt for one of two possible solutions: either he is a victim of an illusion of the senses, of a product of the imagination—and laws of the world then remain what they are; or else the event has indeed taken place, it is an integral part of reality—but then this reality is

> controlled by laws unknown to us. . . . The fantastic occupies the duration of this uncertainty. Once we choose one answer or the other, we leave the fantastic for a neighboring genre, the uncanny or the marvelous. The fantastic is that hesitation experienced by a person who knows only the laws of nature, confronting an apparently supernatural event.[23]

Since the uncanny itself is an experience of hesitation as to whether something is familiar or unfamiliar, Todorov is proposing a doubling of ambiguity. And this, I think, is why Tolkien's enjoyment of "The Juniper Tree" points to a key aspect of his subtle mind.

I do not mean to suggest that Tolkien wrote in Todorov's register of the fantastic. Although, as I will discuss in later chapters, Tolkien did include important passages about the uncanny and the abject, and images such as the barrow-wight and the dead marshes edge close to the horror genre, these are subsumed in an overall project that in Todorov's schema best fits in the register of the marvelous. What I mean to highlight is that Tolkien situates himself at a complex, ambiguous balance point between enchantment—the term I am using that is close to Todorov's "marvelous"—and disenchantment. The uncanny is already akin to but not identical to enchantment; while experiencing the uncanny, we may be uncertain if we are in the presence of enchantment or not.

Thus, by destabilizing us as to whether something is or is not real and familiar, the uncanny prepares us for enchantment, but additional esthetic steps need to be taken to fully produce the enchanted realm: "In fairy tales, for instance, the world of reality is left behind from the very start, and the animistic system of beliefs is frankly adopted . . . in the realm of fiction many things are not uncanny which would be so if they happened in real life."[24] This is why it is not deep time alone, but deep time plus the stew and bones, that made "The Juniper Tree" special for Tolkien: "Without the stew and the bones—which children are now too often spared in mollified versions of Grimm—that vision would largely have been lost." The cannibalism of "The Juniper Tree" balances precariously between enchantment and disenchantment: the uncanny image of the benign cannibal father points to possible enchantment by disorienting us from reality; the fairy-tale form lets us situate the cannibalism more firmly in enchantment, but still with a degree of unease.

In addition to this way that the general tone of "The Juniper Tree" balances between enchantment and disenchantment, its content more specifically balances between enchantment and loss, the theme that I addressed in the previous chapter. We see this first in the straightforward description of the step/mother murdering the boy juxtaposed with the uncanny description of cannibalism. As I discussed above, the murder is plain disenchantment, the cannibalism an ambiguous mixture.

The dialogue between enchantment and loss is also found in the two other elements of the story singled out by Tolkien that I have not yet discussed: the gruesome bones and the gay and vengeful bird-spirit. Up through the father dining on cannibal stew there has been little to mark "The Juniper Tree" as a fairy tale rather than a horror story—only the setting in old time, and the mother's wish for a child seeming to come true by magic. The obvious magic sets in with the bones and the bird-spirit, both of which are images of loss magically transformed into enchantment. When the girl buries her brother's bones beneath the juniper tree where his mother is buried, the tree begins to sway and exude a mist, and out of the mist flies the marvelous bird. Whether one imagines that the mother has become the tree, or simply that the joint burial has somehow magically activated the tree, this is a clear depiction of resurrection through loving merger.

The bird then obtains rewards for sister and father, and the means to kill the evil step-mother, by singing:

> My mother, she killed me,
> My father, he ate me,
> My sister Marlene,
> Gathered all my bones,
> Tied them in a silken scarf,
> Laid them beneath the juniper tree,
> Tweet, tweet, what a beautiful bird am I.

That the bird can sing in words is obviously magical. But we see a subtler enchantment when we consider the words themselves: Not *hocus-pocus,* not *abracadabra,* not *imperio,* not even *mellon,* but a straightforward description of the horrible trauma the little bird has experienced. The bird charms his listeners by speaking the truth directly. Yet only the step/mother, consistent with her role as realistically differentiated without a trace of enchantment, hears the song realistically and is frightened; the others respond to the beauty of the bird and his singing. Thus, this episode embeds in the fairy story an illustration of how this fairy story as a whole transforms horror: by telling a horrible tale enchantingly. It is easy to see how Tolkien, with his love of and fascination with languages, would have appreciated the bird's singing.

In chapter 1, I discussed how Tolkien never resolves whether enchantment or loss "wins," never resolves which of them is primary. In his appreciation of "The Juniper Tree," with its transformation of the murdered boy back to life, its transformation of trauma into a beautiful song, and its happy ending, do we see Tolkien appreciating the simpler circumstance where at the end enchantment is triumphant? I think not—because how happy is this happy ending? It is true that the wicked step/mother has been destroyed and the boy returned to life, and the closing words are, "He [the boy] took his father and Little Marlene by the hand and the three of them were filled with joy. Then they went back in the house, sat down at the table, and dined."[25] Nevertheless, the man has no wife and the children have no mother. Explicit joy is partnered with implicit sorrow. One way to understand fairy tales is that they represent the process of development and maturation. In chapter 1 I discussed how psychological development entails the loss of earlier forms of enchantment and the need to find new forms. "The Juniper Tree" agrees and presents the loss of earlier enchantment in particularly brutal form: older now and happy with their father, the brother and sister nevertheless have lost their mother.

The trope in this fairy tale of women but not men being either idealized like the saintly biological mother or devalued like the horrible stepmother is unmistakable. The transition in "The Juniper Tree" from mother to step/mother to only father as parent can be understood as maturation from blissful merger with mother, to terrifying separation from her, to complete elimination of the mother figure without the possibility of a comfortable, differentiated relationship with her. Many fairy tales share this trope, "Hansel and Gretel" being a very familiar example. Tatar pointed out how such tales can be read as expressing and reinforcing general cultural patriarchal values (and discusses Bettelheims's *Uses of Enchantment* as a case in point), and Jack Zipes added that the Grimms selected and shaped tales to express their personal sociopolitical patriarchal views.[26]

Because it is so widespread in fairy tales, this idealized/devalued-mother trope in "The Juniper Tree" cannot be a reason that Tolkien singled this tale out for special appreciation; nevertheless, this view of women appears to have played a role in Tolkien's life and work that I shall explore in chapter 5. For now, I will close with the observation that the elimination of the adult feminine in the "happy" ending of "The Juniper Tree" is one more way that this enchanting story is about disenchantment.

CHAPTER 3

Bilbo Baggins, the Master of Laketown, and the Fate of Enchantment

One facet of Tolkien's dialogue between enchantment and disenchantment that I looked at in chapter 1 was the plot progression in *The Hobbit* and *The Lord of the Rings* of the hobbits traveling from mundane home life into the enchanted world of Faërie, and then leaving enchantment behind with the return home. In this chapter I will focus on the thematically simpler *The Hobbit* and explore more deeply the nature of developmentally mature enchantment by contrasting Bilbo's journey with the position of the Master of Laketown. After encountering enchantment in the form of dwarves and a wizard dropping in for an unexpected party, Bilbo embarks upon a developmental path wherein he gains enchantment only to lose much of it, and finally learns just how much enchantment he can keep.[1] When the same dwarves (plus Bilbo) wash up in Laketown, another unexpected party begins that gives the Master a similar opening to enchantment. The Master, however, remains stagnantly resistant to this experience until finally falling under the deadly spell of dragon's gold, which precludes mature existence.

The first chapter of *The Hobbit* demonstrates Bilbo's shock and resistance when first confronted by enchantment. In his initial grownup encounter with the wizard Gandalf, Bilbo is comically anxious and tries to shoo this messenger from an enchanted world away from his comfortable mundane life. Throughout the Unexpected Party his main wish is to get it over with and get rid of the dwarves, a wish that he throws over only twice briefly. This happens first when he listens to the dwarves' song: "Then something Tookish woke up inside him, and he wished to go and see the great mountains and hear the pine-trees and the waterfalls, and explore the caves, and wear a sword instead of a walking stick," but when he promptly imagines dragons on his Hill "He shuddered; and very quickly he was plain Mr. Baggins of Bag-End, Under-Hill, again."[2] A little later when Gandalf produces the map of the Lonely Mountain showing its secret entrance, Bilbo grows "excited and interested again. . . . He loved maps," but by the time the party ends and Bilbo goes to bed, "The Tookishness was wearing off, and he was not now quite so sure that he was going on any journey in the morning."[3] Thorin humming the song that had awakened Bilbo's Tookishness now only gives him uncomfortable dreams. These scenes smoothly establish that enchantment is very different from everyday life, and that the Tookish desire for enchantment is very different from the Bagginsish desire for ordinary life.

Soon Bilbo's Tookish side wins out and he is immersed in the wider enchanted world. Even when Bilbo and his companions encounter dangers—and they encounter many because of course Bilbo was right that the world of enchantment contains unfamiliar dangers as well as unfamiliar pleasures—the mood is basically lighthearted at first. For example, Bilbo's confrontation with trolls early on is played for laughs—the trolls themselves are funny with their cockney accents and general loutishness, and they are defeated by clever wordplay—and the Rivendell Elves greet Bilbo and the dwarves with silly songs. The ensuing adventures in the Misty Mountains and Mirkwood are not played for laughs in the same way, but the tone remains one of comedic excitement.

But a powerful shift in mood occurs partway through *The Hobbit,* so that it becomes darker and disillusioning. This change has been widely recognized, beginning with C. S. Lewis's book review in which he referred to "the curious shift from the matter-of-fact beginnings of the story . . . to the saga-like tone of the later chapters."[4] Tolkien himself agreed that "the tone and style change with the Hobbit's development, passing from fairy-tale to the noble and high and relapsing with the return."[5] "Fairy tale" is indeed a good label for the first part of the book, as Bilbo encounters in succession dwarves, trolls, Elves, goblins, the weird underground creature Gollum, sentient wolves and eagles, a were-bear with animal servants that include bipedal dogs, giant spiders, and more Elves, and gradually grows in confidence and competence through his adventures with them.

Paul Thomas discussed stylistic changes that contribute to the change away from fairy-tale mood in the last six chapters of *The Hobbit,* such as the absence of direct address from the narrator to the reader and the general elevation of language.[6] But I think the big change in mood begins even earlier, when Bilbo and the dwarves arrive in Laketown. Prior to Laketown, the many strange creatures with fairy-tale roots whom they encounter contribute to the book's mood of enchantment. But in Laketown they meet a creature that, although very strange indeed, is strange in an opposite way that punctures a first hole in the mood of enchantment: the Master of Laketown. The Master is a duplicitous, self-serving, capitalist merchant politician who personifies some of the worst aspects of our rationalized, disenchanted world. His presence invites the reader to be more concerned with mundane reality than has hitherto been the case.

The slaying of Smaug by Bard, a character who up to that point has not even been in the book, is another blow to the mood of enchantment. In standard fairy tales and adventure tales, the hero accomplishes great deeds that would not realistically be possible for him or her. This may be done with magical assistance, as when the heroine of "Rumpelstiltskin" is able to spin straw into gold only with the aid of the dwarf, or when Jack is able to accomplish his great giant-killing deeds only with the aid of the giant's wife, but the main action still centers on the hero or heroine. At the beginning of *The Hobbit* the first-time reader has every expectation that Bilbo, or at least the dwarves or Gandalf, will kill Smaug, and that this will be the climax of the story. Tolkien himself expected this development as he began the story.[7] But in the finished book the only contributions our heroes make to Smaug's death are accidental: they irritate him so much that he attacks Laketown, and Bilbo's description to the dwarves of Smaug's weak spot is overheard by the thrush, who communicates this weakness to Bard. In fact, Bilbo and the dwarves are so far removed from the actual slaying that they do not even know about it until the raven tells them three days later—and rather than being the climax of the story, Smaug's death is quickly overtaken by other events. In showing a greatly anticipated heroic event occurring completely outside the control of the character we identify with, and then being overcome by other events, Tolkien is again lessening the mood of enchantment by deidealizing Bilbo's role.

The next disenchantment is the change that comes over Thorin when he realizes that the treasure is his for the taking. The leader of the quest, who has always been somewhat regal and pompous but nevertheless has remained approachable and even appreciative of Bilbo as the hobbit saves the dwarves from spiders and from the Elven-King's halls and makes the first forays into Smaug's lair, now becomes angry, jealous, and threatening toward anyone who wants the treasure, and especially anyone who might take the Arkenstone. Ironically, the disenchantment that Bilbo and the reader feel in the changed Thorin is a result of Thorin himself falling under a particular enchantment, "the bewilderment of the treasure."[8] Bilbo had himself briefly felt this enchantment when he first beheld Smaug's treasure: "His heart was filled and pierced with enchantment and with the desire of dwarves."[9] (Tolkien's fullest description of the effects of such "dragon sickness" is in the poem, which took its final form as "The Hoard" in *The Adventures of Tom Bombadil.*) Bilbo and the reader now recognize that enchantment itself can be disenchanting for those who stand outside it.

And then the tale takes a dark turn into moral ambiguity. Bilbo steals the Arkenstone, the treasure that Thorin craves above all others, and betrays Thorin and the dwarves by turning it over to their enemies, the Elves and Lakemen. Bilbo rationalizes his theft by proposing that the Arkenstone serve as his promised fourteenth share of the treasure, but clearly even he is not comfortable with this formulation. Of course, his actions with the Arkenstone have the commendable motivation of trying to stop a war, and he receives Gandalf's praise, which helps the reader feel that Bilbo has done the right thing. But whatever position the reader takes, he or she has been led far from lighthearted enchantment to complex political and moral questions. To complicate the situation further, at least on one level Bilbo's theft was a wasted effort because it does not succeed in preventing war among the "good guys": Dain's troops attack the Elves and men and are met with answering arrow fire. It is only the timely arrival of the goblins, wargs, and bats that leads the good guys to unite against the common enemy.

The Battle of the Five Armies is the last of the major disenchantments that Bilbo encounters. Battle and war can of course play a significant role in enchanting adventure stories because they provide an arena for idealized strength and heroism. But Bilbo's role, far from being heroic, is to experience realistic fear and rapid injury that prevent him from taking part; furthermore, the narrator stays with Bilbo so that the reader receives not an exciting firsthand account of the battle as it unfolds, but only a secondhand description. Upon waking from his head injury and observing that his side was victorious, Bilbo sums things up by saying, "Well, it seems a very gloomy business."[10] Then he learns that three of the dwarves are dead or dying. And here Tolkien has ensured that we feel some of the realistic pain and loss of war because the three dead are Thorin, who gives a moving deathbed speech, and Fíli and Kíli, two of the most likable. Only the loss of Balin would have been comparably painful.

Despite feeling disenchanted by duplicity, moral ambiguity, and war and death, Bilbo will learn that there is still enchantment in his life. To see how this comes about, it will be helpful to first explore the contrasting fate of the Master of Laketown, who in his desire for mundane power personifies disenchantment until he finally falls victim to the power of a spell that is brought on by his disenchanted existence.

The inhabitants of Laketown are regular men, women, and children, not fairy-tale beings like dwarves and Elves, and so they introduce a note of ordinariness into the story. Nevertheless, they are engaged with enchantment: they trade with the Wood-Elves, they know that not far off a dragon sleeps on its hoard, and they dwell in a town constructed on pilings in a lake, reminiscent of archaic European prototypes. But the Master is blind and deaf to these enchantments, caring only about power and wealth, as can be seen by his reaction to the arrival of the dwarves and Bilbo. Their showing up on his doorstep results in a second version of the unexpected party that began Bilbo's adventure, but the Master is unresponsive to this invitation to enchantment. When Thorin announces himself as King Under the Mountain, and then is contradicted by the raft-men of the Elves, "Then the Master hesitated and looked from one to the other. The Elvenking was very powerful in those parts and the Master wished for no enmity with him, nor did he think much of old songs, giving his mind to trade and tolls, to cargoes and gold, to which habit he owed his position."[11] Although his people are genuinely excited by the advent of the King Under the Mountain, singing and cheering for him, "the Master . . . saw there was nothing else for it but to obey the general clamour, for the moment at any rate, and to pretend to believe that Thorin was what he said."[12] In his disbelief and deviousness he could almost have been invented to illustrate Weber's idea that I quoted in the introduction: "in principle, then, we are not ruled by mysterious, unpredictable forces, but that, on the contrary, we can in principle control everything by means of calculation. That in turn means the disenchantment of the world."

The Master's disenchanted status is further confirmed by his contrast with Bard the Bowman when Smaug attacks. The narrative situates Bard in enchantment: "He was a descendant in long line of Girion, Lord of Dale" and when the thrush lands on his shoulder to inform him of the dragon's vulnerable spot, "Marvelling he found he could understand its tongue, for he was of the race of Dale."[13] Meanwhile, "The Master himself was turning to his great gilded boat, hoping to row away in the confusion and save himself."[14] After Bard slays the dragon, and he and the Master gather onshore with the survivors, the people rage at the Master for his cowardice and want to make Bard king. Seeing how things are going, the Master resorts to manipulative rhetoric: "'I am the last man to undervalue Bard the Bowman,' said the Master warily (for Bard now stood close beside him). . . . 'But why O People? . . . Why do I get all your blame?'"[15] He proceeds to shift the people's anger from himself to the dwarves. Bard's response is sympathetic: "Why waste words and wrath on those unhappy creatures? Doubtless they perished first in fire, before Smaug came to us."[16] Bard musters soldiers to the Lonely Mountain, where he will heroically lead them in the Battle of the Five Armies. The Master stays behind to lead the important but unexciting task of building a new Laketown.

Much later, after Bilbo has returned home, he learns of the Master's end: "Bard had given him much gold for the help of the Lake-people, but being of the kind that easily catches such disease he fell under the dragon-sickness, and took most of the gold and fled with it, and died of starvation in the Waste, deserted by his companions."[17] Ironically, after thoroughly resisting all invitations to enchantment, the Master has succumbed to an enchantment that leads to his death; fittingly, the magic power to which this man who was devoted to self-aggrandizement and the pursuit of personal power falls prey is one that causes his death in isolation.

Although we have followed Bilbo Baggins as he traveled a road from light-hearted enchantment to dark disillusionment, he, unlike the Master of Laketown, is able to maintain connection with a form of enchantment appropriate to the more mature status that he has attained by the end of the book. It is his relationship with magical creatures, not magical spells, that has ongoing meaning for him.

The role that magical spells play in *The Hobbit* contributes subtly to the growing sense of disenchantment. The magical spells always feel enchanting but this form of enchantment is restricted from the beginning and disappears completely by the time Bilbo returns to Bag End—except in the delayed notification about the Master's dragon sickness. There are actually very few examples of magical spells in *The Hobbit,* and they don't really accomplish very much. The dwarves' musical instruments and runes are magical, and we have Gandalf's smoke rings; his blast of fire, which kills the goblins trying to seize him in the Misty Mountains; his igniting pinecones to throw at the wargs; and the blast of light that he sends forth to alert the dwarves, Elves, and men that they have other enemies to fight rather than each other. But I imagine many readers, young and old, have longed for Gandalf to do more: "Don't just set pinecones on fire! Blast those wargs!" Perhaps the most powerful magic spell in the book is the one that ironically contributes to the mood of disenchantment: the dragon sickness that temporarily afflicts Thorin and leads to the death of the Master of Laketown.

The way that Tolkien limited the overt magic in *The Hobbit* is consistent with passages in other works where he showed that he valued enchantment but distrusted magic. In *The Lord of the Rings,* Galadriel expresses puzzlement at what the hobbits mean by "magic," since they seem to use it for the evil works of Sauron as well as for beautiful enchantments. In "On Fairy-Stories" Tolkien draws a distinction between magical spells that are basically a labor-saving technology that can readily be used for power and domination, and enchantment that strives for beauty and connection. As quoted in the introduction, "Enchantment . . . in its purity it is artistic in desire and purpose. Magic . . . is not an art but a technique; its desire is *power* in this world, domination of things and will."[18]

In contrast to how the spell of dragon sickness caused the Master of Lake-town to die in complete isolation, abandoned by his companions, Bilbo finds continuing enchantment in his connections with magical companions and is unaffected by magical spells. Not merely able to resist dragon sickness, Bilbo clearly values treasure far less than relationships. Thorin takes note of this in his deathbed speech praising Bilbo for valuing "food and cheer and song above hoarded gold."[19] As he takes leave from the Elvenking, Bilbo gives him a beautiful necklace and in return is named "elf-friend." When they recover the troll-hoard, Bilbo tries to give his share to Gandalf, and although he allows himself to be convinced to keep it, we learn in *The Fellowship of the Ring* that Bilbo gave most of it away, feeling that since it had been stolen it didn't really belong to him.

Bilbo's return journey, although described only briefly, is a period of relational healing after his disenchanting travails near the Lonely Mountain. With Gandalf as his companion, he has a "warm and merry" Yuletide with Beorn, and then many a dance and song with the Elves in Rivendell. Significantly, his second sojourn in Rivendell is described as a chance to "be cured of weariness," and in fact "Weariness fell from him soon in that house."[20] With these experiences Bilbo illustrates Tolkien's descriptions of enchantment as a connection to something Other, which I quoted in the introduction: "Fantasy, the making or glimpsing of Other-worlds, was the heart of the desire of Faërie"; and "'seeing things as we are (or were) meant to see them'—as things apart from ourselves."

Not only are these relationships with people from the enchanted world; the relationships themselves have an enchanted quality: Bilbo is in contact with characters who seem to exist particularly for him at the same time that they have an independent existence. Consider Gandalf, whose explanation for bringing Bilbo along doesn't quite hold water rationally: Bilbo really is more like a grocer than a burglar at the start, and it isn't really clear that a burglar would be much help anyway. But Gandalf likes sending "quiet lads and lasses . . . off into the Blue for mad adventures,"[21] and he correctly senses that if Bilbo participates in the enchanted world, he will do both that world and himself a lot of good. Similarly, Gandalf's absconding when the travelers reach Mirkwood doesn't really make sense within the plot of the expedition but is necessary for Bilbo's growth, and Gandalf's delay in revealing himself before Thorin's gate doesn't make sense within the plot except to emphasize that he is saving Bilbo from Thorin's wrath. Tolkien explains Gandalf's behavior in a somewhat more realistic, rational way in an appendix to *The Lord of the Rings* and more fully in "The Quest of Erebor": he selected Bilbo because of a "foresight" that he would be necessary to accomplish not only Thorin's quest but other unknown but more important things (meaning the finding of the Ring), and Gandalf only accompanied the dwarves as far as he did because Thorin insisted that if Bilbo were to be part of the company, Gandalf had to take care of him. But even this explanation includes the enchanted quality of foresight, and the very fact that Tolkien felt the need long after publishing *The Hobbit*[22] to thus rationalize Gandalf's behavior underlines the entwined, "magical" nature of Gandalf's relationship with Bilbo as depicted in *The Hobbit* itself.

The Elves of Rivendell also seem to have a magical connection to Bilbo. On the outward journey Bilbo and the dwarves are greeted with a song, including the lines "What brings Mister Baggins, / And Balin and Dwalin" And on the return journey Bilbo hears, after lines about the death of the dragon, "O! Whither so laden, / So sad and so dreary? / Here elf and elf-maiden / Now welcome the weary" Somehow the Elves know not only about his adventure but even about his internal state. This special insight creates a feeling of caring and connection between the Elves and Bilbo, as though they are there especially for him at the same time that they are quite independent of him.

In thus partaking of both an independent existence and a special connection to Bilbo, these characters manifest qualities of the transitional object, which I brought up in chapter 1. Winnicott described the transitional object as belonging to an "intermediate area of experience, unchallenged in respect of its belonging to inner or external (shared) reality,"[23] and stated, "It comes from without from our point of view, but not so from the point of view of the baby. Neither does it come from within."[24] In Tolkien's words, "the primal desire at the heart of Faerie [is] the realization, independent of the conceiving mind, of imagined wonder."[25]

The visit of Gandalf and Balin some years later demonstrates that Bilbo's relationships with enchanted characters are enduring. We see the three as old friends pleased to share each other's company again. And Gandalf assures

Bilbo that enchantments are bigger than he: "Surely you don't disbelieve the prophecies, because you had a hand in bringing them about yourself? You don't really suppose that all your adventures and escapes were managed by mere luck, just for your sole benefit?"[26]

So in *The Hobbit* we follow Bilbo Baggins on a path that proceeds from him recoiling from his initial meeting with enchantment, to accepting and engaging with enchantment, to disenchantment, and finally to lasting enchantment in the form of his relationships. The centrality of relationships in forming a mature sense of enchantment is subtly emphasized by contrasting Bilbo's fate with that of the Master of Laketown, who dies alone under an isolating spell.

As discussed in chapter 1, an enchanted worldview is more prominent among children than adults, and partial disenchantment of the world is a normal part of maturing. In depicting Bilbo valuing magical relationships rather than magical spells, Tolkien has provided a metaphor for important aspects of this dialogue between enchantment and loss during psychological development. In the move from childhood to adulthood, people gradually surrender, or at least greatly decrease, their investment in magical thinking and the omnipotence of thoughts—the sense that wishing or thinking something can make it come true like a magic spell. The path of relationships is more complex: a degree of disillusionment in parents and the home they provide is normal as children and teens become increasingly aware of the wider world, but unless very severe, this disillusionment leads not to the giving up of relationships but to seeking relationships with other people. These new relationships have the potential to provide mature enchantment, whether in the quieter forms of meaningful attachment or in the more vivid forms of romantic love, which are described as enchanting in many popular songs and stories.

The Hobbit, conceived as a children's book, is aimed for an age group that is immersed in this process of partial disenchantment. But we also know that *The Hobbit* is enjoyed by adults, and *The Lord of the Rings,* intended for adults, also addresses the theme of enchantment and disenchantment. This makes sense because people are never fully satisfied with the loss of magic as they grow up; in fact, the intermingling between magical thinking and realistic thinking deepens and enriches existence. Genuine maturity is not found in the use of rational thought alone, but in the capacity to shift between and combine rational thought and fantasy. Flexible sensitivity to mood and environmental context creates space for fantasy as well as rationality, and thus for the maintenance of wonder, without which life would become dull, empty, and meaningless, as Weber cautioned with his ideas about the disenchantment of the world.

What I have been focusing on in *The Hobbit* is a commentary on the place of enchantment and disenchantment in modern life. As discussed in chapter 1, Patrick Curry has argued that Tolkien's work is valuable in providing reenchantment for our modern disenchanted world, that it fundamentally provides "*the resacralization (or re-enchantment) of experienced and living nature, including human nature.*"[27] I think that this is true but does not go far enough; what we see in *The Hobbit* (as well as other works by Tolkien) is an exploration of the interplay between enchantment and disenchantment, which is part of modern psychological development.

CHAPTER 4

In Deep with *The Hobbit*

As I discussed in chapter 1, hobbits provide a comfortable entry into Middle-earth because readers can identify with hobbits as symbolic children or Englishmen amid all the strange, exalted, and terrible characters. But I think we can recognize deeper sources of their appeal by going deeper into the hobbit-hole and exploring its links to the holes that contain Gollum and Smaug.

The opening paragraph of *The Hobbit* presents us with oppositions that are crucial to the book as a whole: "In a hole in the ground there lived a hobbit. Not a nasty, dirty, wet hole, filled with the ends of worms and an oozy smell, nor yet a dry, bare, sandy hole with nothing in it to sit down on or to eat: it was a hobbit-hole, and that means comfort."[1] Right away Bilbo's hole has been contrasted with two perils that simultaneously are contrasted with each other: nasty, wormy ooze, and dry sand with nothing to sit on or to eat. By saying what the hobbit-hole is not, Tolkien draws our attention to what is repudiated: if not for good fortune, we would be in one of those other holes.

Let's consider the nasty hole first. For a child, nasty, wormy ooze is both disgusting and fascinating—we can imagine (or recollect) the pleasurably horrified "eewws" upon first encountering that image. Thus it is a fittingly childlike manifestation of the *abject*, which both disgusts and attracts.[2] As discussed in chapter 2, even though it is expelled from the self, the abject may be experienced as fascinating so that one is drawn to relate to it or even own and identify with it, in which case one becomes abject oneself and alienated from validating relationships.

In other words, one becomes Gollum. Gollum's existence as a dangerous abject version of hobbits is clearest in *The Lord of the Rings*, as I will discuss in more detail in chapter 10. But Gollum is already abject in *The Hobbit*, and not only in the later version after Tolkien rewrote "Riddles in the Dark" to make Gollum in *The Hobbit* more like the character in *The Lord of the Rings*. Even in the first edition we can recognize Gollum as both abject and hobbit-like, so that in his rewrite, Tolkien only needed to intensify features that were already there. Gollum's abjection was already apparent in his regressed language, his cannibalism, and his dwelling place on a slimy island. But he was similar to Bilbo, as Gandalf pointed out, in that he knew the Riddle-game and even many of the same riddles as Bilbo.

And they shared two other important similarities that Gandalf did not comment upon, although he surely was aware of them: they lived in holes, and they had unusual feet. Hobbits, of course, have hairy feet that are usually kept bare. Gollum's feet in the first edition are described thus: "He paddled [his boat] with large feet dangling over the side"; "he put his long, webby foot in the water"; "He flapped into the water and paddled to the bank"; and "they went along up the tunnel together, Gollum flip-flapping along."[3] And Gollum isn't the only creature who lives in holes and has such feet. Dwelling in the same Misty Mountains holes are the goblins, who, when singing, are "keeping time with the flap of their flat feet on the stone" and when the pursuing goblins get close, the dwarves "could hear even the flap of the goblin feet."[4] Only when they finally slip on soft shoes are the goblins able to sneak up on the dwarves unawares.

And consider also the Mewlips in their cellars (from *The Adventures of Tom Bombadil*):

> Their walls are wet, their ceilings drip;
> Their feet upon the floor
> Go softly with a squish-flap-flip,
> As they sidle to the door.

So bare feet are a shared feature of hole-dwellers, whether hobbit, Gollum, goblin, or Mewlip. Yet parallel to how hobbit-holes differ from other holes, hobbit feet differ from the feet of other hole-dwellers. Gollum, goblins, and Mewlips have feet that are reptilian or even amphibian in the way they flap and squish, and in the case of Gollum are even webby—these feet belong in nasty, oozy holes. Hobbits have mammalian feet, hairy and warm, that belong in comfy hobbit-holes. And in this way Tolkien has created hobbits as comfortable, cozy figures to identify with, while at the same time showing a link between them and the abject, a possibility of developing abjection.

Bilbo's distance from and yet linkage to the abject is also shown by his experience in the goblin tunnels. He wasn't as bad off as we would have been when he was lost there because even "if [hobbits'] holes are nice cheery places and properly aired, quite different from the tunnels of the goblins, still they are more used to tunneling than we are, and they do not easily lose their sense of direction underground."[5]

So far, I have been discussing nasty, oozy holes. What about the ends of worms? There is one wormy hole in *The Hobbit,* although the worm dwelling therein is the opposite of the small, soft, slimy thing conjured in the first paragraph: Smaug the Magnificent, Chiefest and Greatest of Calamities. And his hole is the opposite of nasty and oozy. As Bilbo first sees it, "stretching away across the unseen floors, lay countless piles of precious things, gold wrought and unwrought, gems and jewels, and silver red-stained in the ruddy light" and Smaug himself is "crusted with gems and fragments of gold."[6]

In creating a worm that is opposite to an abject worm, living in a hole that is opposite to an abject hole, Tolkien has done more than create a great story—he has illustrated a psychological truth: Idealized, glittering beauty can defend against awareness of or contact with the abject. Julia Kristeva states that "In the symptom, the abject permeates me, I become abject. Through sublimation, I keep it under control. The abject is edged with the sublime."[7] She describes the idealizing defense against abjection as a way to "purify" defilement, as "dazzlement" and "fascination."[8] Yet at the same time that glittering treasure defends against the abject by instantiating its opposite, it remains by that very fact linked to and representative of the abject. Kristeva refers to "experience which is rooted in the abject it utters and by the same token purifies."[9]

Freud was thinking along the same lines with his concept of defenses against anality,[10] perhaps particularly relevant here since a nasty, dirty hole can easily be considered an anal metaphor. The psychological importance of anality lies both in the social meaning of toilet training and in the developmental stage during which toilet training typically occurs. Prior to toilet training, babies and toddlers see no reason to control excretion or the body parts involved and often positively enjoy them, but society will not tolerate this attitude in older people. Toilet training is a process during which society's views, as represented by the parents, must replace the child's view. For the very first time, a child is required to define as disgusting or embarrassing a part of his or her body and its productions.

All this takes place approximately at the ages of two to three, when children are going through what has been called the "rapprochement phase."[11] This is when children have developed the motor skills to be able to effectively walk away from their parents, as well as the cognitive skills to recognize how small they are in the great world. It is common for children to feel conflict between exploring the exciting world and running back to their parents for protection from the overwhelming world. This means that the parents are demanding that children repudiate a part of themselves just when they are increasingly aware of how much they need their parents' strength and support. Although all this goes more or less smoothly in healthy development; it creates fertile ground for shame and abjection, and the need to repudiate disgusting things in order to maintain one's self-image as good.

To get back to Smaug's treasure, Freud understood gold, and money more generally, to serve unconsciously as signifiers of purified anality. Children, having been required during toilet training to devalue feces and change their pleasure into the opposite emotion of disgust, can preserve the feeling of pleasure by performing the reverse operation in their unconscious: idealizing feces by representing them as precious gold. But this series of reversals, from pleasurable to devalued to idealized, does not firmly hide the original meaning of feces, so at the same time that gold is experienced as an ideal opposite, it can still be experienced as linked to anality. This is manifested in terms such as *filthy lucre* and *filthy rich,* or in the portable toilet company that goes by the name "Pot o' Gold." Tolkien depicted the continuing existence of slimy abjection amid Smaug's treasure by the way he described Smaug's vulnerability: "there is a large patch in the hollow of his left breast as bare as *a snail out of its shell!*" and "the bare patch in *the old Worm's* diamond waistcoat."[12]

Tolkien also represented the continuing existence of the abject in its opposite in the very character of Smaug. As just mentioned, the magnificent Smaug is at the same time a worm. To emphasize this, the name "Smaug" is derived from the primitive Germanic word *smugan,* meaning to squeeze through a hole.[13] And in earlier drafts of *The Hobbit,* Tolkien named the dragon Pryftan, glossed by Mark Hooker as "Worm [pryf] of Fire [tan]."[14] The online Welsh dictionary *Geiriadur Prifysgol Cymru* gives additional meanings of *pryf* that further emphasize lowness: (1) insect, especially housefly; (2) larva of various insects, maggot, grub, earthworm; (3) maggot, earthworm that devours a body in the grave or in hell; (4) maggot or earthworm breeding in the body, causing illness; (5) reptile, serpent, snake, dragon. All of these definitions, especially that of the maggot devouring the body in the grave or in hell, point to the abject.[15]

Tolkien further showed the continuing existence of the abject in its opposite in his depiction of the trolls' lair, which combines elements of the nasty hole with elements of Smaug's treasure-filled hole. True, it contains pots full of gold, and Glamdring and Orcrist with their "beautiful scabbards and jeweled hilts," but these items were found amid "bones on the floor and a nasty smell was in the air" and Bilbo, the dwarves, and Gandalf finally leave when Fíli says, "'Let's get out of this horrible smell!'"[16] Even the gold itself was contaminated (filthy lucre): years later when the hobbits and Strider encounter the stone trolls, Frodo tells them, "'Bilbo gave [all the treasure] away. He told me he did not feel it was really his, as it came from robbers.'"[17]

Since the idealized defense remains intertwined with the abject that it purifies, it too threatens the integrity of the self. As Kristeva states,

> For the sublime has no object [by which she means human connection] either. When the starry sky, a vista of open seas or a stained glass window shedding purple beams fascinate me, there is a cluster of meaning, of colors, of words . . . that . . . shroud me, carry me away, and sweep me beyond the things that I see, hear, or think . . . transfers that object to the refulgent point of the dazzlement in which I stray in order to be . . . the sublime is a *something added* that expands us, overstrains us. . . . A divergence, an impossible bounding. Everything missed, joy—fascination.[18]

What Kristeva is getting at is the idea that when the self is immersed in the sublime, it loses grounding, definition, and mutual connection with other people, and that this in its own way can be as destructive as immersion in the abject. And just as Tolkien illustrates immersion in the abject in the figure of Gollum, he illustrates immersion in the sublime in Thorin Oakenshield's dragon sickness.[19] To begin with, Thorin and Company are "decent enough people,"[20] but at least for Thorin this changes after encountering Smaug's treasure. The sublimity of the treasure, and especially the Arkenstone, are described through Bilbo's perceptions. "Bilbo had heard tell and sing of dragon-hoards before, but the splendour, the lust, the glory of such treasure had never yet come home to him."[21] After Smaug flies for Laketown and Bilbo sees "the Arkenstone, the Heart of the Mountain . . . he caught his breath. The great jewel shown before his feet of its own inner light, and yet, cut and fashioned by the dwarves, who had dug it from the heart of the mountain long ago, it took all light that fell upon it and changed it into ten thousand sparks of white radiance shot with glints of the rainbow."[22]

Thorin succumbs to the allure of the treasure. Even the raven who brings news that Smaug has been slain advocates that the dwarves give up some of their gold to make peace with the Men of Laketown and the Elves, but Thorin's immediate angry response is that the treasure belongs only to the dwarves. This greedy possessiveness toward treasure to the exclusion of human decency escalates to the point that it would have initiated the Battle of the Three Armies if the goblins and wargs had not arrived just in time. Equally or more destructive is Thorin's desperate fascination with the missing Arkenstone, culminating, when he discovers that Bilbo has given the Arkenstone away, in Thorin banishing Bilbo and nearly casting him to his death, only to be saved by the intervention of Gandalf. Only his own death frees Thorin from fascination and greed so that he can see that one should value "food and cheer and song above hoarded gold."[23]

John Rateliff has pointed out the great difference between Thorin and Company and the evil dwarves that Tolkien had depicted in already existing versions of the Silmarillion—amusingly, Rateliff wrote that the switch from evil to sympathetic dwarves is no less amazing than having a band of wolf-riding goblins arrive at Bag End[24]—and this raises the question of how Tolkien came to make such a radical transformation. Whatever his conscious intention, the new version of dwarves sharpens the depiction of the dangers of idealization by linking the dwarves to "everyman" Bilbo. Dwarves like those in the Silmarillion would have refused companionable interaction with Bilbo and so would have obscured any points of contact with Bilbo's qualities, but several points of contact can be seen with dwarves as depicted in *The Hobbit:* They are linked by their companionship on the journey. They are linked by size—the initial description of hobbits includes that "They are (or were) a little people, about half our height, and smaller than the bearded dwarves."[25] That phrase also links them as remnants from the magical past. And of course dwarves are another people associated with holes, their mines as well as the hole commandeered by Smaug. Therefore, just as Bilbo is linked to the dangers of abjection in the figure of Gollum, he is linked to the dangers of idealization in the figure of Thorin. After all, Bilbo had his own moment approaching dragon sickness when he first glimpsed the treasure: "There are no words left to express his staggerment, since Men changed the language that they learned of elves in the days when all the world was wonderful. . . .

His heart was filled and pierced with enchantment and with the desire of dwarves; and he gazed motionless, almost forgetting the frightful guardian."[26] In his dazzlement he steals a cup and looses the dragon's wrath.

So far I have been exploring the relations between Bilbo's comfortable hole and nasty, oozy holes. Is there anything important to say about the dry, sandy hole? To reach the answer to this question we must travel by way of another opposition in *The Hobbit,* one that is very familiar and often commented upon: that between Bilbo's comfortable, static Baggins life and Tookish adventure.

After Tolkien describes the dull, respectable Bagginses, we read, "This is a story of how a Baggins had an adventure, and found himself doing and saying things altogether unexpected. He may have lost the neighbors' respect, but he gained—well, you will see whether he gained anything in the end."[27] And in the end we find out that he gained a lot. Treasure, of course, but that was the least important. He also gained cheerful insight into his place in the wide world, as we see when Gandalf says, "'You are a very fine person, Mr. Baggins, and I am very fond of you; but you are only quite a little fellow in a wide world after all!' 'Thank goodness!' said Bilbo laughing."[28] And he gained confidence in his curiosity and creativity: "He took to writing poetry and visiting the elves; and though many shook their heads and touched their foreheads and said 'Poor old Baggins!' and though few believed any of his tales, he remained very happy to the end of his days, and those were extraordinarily long."[29] This is a description that remains true enough even with the addition of *The Lord of the Rings.* So unlike abjection and idealization with their dangers of destroying the self, adventure deepened and strengthened Bilbo's self.

But how can adventure have this positive effect when I have been pointing out that Bilbo's adventures were filled with nasty, abject holes? To make this question even more acute, we can look at the distribution of the word *nasty* in *The Hobbit. Nasty* is regularly used in connection with adventures: four times in "Roast Mutton"; Bilbo's dream about the goblins just before goblins actually jump out is nasty; *nasty* is used seven times in "Riddles in the Dark"; three times in "Flies and Spiders"; and eleven times from Laketown through the Battle of the Five Armies. Most importantly, adventures thrice are directly called nasty—Bilbo says, "'We are plain quiet folk and have no use for adventures. Nasty disturbing uncomfortable things!'"; on the return journey, Bilbo and Gandalf reach the spot where "they had turned aside for their nasty adventure with Tom and Bert and Bill"; and Gandalf describes his exploration of the Necromancer's dungeons—an adventure for sure—as "a nasty dangerous business."[30] It appears that adventures are closely akin to the abject. Then how can adventures lead to strengthening of the self?

One answer, of course, is that Bilbo survives his encounters and thus shows that he is stronger than abjection. But I think something deeper is going on here, something that we see more clearly in *The Lord of the Rings,* where Bilbo longs for more adventure and where much is made of his authorship of the Red Book, but which is hinted at in *The Hobbit* with the statement that "some years afterwards Bilbo was sitting in his study writing his memoirs—he thought of calling them 'There and Back Again, a Hobbit's Holiday.'"[31] With his writing, Bilbo was keeping his adventures with the abject alive in his mind. This suggests that abjection is not only something to be defeated but something to be kept in touch with.

But this leads to a further complication because *The Hobbit* also shows us that it matters *how* one stays in touch with the abject. In Bilbo's first version of his memoirs, he lied about how he obtained the Ring, claiming that it was a gift from Gollum. "[Gandalf] thought it important, and disturbing, to find that the good hobbit had not told the truth from the first: quite contrary to his habit";[32] this was a portent of incipient abjection, a first step toward becoming like Gollum, under the power of the Ring. So preliminarily we can say that maintaining *honest* contact with the abject is important.

Aspects of the *form* of *The Hobbit* indicate an additional way to maintain adaptive contact with the abject. Verlyn Flieger has identified a formal similarity, and perhaps a partial derivation, of "adventure" in *The Hobbit* with the French *aventure.*[33] She links *aventure* to French medieval romances in which knights went out and had adventures consisting of a series of disconnected events, simply because that is what knights do. In *The Hobbit,* similarly, prior to the change to a more serious tone that sets in at Laketown, Bilbo has a series of disconnected adventures: trolls, goblins, Gollum, wargs, eagles, Beorn, spiders, and Elves happen one after another without in any essential way leading into one another. The intention of the companions is to wrest the treasure from Smaug, and none of the adventures they have along the way have any direct effect on this, except in the simple sense that if they were killed by, say, trolls, they would not reach the treasure. If the Gollum episode were removed, and Bilbo went straight from goblins to wargs and eagles, nothing would be lost in terms of continuity. True, Bilbo gets the magic ring, which he uses in his later adventures, from Gollum, but there is nothing essential in this—he could have found it in the goblin tunnels, say, or at the edge of

Mirkwood, with no other essential change in *The Hobbit*. The distinction I am making becomes clearer if we compare this to the impact of the Gollum episode in the context of *The Lord of the Rings*, where the ring has become the Ring, and the Gollum episode has changed from an *aventure* to an essential element that begins to establish our understanding of Gollum's abject character and the power of the Ring.

Of course, something would be lost if "Riddles in the Dark" were removed: an enormously entertaining episode. And this gets us to something about the basic nature of *aventures:* they are playful. Play can be defined as *activity* that is *pleasurable*, relatively *unconstrained by reality*, and *noninstrumental* (it does not have a goal other than its own process),[34] and Bilbo's *aventures* partake of all these qualities.

Let's take a closer look at the *aventure* of Beorn, which in its idiosyncracy manifests the playfulness of *The Hobbit* especially strongly. The Beorn episode could have been removed without even the complication of having to explain the discovery of the ring in some other way. True, the companions receive provisions from Beorn, and ponies to ride to the Forest Path, but Tolkien could have had the eagles fly them directly to the Forest Path, and placed friendly farmers nearby to provide provisions. Or they could have gone from the Carrock to a completely different helpful personage, maybe one of Gandalf's "more or less decent giant[s]."[35] Why a were-bear? And especially, what is going on with the bipedal dogs, and livestock who understand human speech?

Like the Gollum episode, removal of the Beorn episode would have deprived us of an enormously entertaining event. But here we can add that the Beorn episode had the special importance of playfully pleasing Tolkien's children, and playfully pleasing the child in Tolkien. Tolkien's children loved bears. They had stuffed bears—Priscilla had so many that she took on holiday that someone once asked her father if he was a traveling salesman in teddy bears[36]—and they wanted bears in their stories, at least partly accounting for not only Beorn but the North Polar Bear in the *Letters to Father Christmas*, and the troublesome bears in "Mr. Bliss." (It is probable that Tolkien, with his interest in Beowulf, also had a liking for bears.[37]) And in "On Fairy-Stories," Tolkien referred to the wish to communicate with animals as one of the fundamental desires of childhood. Thus we get not only Beorn's quasi-human beasts, but the thrush and ravens of the Lonely Mountain, and perhaps even the fox who observes the camping hobbits early in *The Lord of the Rings*—he doesn't speak, but clearly has a verbally accessible mind. And Beorn himself, a man who is also a bear, can be thought of as an animal who speaks.

Beorn and his animals are so idiosyncratic that he is hard to account for, either by characters within the story or by Tolkien and readers. Bilbo and the dwarves have no knowledge of him, and upon querying Gandalf, learn only that "Some say that he is a bear descended from the great and ancient bears of the mountains that lived there before the giants came. Others say that he is a man descended from the first men who lived before Smaug . . . I cannot say, though I fancy the last is the true tale."[38] Unlike the ring, which Tolkien found a way to seamlessly and essentially work into *The Lord of the Rings,* he did not find any way to incorporate the were-bear and his animals. True, we hear of Beorn's grandson Grimbeorn and other Beornings, but even though at the end of *The Hobbit* we learn that many generations of Beorn's descendants could turn into bears, there is no suggestion of this in *The Lord of the Rings;* in Glóin and Gimli's words, they are merely "valiant men" and "the best bakers that I know of."[39] It was honey-cakes that Gimli praised, and in this there is a hint of the ursine, but that is all. And the bipedal dogs and the livestock that understand human speech simply disappear from later writings.

Idiosyncracy so extreme that the character is hard to account for either by other characters or by Tolkien and readers is also found in *The Lord of the Rings*'s Tom Bombadil. When queried who Tom is, Goldberry gives the wonderfully accurate and imprecise response, "He is." Since Bombadil does not fit into any of the clearly defined races in Tolkien's oeuvre, readers have struggled to fit him in anyway, perhaps as a Maia.[40] These efforts are unconvincing. Bombadil does not fit because Tolkien did not want him to fit, stating that Bombadil might be thought of as "the spirit of the (vanishing) Oxford and Berkshire countryside," and also that "even in a mythical Age there must be some enigmas, as there always are. Tom Bombadil is one (intentionally)."[41] Some people consider the Bombadil episode to be an *aventure* that could easily be discarded, as Peter Jackson did in his film adaptation. In fact, Tom is extremely important in providing a counterpart to Sauron and the Ring (see chapter 10), but there is a sense in which his importance is consistent with Tom being an *aventure* because paradoxically, his purpose is that he has no purpose—as Goldberry says, "He is."

Of course, Bombadil does not exist in *The Hobbit,* but he is relevant to my argument because like Beorn, Bombadil originated in the play of Tolkien's children: his first incarnation was as a Dutch doll. Beorn and Bombadil, who were birthed in childlike play, epitomize the *aventure* qualities of being *pleasurable,* relatively *unconstrained by reality,* and *noninstrumental.*

We can see the link to childhood again in Tolkien's artworks *Undertenishness* and *Grownupishness.* Done at the same time on similar paper, they seem to be companion pieces that comment on each other. In Hammond and Scull's description,

> *Undertenishness* . . . is attractive . . . because it is abundantly coloured like a flower garden in summer. . . . The lines at centre are like a directional arrow, pointing the viewer's way along the central path. One is invited into the landscape, to walk between the trees and up the hill to see what lies beyond. But stand back and look carefully at the painting, and it dawns that Tolkien has played a visual trick. The "forest" is also a butterfly, the "trees" in the distance its "antennae" and "eyes."[42]

Grownupishness, on the other hand, is in black and white, and it is a "strange amalgam of an elongated, tonsured head with blank eyes, shoes, circles, squares, exclamation and question marks, and two long-fingered hands, above the inscriptions 'Sightless : Blind : Well-Wrapped-Up.'"[43]

Of course, interpretations of art are inevitably subjective, but it is hard not to see this pair of paintings as associating a joyful mood with childhood, and a grim and dark mood with adulthood. Not only is the one colorful and the other lacking color, but *Grownupishness* includes the words "sightless, blind," making it a condition of being impervious to any color that might be present. *Undertenishness* is expansive and playful, with the path into the distance and the visual transformation between trees and butterfly, whereas *Grownupishness* is constricted, with the central figure imprisoned by the geometric figures and punctuation marks. We should not take these contrasts as providing an accurate picture of Tolkien's overall view of his life; we know that he described his childhood as "sad and troublous,"[44] as well as including much joy, and that his adulthood included good moods as well as depressions. Rather, they appear to depict a contrast of moods that was vivid for him when he painted them in 1913 when he was twenty-one. On the cusp of adulthood, it appears that Tolkien was worried that expansive play could be constrained by aspects of adulthood.

Color is a primary signifier of expansive play in *Undertenishness,* and color is also an important signifier in *The Hobbit.* After the first paragraph description of the hobbit-hole that I quoted above, the second paragraph begins "It had a perfectly round door like a porthole, painted green, with a shiny yellow brass knob in the exact middle."[45] A little later Bilbo is upset when there comes "a hard rat-tat on the hobbit's beautiful green door," and a little later again he incorrectly denies that there are any signs on his door " . . . it was painted a week ago."[46] Hobbits themselves "dress in bright colours (chiefly green and yellow) . . . their feet grow . . . thick warm brown hair like the stuff on their heads . . . [and] have long clever brown fingers."[47] Bilbo's first recall of Gandalf is of his fireworks, which "used to go up like great lilies and snapdragons and laburnums of fire." This signifier is also central to the first arrival of the dwarves, where we learn the colors of their hoods, belts, and tassels, and the importance of their colors is emphasized when in Laketown the bedraggled dwarves are "fitted out in fine cloth of their proper colours."[48]

All these colors were important at least to Christopher Tolkien as a four- or five-year-old, as he reports his father's memory "that on one occasion I interrupted: 'Last time, *you said* Bilbo's front door was blue, and *you said* Thorin had a golden tassel on his hood, but you've just said that Bilbo's front door was green, and the tassel on Thorin's hood was silver'; at which point my father muttered 'Damn the boy,' and then 'strode across the room' to his desk to make a note."[49]

Tom Bombadil is famously colorful, with his bright blue jacket and his yellow boots. Similarly, upon first approaching Beorn's house, "they noticed that great patches of flowers had begun to spring up, all the same kinds growing together as if they had been planted. Especially there was clover, waving patches of cockscomb clover, and purple clover, and wide stretches of short white sweet honey-smelling clover"; and on the return journey Bilbo leaves Beorn's house "with regret, for the flowers of the gardens of Beorn were in springtime no less marvelous than in high summer."[50]

If my understanding of color as a signifier of playful expansiveness is correct, then all these colors support reading *The Hobbit* as a series of playful encounters with the very serious subject of abjection. Earlier I mentioned the importance of facing abjection honestly in order to deepen the self; now I add the importance of facing abjection playfully.

At last I am ready to get back to the dry, sandy hole, which the first paragraph presents as a second danger alongside the nasty, oozy hole. Although Bilbo's adventures take him to a few nasty holes (the troll cave, the goblin tunnels, and Gollum's lair) and one idealized nasty hole (Smaug's lair), he encounters no dry sandy holes. And although the word *nasty* is used numerous times to describe adventures or in the context of adventures, neither "dry" nor "sandy" is applied to adventures. *Sandy* does not occur at all in the text after its appearance in the first paragraph. *Dry* is used thirteen times after its original appearance, and eleven of those uses describe comfort that is lost, longed for, or found. For example, after Thorin sends Fíli and Kíli ahead to find a safe spot during the mountain thunderstorm, they return and report,

"'We have found a dry cave,' . . . it had a dry floor . . . Óin and Glóin wanted to light a fire at the door to dry their clothes . . . they spread out their wet things on the floor, and got dry ones out of their bundles."[51] (The uses of *dry* that do not seem to imply comfort are a "dry little watercourse" that Bilbo encounters in Mirkwood, and the "wall of squared stones laid dry" that the dwarves build at the entrance to the Lonely Mountain.[52])

So just as a dry, sandy hole is the opposite of a nasty, oozy hole, dryness appears to be the opposite of adventure. Dryness is an aspect of comfort, something to appeal to Bilbo's Baggins side, not his Took side. But it is very important to note that the comfort signified by dryness can be false. After all, the dry hole in which the company shelters in the Misty Mountains turns out to be an opening into the goblin tunnels and Gollum's lair. It is as though the dry comfort is built on top of, and hides, abject horror. And this points us to an understanding of the danger represented by the dry, sandy hole: the dry, sandy hole signifies an attempt to deny the existence of the abjection represented by the nasty, oozy hole. Abjection threatens to overthrow and destroy the self. Defending against abjection by purifying and idealizing it threatens another kind of diminishment of the self. But completely turning away from abjection creates an impoverished, dry, sandy life of Grownupishness.

The dynamic between beauty, abjection, and empty, dry refusal to engage with abjection plays out during an interchange in the Riddle-game.[53] Bilbo asks:

> An eye in a blue face
> Saw an eye in a green face.
> "That eye is like to this eye"
> Said the first eye,
> "But in low place,
> Not in high place"

After a mental struggle, Gollum correctly answers "'Sun on the daisies it means, it does.' But these ordinary aboveground everyday sort of riddles were tiring for him. Also they reminded him of days when he had been less lonely and sneaky and nasty, and that put him out of temper. What is more they made him hungry; so this time he tried something a bit more difficult and more unpleasant." In this description we see Gollum being wearied by the thought of sun on daisies with all their colors, and especially being upset because this image reminds him of when he was less abject. Perhaps it is not only the image of colorful nature in the riddle but also the contrast between "low" and "high" that sharpens his pain at his abjection. Gollum responds with:

> It cannot be seen, cannot be felt,
> Cannot be heard, cannot be smelt.
> It lies behind stars and under hills,
> And empty holes it fills.
> It comes first and follows after,
> Ends life, kills laughter.

Bilbo easily comes up with the answer "dark" because darkness is all around him, but the empty hole at the center of the riddle is not really like Gollum's hole. It lacks all sensation; it does not even contain food, whether hobbit or fish, to assuage Gollum's hunger. Although it even lacks sand, in the feeling it evokes it is the apotheosis of the "dry, bare, sandy hole with nothing in it to sit down on or to eat." In presenting this riddle, Gollum tried to quash both the colorful joy depicted by Bilbo's riddle and his awareness of his own abjection that Bilbo's riddle had intensified.

I will close this chapter with Tolkien in his moment of inspiration when the first line of *The Hobbit* came to him. Here are two of his descriptions of that moment. The first comes from a 1967 interview for the *Daily Telegraph Magazine:* "It all began when I was reading exam papers to earn a bit of extra money. That was agony. One of the tragedies of the underpaid professor is that he has to do menial jobs. He is expected to maintain a certain position and to send his children to good schools. Well, one day I came to a blank page in an exam book and I scribbled on it. 'In a hole in the ground there lived a hobbit.'"[54]

The second description comes from the 1968 *Tolkien in Oxford* BBC television program: "I had an enormous pile of exam papers there. Marking school examinations in the summertime is very laborious and unfortunately also *boring*. And I remember picking up a paper and actually finding—I nearly gave an extra mark for it; an extra five marks, actually—there was one page of this particular paper that was left blank. Glorious! Nothing to read. So I scribbled on it, I can't think why, In a hole in the ground there lived a hobbit."[55]

Tolkien cannot think why that sentence came to him, but we can. In a moment when he was almost overwhelmed by bleak grownupishness, in a moment when he was feeling controlled and diminished by the need for filthy lucre, he played with the sources of those pains by going on an adventure.

CHAPTER 5

Mother Music

Although mothers and children play relatively minor direct roles in Tolkien's legendarium, I will explore in this chapter the idea that certain of Tolkien's songs and music that were especially important to him depict maternal relationship themes indirectly, and that these themes play a significant part in establishing the mood of loss and longing and the threat to enchantment in his works, which I have described in previous chapters. I will further suggest that recognition of these themes may contribute to understanding the mixture of idealization and devaluation found in Tolkien's female characters, as well as what appears to have been an idealized view that he held of his mother. It appears that Tolkien lived the dialogue between enchantment and loss in his relationship with his mother.

I will be interrogating particular interpersonal relationships expressed in the songs and music, rather than particular individuals who perform the songs or are sung about. By focusing on relationships rather than individuals, we can recognize forms of interacting that have characteristics of the mother-child relationship even if Tolkien depicts the particular musical exchange as taking place between male characters.[1] Of course not all relationships enacted in Tolkien's songs are maternal in nature, but maternal relationship themes appear to have been especially important to Tolkien because he used them especially prominently and/or repeatedly in his work. I will focus on two such themes: songs that demonstrate interpersonal disruption and repair; and songs that enchant the individual self into oblivion or awareness.

The importance to Tolkien of the theme of interpersonal disruption and repair is apparent in its providing a central dynamic in "The Music of the Ainur." As a depiction of the creation of the world, "The Music of the Ainur" is a foundational myth that underlies all of Tolkien's legendarium. Jonathon McIntosh makes the case that Tolkien expressed fundamental aspects of his worldview in this work.[2]

To create Arda, Ilúvatar reveals to the Ainur a great musical theme and requests that they join him in elaborating it with their own voices. Magnificent angelic music ensues until Melkor, envious of Ilúvatar's power, introduces a discordant theme. Ilúvatar responds by lifting his left hand and creating a second theme more powerful than the first, which integrates Melkor's contribution. Melkor then creates even uglier discord, and Ilúvatar responds by lifting his right hand and creating a third theme, soft, sweet, powerful, and profound. This theme and Melkor's loud, vain, repetitive theme seem to war with each other, and Melkor's tries to drown out Ilúvatar's music, but Ilúvatar's music weaves in even the most triumphant of Melkor's notes. Then Ilúvatar raises both hands, his face terrible to behold, and a final, utterly powerful chord ends the music. Ilúvatar then states that he himself is the uttermost source even of Melkor, and Melkor's efforts to alter the music from what was in the mind of Ilúvatar will only make it more beautiful. A specific example of this is that Melkor's bitter cold makes water more beautiful by creating ice and frost.

The relational theme in this story is one of striving to establish and maintain a sense of mutuality through cycles of disruption and repair. Ilúvatar does not want to create Arda by himself but with the free assistance of the Ainur. This shows a longing for mutuality wherein each being participates in a joint activity according to his or her own power, interest, and ability. Melkor consistently responds by trying to disrupt mutuality and aggrandize his individual self. Each time he does this, Ilúvatar attempts to reestablish mutuality by integrating Melkor's contributions into the larger theme.

This kind of interaction is prominent in human relationships throughout the life span; for example, when couples or friends who are generally in a mutually respectful and affectionate relationship find themselves at odds with one another and then try to find a way to see each other's point of view and heal the disruption. It is especially important in intensely meaningful relationships, such as those between parents and children, between lovers, and during psychotherapy.

This interaction pattern has its roots in the relationship between infant and mother, and the way it plays out in this relationship is crucial in the development of the self.[3] Emotional bonding is part of the inborn biological apparatus of humans: babies at birth preferentially pay attention to human faces; they show "reflex smiles" from birth that do not appear to be reactive to other people but which attract affection from caretakers; and they begin "social smiling" in response to the smiles of others in their second month. Mutual smiling, babbling and baby-talk conversations, and physical touch/holding are the roots of loving mutuality.

Disruption and repair of this mutuality also begin at birth. To clarify what is meant by this phenomenon, consider dramatic instances of disruption and repair seen in experiments wherein a mother gazes at her infant but stops smiling and presents a "still face."[4] The infant will briefly increase her smiling to try to elicit a response, will then protest, and eventually will give up and show a still face herself. When the mother resumes smiling, the baby will feel that the disruption has been repaired and smile back. A more familiar example occurs when the mother leaves the baby's or toddler's sight, the child stops whatever activity he or she is engaged in and begins to cry, the mother returns, and the child smiles and resumes his or her activity.

Disruption between mother and child is inevitable since no parent can be perfectly attentive. In fact, mild amounts of disruption followed by effective repair are optimal for development, facilitating the child's gradual development of self-reliance and of the understanding that relationships can continue and be trusted even during the temporary absence of the other person.[5] Repeated experiences of too-strong disruption and/or disruption without repair, on the other hand, have destructive developmental effects, including difficulty forming attachments, low self-esteem, insecurity, and basic mistrust of the world. In the extreme, babies who are never engaged with in a personal affectionate manner will show failure to thrive and perhaps die, even if they have been offered adequate food and shelter.[6]

Experiences of disruption depend not only on the behavior of the mother but also on the child's inborn temperament. Some children exhibit more intense or longer lasting distress at relatively mild maternal misattunements, whereas other children are more robust and exhibit relatively little distress in the same situations.

In the light of this we can see that in "The Music of the Ainur," Tolkien has simultaneously depicted successful and unsuccessful repairs of the disruption of mutuality. If we consider the metaphoric "child" to be the music as a whole, then Melkor's disruptions are successfully repaired in such a way that the music becomes more profound by integrating the disruption—this parallels healthy child development in which the child becomes more mature as a consequence of living through and integrating experiences of disruption. But if we consider the "child" to be Melkor, the repair was a gross failure. Even before the Music began, something went wrong that highlights Melkor's relational isolation: he traveled in the Void searching fruitlessly for the Fire, and "being alone he had begun to conceive thoughts of his own unlike those of his brethren."[7] Once the Music starts, Melkor's envy and hatred simply grow worse each time Ilúvatar responds to his disruptions, and never abate until he is finally cast out of Arda entirely; this parallels disastrous child development in which the child is never able to establish any relationship with any degree of mutuality.

In three additional scenes that resemble each other closely, Tolkien depicted repair occurring through music after disruption so severe that repair seemed impossible. These are the scenes in which two characters who love each other have been separated, and after great travail find each other again only after one starts to sing and the other responds by singing back. Tolkien's use of this trope three times demonstrates its importance to him.

One occurrence is the scene wherein Fingon determines to free Maedhros whom Morgoth has chained to an unclimbable cliff of Thangorodrim. Fingon seeks Maedhros through great danger, but finally is defeated by the crags: "Then in defiance of the Orcs, who cowered still in the dark vaults beneath the earth, he took his harp and sang a song of Valinor that the Noldor made of old, before strife was born among the sons of Finwë; and his voice rang in the mournful hollows that had never heard before aught save cries of fear and woe. Thus Fingon found what he sought. For suddenly above him far and faint his song was taken up, and a voice answering called to him. Maedhros it was that sang amid his torment."[8] Thorondor, king of eagles, then carries Fingon to Maedhros whom he frees from his shackle by slicing off his hand.

The poignancy of the repair of their relationship is emphasized by Tolkien representing the disruption between the two as resulting not only from evil external forces separating them, but also from emotional conflict on both a personal and political level. Fingon had great love for Maedhros, but he did not know that Maedhros still loved him after the confusion of the kinslaying—Fingon and his people had been left without passage over the sea after Fëanor burned the ships, and he did not know that Maedhros had opposed the burning. Politically, he undertook to save Maedhros in order to heal the rift between the houses of Fëanor and Fingolfin. And in this he was successful: Maedhros forswore the kingship and said that since the death of his father Fëanor, the kingship rightly belonged to Fingon's father (Maedhros's uncle) Fingolfin as the eldest heir.

Tolkien also used this musical trope in *The Lord of the Rings*. As Sam seeks Frodo in the Tower of Cirith Ungol, the hidden trapdoor at the top thwarts him. He despairs of locating Frodo. "And then softly, to his own surprise, there at the vain end of his long journey and his grief, moved by what thought in his heart he could not tell, Sam began to sing. . . . He murmured old childish tunes out of the Shire, and snatches of Mr. Bilbo's rhymes. . . . And then suddenly new strength rose in him, and his voice rang out, while words of his own came unbidden to fit the simple tune."[9] The lyrics are hopeful, and Frodo faintly responds, attracting an orc who inadvertently shows Sam the way. As with Fingon and Maedhros, the preceding disruption is especially poignant because it is represented not only by the separation imposed by evil external forces, but also by emotional conflict: Sam feels that he has failed Frodo by mistaking him for dead after Shelob stung him, and Sam has taken the Ring, creating an inevitable rift even though it does not become manifest until Frodo realizes Sam has the Ring.

The other example comes from the tale of Beren and Lúthien. The two lovers are separated by multiple external forces: Thingol forbidding their love unless Beren can recover a Silmaril, Thingol imprisoning Lúthien in a tree house to enforce his ban, Celegorm and Curufin capturing Lúthien in turn after her escape, and Thû intercepting Beren on his quest and imprisoning him in a hopeless dungeon. Eventually Lúthien with Huan's help is freed and brought to Thû's castle, where she begins to sing; Beren thinks he is dreaming but sings back, and so the lovers recover each other. This version is less psychologically developed than the other two in that it does not involve internal emotional disruption, but it still contributes to our recognizing the importance of disruption and repair to Tolkien.

In the meeting of Melian and Elwë (Thingol), and then repeatedly in the story of Lúthien and Beren, Tolkien depicts a woman singing so wondrously that listeners are enchanted to the point that they lose their sense of self and individuality, or recover it again after having first lost it. This theme is worth highlighting both because of its frequency and because Tolkien considered the story of Lúthien and Beren to be at the center of his legendarium.

As he leads his people the Teleri to Valinor, Elwë goes by himself to seek his friend Finwë:

> Suddenly he heard the song of nightingales. Then an enchantment fell on him, and he stood still; and afar off . . . he heard the voice of Melian, and it filled all his heart with wonder and desire. He forgot then utterly all his people and all the purposes of his mind, and . . . he . . . was lost. But he came

> at last to a glade open to the stars, and there Melian stood. . . . She spoke no word; but being filled with love Elwë came to her and took her hand, and straightway a spell was laid on him, so that they stood thus while long years were measured by the wheeling stars above them; and the trees . . . grew tall and dark before they spoke any word.[10]

Notice the emphasis on wordlessness in the description of their enchantment, suggesting kinship with early preverbal experience before learning language.

Lúthien's song plays an opposite role in her meeting with Beren. After her dancing has lulled him into a state of dumbness with "a chain . . . upon his limbs," her song finally returns speech to him, as well as awakening the world to springtime life: "suddenly she began to sing. Keen, heart-piercing was her song as the song of the lark that rises from the gates of night and pours its voice among the dying stars, seeing the sun behind the walls of the world; and the song of Lúthien released the bonds of winter, and the frozen waters spoke, and flowers sprang from the cold earth where her feet had passed. Then the spell of silence fell from Beren."[11] Here language loss and gain are also emphasized to show Beren shifting from less to more mature self-states.

But like Melian, Lúthien does use her power to sing people into oblivion. In the early "Tale of Tinúviel,"[12] with details not described in the *Silmarillion* version, Lúthien escapes from her tree prison first by weaving a cloak, which she imbues with powers of sleep and darkness in part by singing, then sings to sleep the guards beneath her tree, and then puts other guards to sleep by brushing them with the cloak. More crucially, she overcomes Morgoth by singing "a song of such surpassing loveliness, and of such blinding power, that he listened perforce; and a blindness came upon him. . . . All his court were cast down in slumber, and all the fires faded and were quenched; . . . her voice came dropping down like rain into pools, profound and dark . . . and set upon him a dream, dark as the Outer Void where once he walked alone. Suddenly he fell. . . . The iron crown rolled echoing from his head. All things were still."[13]

Lúthien's song to Mandos has its effect at a more verbally, conceptually communicative level; semantics are emphasized by the double use of *words* in the passage describing this song: "the song most fair that ever in *words* was woven, and the song most sorrowful that ever the world shall hear . . . Lúthien wove two themes of *words,* of the sorrow of the Eldar and the grief of Men . . . and Mandos was moved to pity."[14] Rather than being lulled into unconsciousness, Mandos shows a less profound but still important change of consciousness in his deep emotional response. Yet even here the ultimate effect of her song was more profound changes in states of consciousness: First Beren was returned to life, and later Lúthien had to join him in death.

In sum, Melian sings Elwë into a state of wordless, timeless, selfless bliss, in which all responsibility is forgotten. Lúthien sings her guards to sleep, and sings Morgoth into a dark unconscious dream in which he is unable to exert his will to protect his stolen Silmarils. She sings Beren out of a state of wordless agony and returns him to his usual effectively functioning adult self, and later she sings him out of death and again returns him to his usual effective self, until finally Lúthien and Beren enter death together.

Although there are differences among these changes, they are all profound alterations in the state of consciousness in one or the other opposite direction: either into a state of preverbal/nonverbal/oblivion/merger, or out of such a state into alert/verbal/individual consciousness. The shifts of consciousness in these stories resemble shifts in consciousness that mothers can induce in their babies and toddlers. This is most obvious in the songs Lúthien sings to her guards, to Morgoth, and to Beren: basically, she lullabies the guards and Morgoth to sleep, and she awakens Beren from sleep. The sleep of the guards and Morgoth is literally depicted; Beren's sleep and awakening is metaphorically represented by his speechlessness and "chained limbs" followed by his return to language and activity, and by the parallel wintry slumber of the world followed by its springtime awakening. Beren's return from death, and Lúthien's acceptance of death, may also represent awakening and sleep.

The importance to Tolkien of song that regulates sleep is shown yet again in his use of a similar trope for the first encounter of the Eldar with men. Finrod hears strange singing and follows it and beholds that the singers are men. He waits until they fall asleep, and then "He went among the sleeping people, and sat beside their dying fire where none kept watch; and he took up a rude harp which Bëor had laid aside, and he played music upon it such as the ears of Men had not heard. . . . Now men awoke and listened to Felagund as he harped and sang, and each thought that he was in some fair dream, until he saw that his fellows were awake also beside him."[15]

The effect of Melian's song on Elwë is somewhat different. He does not go to sleep but loses his individuality in a state of blissful merger with Melian. This is reminiscent of mystical experience or oceanic experience, which Freud understood as being a reexperiencing of a state similar to the infant's state of merger with the mother.[16] Although infants have brief periods of alert wakefulness in which they appear to experience themselves as separate from the world around them, much of their time is spent in less alert states of consciousness in which they appear to feel as though they are unbounded from the rest of the world and not separate from the mother.[17] It is this state that is gradually left behind when it is optimally disrupted by awareness of separation.

But to more fully understand the maternal relationships expressed in these songs, we must consider another of their aspects: in all of them joy is imbued with loss and sorrow. Although joined in bliss with Melian, Elwë temporarily loses his self and permanently loses his quest for Valinor. Sorrow is interwoven with triumph throughout the tale of Lúthien and Beren; as Aragorn says, "it is sad, as are all the tales of Middle-earth, and yet it may lift up your hearts."[18]

Middle-earth is bounded by the sea, and for Tolkien the sea itself sings a song of allurement and sorrow. "In the deep places [Ulmo, Vala of the sea] gives thought to music great and terrible; and the echo of that music runs through all the veins of the world in sorrow and in joy; for if joyful is the fountain that rises in the sun, its springs are in the wells of sorrow unfathomed at the foundations of the Earth. The Teleri [called the Shoreland Pipers—another musical reference—in their earlier incarnation as the Solosimpi] learned much of Ulmo, and for this reason their music has both sadness and enchantment."[19] The sea's music creates a permanent state of unrequited longing; for example, when Tuor came upon the Great Sea, "he was enamoured of it, and the sound of it and the longing for it were ever in his heart and ear, and an unquiet was on him."[20] Or as Galadriel says,

> "Legolas Greenleaf, long under tree
> In joy thou hast lived. Beware of the sea!
> If thou hearest the cry of the gull on the shore,
> Thy heart shall then rest in the forest no more."[21]

The theme of music that lulls the listener into a longed-for loss of self and merger that is simultaneously painfully out of reach was already in Tolkien's mind at the origins of his legendarium. The following excerpt is from a 1927 revision of "Over Old Hills and Far Away," a poem that Tolkien originally wrote in late 1915 or early 1916:

> . . . something alluring, aloof and queer,
> Like perfume of flowers from the shores of the mere
> . . . or was it a sound?

I listened and marveled with eyes on the ground.
For there came from afar a filtered note
Enchanting sweet, now clear, now remote,
As clear as a star by the reeds,
As faint as the glimmer of dew on the weeds.
. . .
He is gone, and the valley is empty and bare
Where lonely I stand and lonely I stare.
Then suddenly out in the meadows beyond,
Then back in the reeds by the shimmering pond,
Then afar from a copse where the mosses are thick
A few little notes come trilliping quick.

I leapt o'er the stream and I sped from the glade,
For Tinfang Warble it was that played;
I must follow the hoot of his twilight flute
Over reed, over rush, under branch, over root,
And over dim fields, and through rustling grasses
That murmur and nod as the old elf passes,
Over old hills and far away
Where the harps of the Elvenfolk softly play.[22]

After Eriol hears Tinfang Warble's piping, Vairë tells him that "'such is the eeriness of that sprite, you will ever love the evenings of summer and the nights of stars, and their magic will cause your heart to ache unquenchably,'" and she adds that at times, "'Tinfang Warble has gone *heartbreaking* in the Great Lands.'"[23] Tinfang Warble's is a siren song, one that does not lead to physical death but to the death of simple joy; after hearing his flute, the connection that is most desired will always pierce with pain because it is utterly unattainable.

In addition to elucidating important relationships and moods in Tolkien's legendarium, recognition of maternal themes in his music may contribute to understanding biographical roots of the mixture of idealized and devalued qualities in Tolkien's female characters, as well as the idealization that is apparent in his published memories of his mother.

Many authors have tried to understand Tolkien's view of women by studying his depiction of women in his fiction; this literature has been summarized by Leslie Donovan and especially by Robin Reid.[24] Early scholarship often pointed to a devaluation of women in that so few are depicted, especially in works published during Tolkien's lifetime. More recent scholarship has countered that Tolkien's women play highly important and effective roles. However, the most prominent women (Lúthien, Arwen, Galadriel, Goldberry, Éowyn) are idealized in beauty, goodness, and power, whereas the females Ungoliant and Shelob are devalued monsters of gross evil. Among the minor women characters in *The Lord of the Rings,* Ioreth is a bit of a fool, and Rosie Cotton is all good; ironically, it is Lobelia Sackville-Baggins who becomes the fullest character after she redeems her previously one-sided greed by standing up to Sharkey. Tolkien showed that he could also create more well-rounded female characters in, for example, his depictions of Erendis's attempt to cope with her mismatched marriage and Andreth's sophisticated conversation with Finrod.[25] Nevertheless, the qualities that stand out more clearly in his depiction of female characters are devaluation both in the paucity of females and in the embodiment of grossness in the giant spiders, together with idealization of the most important women.

The dynamics of idealization also appear in the record of Tolkien's relationship with his mother. Several passages in Tolkien's letters indicate that he remembered his mother very positively, to the exclusion of any negative views. He attributed to her what were perhaps the central passions of his intellectual life, and partly because of this considered himself more a member of her family than his father's ("I am in fact more of a Suffield [his mother's family, rather than a Tolkien] . . . and it is to my mother . . . that I owe my tastes for philology, especially of Germanic languages, and for romance"[26]). Tolkien's intense positive feelings for his mother are also indicated by the intense grief he felt about her death when he was twelve years old ("I remember . . . when I was not yet thirteen after the death of my mother, and vainly waving a hand at the sky saying 'it is so empty and cold'"[27]), and that he continued to suffer throughout his life ("When I think of my mother's death . . . worn out with persecution, poverty, and, largely consequent, disease, in the effort to hand on to us small boys the Faith . . . I find it very hard and bitter, when my children stray away"[28]).

As the latter quote indicates, Tolkien also attributed his Catholic faith to his mother. He emphasized the depth of his gratitude for this in two other statements in his letters: "I . . . should chiefly be grateful for having been brought up (since I was eight) in a Faith that has nourished me and taught me all the little that I know; and that I owe to my mother," and "I witnessed (half-comprehending) the heroic sufferings and early death in extreme poverty of my mother, who brought me into the Church."[29]

All in all, the picture of Tolkien's relationship with his mother that emerges from his letters is one of idealization. He remembered her as not only good, but as the source of much of what was most important in his life, and as a "heroic" martyr who died to give her children the true faith. He lionized both her qualities and her suffering: "she was a gifted lady of great beauty and wit, greatly stricken by God with grief and suffering."[30] These appreciations were not tempered by any critical or even neutral descriptions.

Idealization of one's parents is a normal part of child development that is important for psychological health, and is often based upon actually commendable qualities.[31] However, such healthy, "realistic" idealization does not preclude realistic recognition and criticism of imperfections in one's parents, and usually eventuates in a more measured positive assessment than we see in Tolkien's letters. With people other than his mother Tolkien was quite capable of this sort of recognition of flaws in conjunction with esteem, whether toward someone as central to him as C. S. Lewis ("Yes C. S. L. was my closest friend from about 1927 to 1940, and remained very dear to me. His death was a grievous blow. But in fact we saw less and less of one another after he came under the dominant influence of Charles Williams, and still less after his very strange marriage";[32] "C. S. L. of course had some oddities and could sometimes be irritating. . . . But he did nothing for effect. . . . He was generous-minded, on guard against all prejudices."[33]) or as peripheral as Dante ("My reference to Dante [in an interview where Tolkien had said Dante was unattractive because of his spite and malice] was outrageous . . . I do not seriously dream of being measured against Dante, a supreme poet. . . . It remains true that I found the 'pettiness' that I spoke of a sad blemish in places."[34]).

Therefore, it appears to have been important to Tolkien to maintain an idealization of his mother in particular. Such ongoing idealization often defends against awareness of unsatisfying qualities that would lead to anger or disappointment that are too painful to bear consciously. This dynamic is not only very familiar to psychologists but is widely recognized in our society.[35] Tolkien himself showed a keen awareness of it in his evaluation of romantic love in his letter to his son Michael, when he stated,

> There is in our Western culture the romantic chivalric tradition still strong. . . . It idealizes "love" . . . combined and harmonized with religion it can be very noble. . . . Yet I still think it has dangers. It is not wholly true. . . . It takes . . . the young man's eye off women as they are, as companions in shipwreck not guiding stars. (One result is for observation of the actual to make the young man turn cynical.) . . . It inculcates exaggerated notions of "true love," as a fire from without, a permanent exaltation, unrelated to age, childbearing, and plain life. . . . (One result of that is to make young folk look for a "love" that will keep

them always nice and warm in a cold world, without any effort of theirs; and the incurably romantic go on looking even in the squalor of the divorce courts).[36]

What experiences with his mother could have created for Tolkien a need to defensively idealize her? First, of course, is the simple yet dreadful fact of her death, on top of the death of his father several years earlier. Tolkien's sense of isolation and despair at this event, depicted in the letter quoted above, is in no way unusual except perhaps in its poignantly evocative phrasing. Mabel's death left Tolkien without a parent at the young age of twelve, and although obviously unintentional, this would likely have been experienced as an abandonment with accompanying disappointment and anger. Yet a child in this situation will often feel the need to think only positively of the lost parent, so as to have a comforting companion at least in memory and fantasy, and this desire can lead to conscious idealization that keeps anger and disappointment unconscious.

It is not clear, however, that this dynamic by itself would lead to the idealization being maintained for the duration of a long life, raising the question of whether other factors were at play. Nancy Bunting's reading of Tolkien's biography and art have led her to propose that Mabel was emotionally and physically abusive to Tolkien and his brother, even attacking them murderously during the final year of her life;[37] if this were true, it would be a blatant source of negative feelings toward his mother that Tolkien might have been motivated to hide behind idealization. But as I have stated elsewhere, I believe Bunting's proposal to be unduly speculative, unsupported by currently available data.[38] (Bunting agrees that her thesis would require the release of additional archival information to determine whether or not it is true.[39])

I think that the maternal relationship themes in Tolkien's writings provide a more plausible picture of what factors other than Tolkien's orphaning may have motivated him to defensively idealize his mother: a mixture of positive and painful experiences with his mother that do not reach the level of abuse or neglect. Since taking this interpretive step requires the assumption that the maternal relationship themes in Tolkien's writing have biographical import, I will first delineate aspects of Tolkien's musical development that make this assumption reasonable before describing in more detail what the maternal relationship themes might reveal about his biography.

Tolkien's musicality was always embedded in feelings about his mother because it developed in the matrix of his early relationship with her.[40] Hargreaves and Lamont summarize extensive research indicating that musicality generally originates in the matrix of mother-infant relationships.[41]

Music appears to be a primary source of pleasure and emotional regulation during this phase. Even in the womb babies attend to the music of their mother's voices, so that after birth they show preferences for songs sung to them prenatally. Mothers singing to and rocking their babies appears to be cross-culturally universal. Colwyn Trevarthen discusses how the essentially musical nature of the earliest communications between mother and child forms the core of intersubjectivity, personality, and intelligence. Martin Nass interviewed twenty prominent American composers and reported that during the inspiration phase of creativity they utilized multiple sensory modalities, visual, kinesthetic, and tactile as well as auditory, and he linked this multisensory capacity to the retention of openness to the sensorimotor experience of the early relationship to the mother. Nass concluded that in the process of composition, many of his interviewees revisited and transformed early separation-individuation trauma with their mothers.[42]

In addition to these general developmental factors, Tolkien's letters and biography show that he personally associated his musical development with his mother. She tried to teach him the piano, and although we do not know at what level she could play, this suggests at a minimum that there was musical interest in the household he was born into. But the musicality that Tolkien derived from his mother did not lead to him become a musician—Mabel's attempt to teach him the piano was the one area of her pedagogy at which he failed; rather, it appears instead to have contributed to his unusual degree of appreciation for the musical qualities of language. "Early in his Sarehole days his mother introduced him to the rudiments of Latin, and this delighted him. He was just as interested in the sounds and shapes of the words as in their meanings, and she began to realize that he had a special aptitude for language . . . the sounds [of French] did not please him as much. . . . She also tried to interest him in playing the piano, but without success. It seemed rather as if words took the place of music for him, and that he enjoyed listening to them, reading them, and reciting them, almost regardless of what they meant."[43] Or as Tolkien stated, "Though I come of a musical family, owing to defects of opportunity and education as an orphan, such music as was in me was submerged . . . or transformed into linguistic terms."[44]

We see this appreciation of the music in language clearly when Tolkien sets forth his theory of linguistic esthetics in "English and Welsh" (in *The Monsters and the Critics*). He uses a musical analogy to illustrate the pleasure he takes in the Welsh language: "the pleasure is not solely concerned with any word, with any 'sound-pattern + meaning,' by itself, but with its fitness also with a whole style. Even single notes of a large music may please in their place, but one cannot illustrate this pleasure (not even to those who have once heard the music) by repeating them in isolation."[45] He later makes clear that it is particular sounds in Welsh that especially give him pleasure: "I should mention the fondness for nasal consonants, especially the much-favoured *n*, and the frequency with which word-patterns are made with the soft and less sonorous *w* and the voiced spirants *f* and *dd* contrasted with the nasals." And again: "For many of us it [Welsh] rings a bell, or rather it stirs deep harp-strings in our linguistic nature."[46] In his draft manuscript "On 'The Kalevala' or Land of Heroes" he spoke similarly about the musicality of Finnish: "Finnish . . . suffers like many languages of its type from an excess of euphony: so much so that the music of language is apt to be expended automatically and leave no excess with which to heighten the emotion of a lyric passage. Where vowel harmony and the softening of consonants is an integral part of ordinary speech, there is less chance for sudden unexpected sweetnesses."[47]

Language learning typically takes place in interactions with the mother—it is no accident that we refer to the language we grew up speaking as our "mother tongue." Baby talk and "motherese" are found across cultures and languages and appear to be part of our biological makeup that facilitates language learning. And as the above quotes show, the emotional link between language and mother was especially close for Tolkien. He believed that he had inherited an affinity for the version of Middle English spoken in the ancestral location of the Suffields, his mother's family.[48] And he further stated, "My interest in languages was derived solely from my mother," and he dated the origin of his love for the musicality of language to his earliest days: "[As to when his work started] That is rather like asking of Man when language started. It was an inevitable, though conditionable, evolvement of the birth-given. It has been always with me: the sensibility to linguistic pattern which affects me emotionally like colour or music."[49] Note the word "conditionable," which shows that Tolkien is thinking not of something completely inborn but something that develops from experience.

Tolkien's various metaphors for the appeal of Welsh conjure an overall bodily-sensory experience that implicates the mother-child relationship. These metaphors include taste: "I have, in this peculiar sense, studied ('tasted' would be better) other languages since" and touch and sight: "The fluidity of Greek, punctuated by hardness, and with its surface glitter."[50] Tolkien invested Tinfang Warble's music that I cited earlier with the same multisensory effect: it implicated sound, of course, but also smell ("like perfume of flowers")—and here we can note that Lúthien's song to Morgoth as well filled his dungeon with subtle odors—vision ("as clear as a star," etc.), and kinesthetics ("I leapt o'er the stream and I sped from the glade").[51] Indeed, although Tolkien disavows the jargon in the subsequent sentence, he summarizes what he is talking about thus: "Language is related to our total psycho-physical make-up." Our total psycho-physical makeup originates in earliest development as our minds and selves are formed from body experiences interpersonally mediated by the mother.[52] Infant learning crosses sense modalities—for example, infants can visually identify shapes that they have touched but never before seen,[53] and Nass noted that some composers retain the ability to access different sense modalities as they create.

Throughout my discussion so far I have noted the intense and nearly exclusive involvement of Tolkien's mother in the early development of his musicality and his mind more broadly. To be able to teach him in this way, she herself had to have been talented and creative.[54] It is not a great leap to suppose that as a woman in her time, she was unable to develop her talent and instead fulfilled herself through her sons. Perhaps on some level Tolkien even thought that it was as though he himself "had horses and deeds of arms, and the free fields, but she, born in the body of a maid, had a spirit and courage at least the match of [his]. Yet she was doomed to wait upon an old man,"[55] or in Tolkien's case, on two young children. However this may be, it is likely that Tolkien's mother had powerful hopes for him that would have given particular intensity to their relationship.

To summarize these thoughts about the development of Tolkien's musicality, it appears that both his musical sense per se and his sensitivity to the musicality of language were embedded in feelings for his mother. This linkage suggests that maternal relationship themes that are manifested in Tolkien's songs and music represent his early relationship with his mother.

What might all this tell us about Tolkien's experience of his own relationship with his mother? The Music of the Ainur and the trope of repairing a disrupted love relationship through song reflect a great sensitivity to the importance of mutuality, to how it can be threatened by disruption, and to the possibilities both of successful and unsuccessful repair. This suggests that through a combination of temperamental sensitivity and mothering behavior, Tolkien keenly experienced mutuality with his mother together with its loss through disruptions, as well as both successful and unsuccessful repairs of its disruption. Tolkien's fictional relationship schemas of maternally effected alteration in states of consciousness composed of love and enchantment saturated with sorrow, loss, and longing, suggests that he had intensely painful separation feelings as well as intensely loving feelings toward his mother. These separations and disruptions of love might have resulted either or both from differences in behavior between caretakers (nurses and mother) and from fluctuations in the responses of his mother and other caretakers. It is also likely that Tolkien was born with an emotionally sensitive temperament that facilitated him experiencing his relationship with his mother intensely.

Since Tolkien wrote all his fictions after his mother died, examination of his fictions alone cannot determine whether the degree of pain in Tolkien's relationship with his mother that the fictions appear to express was present before she died. Until we have more complete biographical data, we are left with two possible understandings of this aspect of his development. First, his maternal relationship themes are consistent with his having experienced what has been called "strain trauma" or "cumulative trauma" during his early years.[56] Unlike shock traumas such as the death of a loved one, rape, or combat experience where a single event overwhelms a person's capacity to cope, the effects of strain trauma become pathological because they occur so frequently.[57] Tolkien's maternal relationship themes suggest the possibility that he experienced relatively minor separations and disruptions of his relationship with his mother that were not at the level of abuse but had lasting effect on his personality because they occurred too frequently to be comfortably tolerated.

Alternatively, Tolkien's mother music is consistent with the possibility that his early experiences with his mother did not constitute cumulative trauma, but that after Mabel died Tolkien's early separation experiences with her were retrospectively experienced as harbingers and signifiers of that final separation, and in this way became imbued with greater pain than they had carried before. (This phenomenon, of earlier experience gaining new meaning under the influence of later experience, has broader psychological applicability than to separation experiences alone; it was studied by Freud under the term *nachtraglicheit* and by Lacan as *après-coup,* both rendered in English as *deferred action.*) When *nachtraglicheit* occurs, the later experience is also colored by the earlier; they have conjoined psychological impact. Whether Tolkien already felt a high degree of separation pain in his early childhood, or whether less intense early separation pains were intensified by *nachtraglicheit* when his mother died, in the songs I have discussed he expressed the admixture of separation pain with love in the form of early maternal relationships.

In closing this chapter, I want to consider what bearing this understanding of Tolkien's mother music might have on his concept of eucatastrophe. "I coined the word 'eucatastrophe': the sudden happy turn in a story which pierces you with a joy that brings tears (which I argued it is the highest function of fairy-stories to produce). And I was there led to the view that it produces its peculiar effect because it is a sudden glimpse of Truth, your whole nature chained in material cause and effect, the chain of death, feels a sudden relief as if a major limb out of joint had suddenly snapped back."[58] Eucatastrophe is not simply a moment of powerful joy; like repair of disruption, it can only occur as a corrective to pain: "It does not deny the existence of *dyscatastrophe,* of sorrow and failure: the possibility of these is necessary to the joy of deliverance."[59]

In light of what I have discussed above we can see possible roots of these statements in early experiences of disruption and repair in Tolkien's relationship with his mother. Hopeless pain described as physical suffering is healed by physical ministration, resulting in a sense of freedom and joy that brings tears. It is easy to hear this, with its metaphors of physical ministration and tears, as a description of a young child unbearably distraught at separation from the mother and then healed by her loving return.

Tolkien singled out a musical passage from *The Lord of the Rings* as one that moved him most years after the writing: the moment when the Rohirrim arrive at the Pelennor fields: "I am most stirred by the sound of the horses of the Rohirrim at cockcrow" and "the passages that now move me most . . . are the end of the chapter Lothlórien and the horns of the Rohirrim at cockcrow."[60] Music—whether from nature (sound of horses; a cockcrow) or humankind (horns of the Rohirrim)—with its special access to feelings about his mother, gave Tolkien his most acute experience of joy replacing sorrow.

We see links to mother music as well in Frodo's dream, which foreshadows the eucatastrophe of him reaching Elvenhome to be cured of his physical and emotional traumas, a dream that is musical and multisensory: "Frodo heard a sweet singing running in his mind: a song that seemed to come like a pale light behind a grey rain-curtain, and growing stronger to turn the veil all to glass and silver, until at last it was rolled back, and a far green country opened before him under a swift sunrise."[61]

For Tolkien, the experience of eucatastrophe was existentially fundamental, a part of human nature that was central to his Catholic faith: "this is indeed how things really do work in the Great World for which our nature is made . . . the Resurrection was the greatest 'eucatastrophe' possible."[62] The fundamental nature of eucatastrophe echoes relational disruption and repair, fundamental psychological building blocks of the self that are of crucial importance during the early mother-child relationship and remain important throughout life. By tapping into mother music, Tolkien expressed and reached out to this basic human experience.

CHAPTER 6

The Man-Maiden and the Spider with Horns

I have been proposing that Tolkien's sensitive understanding of the dynamic between enchantment and loss grew out of his struggle to preserve hope and meaning in the face of the severe losses that he experienced in his own life. In this chapter I will further investigate loss in Tolkien's writings and its connection to loss in his life by exploring one of Tolkien's most important female characters, Galadriel, together with her shadow side, Shelob. We recognize that Tolkien found great significance in Galadriel by the way that he continued to ponder and rewrite this character until the end of his life; one of his very last, fragmentary writings concerns her. I believe that this significance derives in part from the way this character memorialized Tolkien's lost mother and, in subtler ways, his lost father too, as well as expressing his effort to process these losses. This understanding can in turn enlarge our understanding of the meanings that Galadriel potentially carries for readers.

It is impossible to comprehend the psychological meaning of Galadriel without considering Shelob alongside her. Galadriel and Shelob are opposite images of women: Galadriel (and her phial) are idealized, positive, beautiful, caring, and characterized by light, whereas Shelob is degraded, negative, hideous, selfish, and characterized by darkness.[1] Despite being opposites, they are intricately involved with each other during Frodo and Sam's battle with Shelob: it is Galadriel's phial, and even more importantly (as I discuss below) Frodo's and Sam's memories of Galadriel, that enable them to survive. It is almost as though Galadriel had foreknowledge of the encounter with Shelob when she gave Frodo "A light to you in dark places.

. . . *A light when all other lights go out*."[2] Galadriel and Shelob thus represent opposite sides of the same symbol.

Although it is obvious enough that Galadriel and Shelob are female characters, it is important to note that Tolkien emphasized both their femininity and their specifically maternal qualities. Galadriel's traditional femininity is shown by her great physical beauty, and by the medieval romantic relationship she establishes with Gimli, to whom she gives a lock of her hair and who then champions her beauty like a knight, even challenging Éomer with a duel to the death if Éomer does not agree upon first espying Galadriel that she is the most beautiful of women. (In the event, Gimli accepts Éomer's different opinion, but only because he honors Éomer's choice of Arwen.) Shelob's femininity is emphasized by descriptions of her sexuality and her body: She spawns many other giant spiders, including those of Mirkwood, and her particular ugliness is described in language that conjures images of sexuality and pregnancy seen as a degraded and devalued state: "lust" for food that makes her "bloated," "huge," and "swollen."[3] Joyce Lionarons has helpfully discussed an interpretation put forward by previous writers according to which Shelob's impaling herself on Sam's sword represents a perverse sexual intercourse. Lionarons correctly understands that this does not mean (as others have proposed) that Tolkien's true, primary experience of female sexuality is thus expressed, but rather that this form of female sexuality is one aspect of "bad" femininity that Tolkien depicts as split off from the good Galadriel.[4]

The femininity of Galadriel and Shelob is also emphasized by the name "She." Tolkien liked the "noisome" effect of giving his giant spider a name that combines "She" with "lob," which is an archaic word for *spider*.[5] The pronoun *she* was also in Tolkien's mind behind Galadriel; the character Ayesha from H. Rider Haggard's "She," one of Tolkien's favorite books in childhood, contributed qualities to Galadriel.[6] Both characters are exceptionally beautiful with an appearance of both youth and age; both are literally luminous; and both have vessels filled with water that provide visions. Although Ayesha is very different from Galadriel in her unabashed grasping for domination and power, Galadriel would have become very like Ayesha if she had not rejected the One Ring.

Galadriel and Shelob may be seen not only as opposite images of femininity, but more specifically as opposite maternal figures. Galadriel, as the Lady of Lórien, is the symbolic mother of her people. She stands for family ties: Aragorn praises her as "'O Lady of Lórien of whom were sprung Celebrían and Arwen Evenstar.'"[7] She offers appropriate support to him as her future grandson-in-law in several ways: in addition to an Elven cloak, she gives him the Elfstone and names him Elfstone (Elessar) as had been foretold; and later through a message sent with Gandalf urges him to travel the Paths of the Dead with the Dúnedain. Galadriel's maternal qualities are also seen in her association with Mary Mother of Jesus. Tolkien acknowledged that he derived some of her features from Mary, and Michael Maher has traced many of Galadriel's qualities to medieval Marian imagery.[8] A simple example is that Lothlórien, Galadriel's land, was "without stain," which is a central attribute of Mary.

Tolkien emphasizes Galadriel's gaze and that of Shelob in a way that makes clear their opposite maternal qualities. Eyes are a channel for deep emotional communication, as is captured in the variously attributed adage "The eyes are the window to the soul." This importance of the eyes has roots in parent-infant gaze and attachment,[9] as I shall develop further in the next chapter, and Galadriel's gazing deep into the eyes/souls of the Fellowship resembles a mother knowing the minds of her little children. This is made especially clear by Sam blushing so that Pippin accuses him of a guilty conscience, and Sam then asserting that that was not so but he felt as if he had no clothes on.[10] But each of the Fellowship experienced something similar, since only Aragorn and Legolas could hold Galadriel's gaze, and all wanted to keep secret what had passed between them and Galadriel. A similar child-in-relationship-with-mother moment occurs when Gimli, upon receiving Galadriel's greeting from the newly met Gandalf the White, "capers,"[11] a verb that connotes childish pleasure at maternal recognition.

Shelob represents a perversion of motherhood. She is a monstrous mother who mates with her own offspring and then devours her mates. And compare Galadriel's soul-searching but caring gaze with Shelob's eyes glinting maliciously in the dark, the only part of her illuminated by the light from Galadriel's phial during the contest within Shelob's lair. Under Galadriel's illumination, Shelob's wicked soul shines through her eyes:

> [Frodo] was aware of eyes becoming visible, two great clusters of many-windowed eyes. . . . The radiance of the star-glass was broken and thrown back from their thousand facets, but behind the glitter a pale deadly fire began steadily to glow within, a flame kindled in some deep pit of evil thought. Monstrous and abominable eyes they were, bestial and yet filled with purpose and with hideous delight, gloating over their prey trapped beyond all hope of escape . . . [Frodo's and Sam's] own gaze held by the dreadful stare of those baleful eyes; but as they backed so the eyes advanced . . . released from the holding spell

> to run a little while in vain panic for the amusement of the eyes . . . the eyes came leaping up behind. . . . Slowly the eyes crept nearer. . . . [Frodo lifts the phial] The eyes halted . . . as if some hint of doubt troubled them . . . Frodo . . . walked steadily down to meet the eyes. They wavered. Doubt came into them as the light approached. One by one they dimmed, and slowly they drew back . . . the eyes began to quail. One by one they all went dark; they turned away. . . . They were gone.[12]

Shelob is present much more briefly than Galadriel in *The Lord of the Rings,* but we can learn more about her as a perverse mother by considering her as a variant of Ungoliant. (This interpretive move is justified by how close Shelob was to Ungoliant in Tolkien's mind: in early drafts of *The Lord of the Rings* he named the creature Ungoliant before coming up with the name Shelob, and they are very similar in physical characteristics and in the webs they spin and their desire to devour light and vomit up darkness.) Especially interesting in the current context is Ungoliant's relationship with Melkor. Each of them is for the other the only partner with whom they ever have a relationship of near-equals. And the way that Ungoliant and Melkor were briefly partners-in-evil evokes a perverse parental couple: rather than creating love and children and family, they are dedicated to destroying the creations of Ilúvatar and the Valar, and their own relationship is characterized by hate and selfishness rather than love. The depiction of Ungoliant and Melkor as a perverse couple is strongest in the chapters of *Morgoth's Ring* describing the Thieves' Quarrel;[13] they come across as an almost human pair as they bicker and backstab. Their relationship culminates in a nearly fatal battle with each other over the Silmarils, during which Ungoliant would have destroyed Melkor except that the balrogs came to save him in response to him crying the loudest cry for help ever heard. Thus, we see what is perhaps Melkor's most vulnerable moment growing out of his relationship with the monstrous mother figure.

But Galadriel and Shelob are not simple signifiers of the feminine; despite all the emphasis on their prominent femininity and maternal qualities, these characters also share subtler masculine features. Tolkien's writings about Galadriel demonstrate fluidity in his thought about her gender, so that he progressively ascribed more masculinity to her. From drafts of *The Fellowship of the Ring* we know that the Celeborn character was originally conceived of as being equally or more powerful than the Galadriel character; Tolkien initially even endowed him with the Mirror, before transferring it with the wisdom and power it entails to Galadriel.[14] Christopher states, "it was while my father was writing the 'Lothlórien' story *ab initio* that the

Lady of Lothlórien emerged; and it is also seen that the figure of Galadriel as a great power in Middle-earth was deepened and extended as he wrote."[15] It is as a survivor of earlier drafts that we hear Galadriel say that Celeborn is wisest among the Elves of Middle-Earth and a giver of gifts beyond the power of kings, even though Galadriel has just shown herself wiser than he by welcoming Gimli with kindness,[16] and even though it turns out to be she who gives the parting gifts.[17] As finally published, Galadriel's power clearly surpasses that of Celeborn, implicating traditional masculinity; by conventional patriarchal standards, Galadriel "wears the pants" in the family.[18]

Tolkien also increasingly ascribed traditional masculine physical qualities to Galadriel: Already in *The Fellowship of the Ring* she had a deep voice, and in Tolkien's last writings he stated that "she grew to be tall beyond the measure even of the women of the Noldor; she was strong of body, mind, and will, a match for both the loremasters and the athletes of the Eldar in the days of their youth." For these reasons even the Noldor recognized her masculine traits and gave her the name Nerwen, meaning *Man-maiden.*[19] Tolkien further described Galadriel as being "of Amazon disposition."[20] All these qualities are described with admiration, so that Galadriel is idealized in her masculine as well as her feminine attributes.

Shelob's masculinity was represented by physical features. Shelob was not truly a spider, but "an evil thing in spider form," and most of the ways that she varied from spider form signify masculine attributes: Shelob possessed horns, claws, and a sting. (Her other unspiderlike features were her compound eyes, discussed above, and her thick hide.) Although a few species of spiders have horn-like appendages, this is uncommon and more likely on the body than the head; spider claws are so small as not to be normally visible to the naked eye; and spiders do not sting. It is difficult to think of any clearer phallic symbols than horns, claws, and a sting—pointed, penetrating body parts. Tolkien mistakenly believed that real spiders have stings, as we know because he refers to having been "stung" by a tarantula as a child,[21] but as a careful and loving observer of nature, he probably knew that real spiders do not share the full array of phallic features that he gave Shelob, suggesting that he put them in intentionally for effect.[22] But whether a conscious artistic choice or not, the presence of these features partially masculinizes Shelob. And Shelob's sting is deadlier than her bite; she intends to give Sam: "a sting to death: no little bite of poison"[23] Thus, Shelob's masculine body is evil just as is her feminine body.

I propose that by imbuing the Galadriel/Shelob symbol with masculine as well as feminine features, Tolkien created a memorial to both his lost parents. To support this idea, I will next explore how Galadriel and Shelob are imbued with a mood of melancholy and experiences of loss extending into the deep past.

Even in the context of Tolkien's generally elegiac tone, Galadriel and Shelob stand out. Galadriel is perhaps the character in *The Lord of the Rings* around whom a mood of melancholy loss looms most powerfully, in the form both of the protagonists' loss of her as the Age of Men approaches, and her own loss of Middle-earth and possible loss of Elvenhome. The chapters of *The Lord of the Rings* dealing with Lothlórien are filled with the hobbits' (and the reader's) increasing awareness that its enchantment has already faded and will continue fading irrevocably; as Galadriel says about herself and Celeborn, "together through the ages of the world we have fought the long defeat."[24] This tantalizing mention of the ages of the world links Galadriel to inaccessible memories of ancient times—although various versions of Galadriel's origins in the First Age are known to readers of *The Silmarillion* and Tolkien's posthumous publications, to the hobbits' knowledge, her origins are lost far back in time. Galadriel further reveals her personal sense of loss when she sings that there may be no ship to carry her back to Elvenhome. As has been pointed out by Romuald Lakowski, Galadriel's song as well as her later lament in Elvish create a plot inconsistency, since previously she had stated (upon refusing the Ring) that she will pass into the West.[25] But although her lament is inconsistent with the plot, it is consistent with and enhances the mood, piling sadness upon sadness, as though Galadriel will lose both Middle-earth and the West.

Tolkien demonstrated that Galadriel had a special importance for him by continuing to explore and alter her character throughout his life, and much of this later development shows him struggling with the vicissitudes of whether and why Galadriel lost the right of return.[26] Tolkien proposed at various times that Galadriel fell under the Doom of Mandos and even was specifically banned from returning because out of pride she refused the pardon of the Valar; it was only in honor of her refusal of the Ring that she was at last allowed to return. In a final development, Tolkien proposed that although Galadriel fell under the ban against returning, she was blameless all along. All these changes circle around the question of whether and why Galadriel was bereft, and demonstrate that Tolkien deeply imbued Galadriel with his emotional concerns about separation and loss.

Since Shelob is an evil character whose defeat is necessary for the plot, the feeling of loss around her is less prominent than that around Galadriel. Nevertheless, of all the evil characters in *The Lord of the Rings,* Shelob stands out as one we may mourn despite her horror. Douglass Parker pointed out that she is the evil character with the most clearly differentiated personality.[27] Similarly, as I indicated above, her ancestor Ungoliant is almost human during the Thieves' Quarrel with Melkor. Even in her evilness Shelob, like Galadriel, is a revenant from ancient times that are gone: "There agelong she had dwelt, an evil thing in spider-form, even such as once of old had lived in the Land of the Elves in the West that is now under the Sea, such as Beren fought in the Mountains of Terror in Doriath and so came to Lúthien upon the green sward amid the hemlocks in the moonlight long ago. How Shelob came there, flying from ruin, no tale tells, for out of the Dark Years few tales have come."[28] Her relative Ungoliant emphasizes the feeling of deep time even more than Shelob, since even the Valar were uncertain of her origins. She was some kind of primordial spirit, but no one was certain whence or when she entered Arda.[29] And so Tolkien's description of Shelob as "the last child of Ungoliant to trouble the unhappy world" gives a pang of sorrow to the reader, and we are left longing to be told more when Tolkien writes that whether or not she recovered to hunt again, "this tale does not tell."[30] Even if we don't want to meet her, maybe we wish she were still there, somewhere.

We can summarize the qualities of the Galadriel/Shelob symbol as follows: Galadriel and Shelob are opposite images of women that are nevertheless similar to each other in that both are powerful maternal figures, both are associated with mournful loss, and both have histories stretching into the deep past. More subtly, they share masculine attributes. We can add to this that Galadriel at least was of special importance to Tolkien. All these qualities resonate psychologically with early childhood experiences of parental loss. Since Tolkien lost his father as well as his mother, Galadriel and Shelob's combined gender attributes point to them as conjoined images of the lost parents.

The question immediately arises as to why the lost-mother side of the Galadriel/Shelob symbol is manifestly more obvious, whereas the lost-father side is manifestly subtle and obscure and must be teased out. In fact, this difference in surface visibility strengthens my interpretation that the symbol represents father as well as mother because it is what we would expect from Tolkien's life history and is consistent with his conscious memories as seen in his letters, where mother is mentioned much more than father. Tolkien's father died when he was only four years old, and Tolkien's last contact with him was even earlier, at the age of three, when he, with his mother and brother, left South Africa for England. Tolkien's mother died when he was twelve. His mother would therefore have been a much stronger presence in his conscious life: she was there longer, she had to do all the parenting for many years, and she was there during the time of life when conscious memories are formed.

His father, on the other hand, died during the time of life that is still cloaked by "childhood amnesia"; most people have very few if any conscious, explicit, episodic memories prior to the age of four. In these earlier years, memory and experience are not yet firmly structured by language in a way that can be retrieved by our adult minds; instead, experience appears to be more sensorimotor and relational, and implicit memories are formed that are difficult to access consciously. Any conscious memories that are retained tend to be brief and disconnected. Tolkien's reported memories of Africa and the voyage to England are typical of this pattern: blazing heat; dark people diving into the water to collect coins thrown from the ship; a city on a hill, which later in life he realized must have been Lisbon—and yet on the other hand *feeling* deeply moved whenever he heard stories about Africa.

Of course, I do not mean to suggest that Tolkien had no conscious, explicit thoughts and memories about fathers. In addition to the kind of cultural knowledge of fathers that he would have picked up from knowing about fathers of friends, reading about fathers, and having male schoolmasters, Tolkien had at least one extremely important father figure: Father Francis Morgan. Father Francis had already begun helping Tolkien and his mother and brother by the time Tolkien was ten, and took on true parental responsibilities after the death of Tolkien's mother. Tolkien's honoring Father Francis as a father is seen clearly in his feeling that he owed Father Francis everything and so needed to obey his stricture to stay away from his beloved Edith until he was twenty-one. (And it does not diminish the extent to which Francis fit in the father role when we recognize that Tolkien was partly motivated by financial dependency on him.) Tolkien himself was a caring and generous father, as is evident from his children's recollections and from his having first composed a number of his fictions by telling stories to his children.

But these experiences and memories come from later in life than the death of Tolkien's father. What I believe we see in the masculine features of the Galadriel/Shelob symbol is an image of the lost father formed prior to explicit memory. To strengthen this inference, I want to look at two places in Tolkien's minor writings that I think show a similar image of the father. These examples are very different from each other and from Galadriel/Shelob in content; what I am looking for are their similarities in formal qualities: preverbal, shadowy, dreamlike, obscure, prone to merger with other images.

First, let us turn to what I believe to be Tolkien's most sustained attempt to depict the father-son relationship: "The Lost Road." Ostensibly about the downfall of Númenor, "the thread was to be the occurrence time and again in human families . . . of a father and son called by names that could be interpreted as Bliss-friend and Elf-friend."[31] The autobiographical relevance of the story is overt, as has been noted by Christopher Tolkien:[32] Alboin, the son in the first pair, has language interests, school career, and professional interests very like Tolkien's own.

Right away in Tolkien's proposed thread we notice an indefinite quality to these characters: each father-son pair was to merge with each in name and motivation, rather than being whole, clearly defined individuals. This merging is especially noticeable between the first son, after he grows up, and his own son. Their names are even hard to distinguish visually and phonetically: Alboin and Audoin. They have similar experiences hinting at the downfall of Númenor. And tellingly, they have these experiences while dreaming. Eventually, Alboin has a dream come true in which he encounters the Númenorean Elendil, who gives him the choice whether to travel back in time or not. Alboin chooses to travel back and in doing so becomes Elendil, while Audoin becomes Elendil's son Herendil. Thus, Alboin's dream seems to change both him and his son in reality. Lurking behind all this is the ominous sense of the impending destruction of Númenor. All these features are consistent with a largely preverbal, unrealistic experience of the lost father.

Things look different between the other father-son pair that we read about, Elendil and Herendil. Instead of being so similar to each other that they almost merge or sound interchangeable, Elendil and Herendil have a stiff, detached relationship. The scene between Elendil and Herendil takes place when Sauron's corruption of Númenor is near fruition, and the king is about to attack Aman. Elendil seeks out Herendil. "I must see him and speak to him, more clearly than we have spoken yet."[33] He finds Herendil lying on top of a wall, the same position in which Oswin first found Alboin. But when Elendil asks if he has been dreaming. Herendil repudiates this as an accusation of immaturity, saying that he is not dreaming because he is a grown man. He thus positions himself very differently from the other father-son pairs who were immersed in dreams. Elendil and Herendil then have a long discussion about the state of affairs, during which Herendil largely champions Sauron's viewpoint and is fearful that Elendil will get them in trouble by speaking against Sauron. Elendil summarizes the creation and history of the world to demonstrate Sauron's evil. The only thing for which Herendil definitely faults Sauron is Sauron's encouragement that the Númenoreans reject the Eressëan language and return to the old language of men. Then Elendil reveals that he is a leader of faithful men and Herendil must choose between Sauron and him. Herendil anxiously chooses his father because he loves him.

The whole discussion reads as though Elendil had said little or nothing of this to his son before, and Herendil never responds with any version of "Yeah, yeah, Dad, you always say that." Even keeping in mind that this is not yet the Elendil of the Last Alliance (Tolkien was not yet working on *The Lord of the Rings*), and keeping in mind that Elendil would want to protect his son by keeping his involvement with a clandestine group secret, the fact that this great leader seems to be ignorant of his son's wandering allegiance suggests a wide emotional gap between them. Or if Elendil was already aware of his son's wandering allegiance (the text is not clear on this point), his not already having engaged Herendil in discussion about these fundamental attitudes suggests the same emotional gap. Herendil, after all, is forty-eight years old, and even if Númenoreans matured more slowly than we do, that gives plenty of time for his father to have spoken about these matters. Then Herendil abruptly agrees to go with his father without really engaging any of his father's arguments. Unlike the other father-son pairs who are so closely attuned as to be almost indistinguishable, Elendil and Herendil come across as unrealistically misattuned to each other.

These look like two sides of the same coin. Whether merged or oddly distant from each other, the father-son pairs in "The Lost Road" reflect an uncertainty about how to relate as two whole people. I believe this reflects Tolkien's lack of conscious experience of his own father, and is in accord with the latent form of his father representation in the Galadriel/Shelob symbol.

My next example is Tolkien's poem "Shadow Bride" from *The Adventures of Tom Bombadil,* together with its earlier model "The Shadow Man," originally published in 1936. The poems resemble each other so closely that they are best considered variants of one poem, and so the alternate titles "The Shadow Man" and "Shadow-Bride" create gender ambiguity like that in the Galadriel/Shelob symbol: the poem is identified as centering on male and female both. And although not overtly about fathers at all, imagery in these poems has formal similarities with the Galadriel/Shelob symbol.

Shadow-Bride
There was a man who dwelt alone,
as day and night went past
he sat as still as carven stone,
and yet no shadow cast.
The white owls perched upon his head
beneath the winter moon;

The Shadow Man
There was a man who dwelt alone
beneath the moon in shadow.
He sat as long as lasting stone,
and yet he had no shadow.
The owls, they perched upon his head
beneath the moon of summer;

they wiped their beaks and thought him dead under the stars of June.	They wiped their beaks and thought him dead who sat there dumb all summer.
There came a lady clad in grey. in the twilight shining: one moment she would stand and stay, her hair with flowers entwining. He woke, as had he sprung of stone, and broke the spell that bound him; he clasped her fast, both flesh and bone, and wrapped her shadow round him.	There came a lady clad in grey beneath the moon a-shining. One moment did she stand and stay her hair with flowers entwining. He woke, as had he sprung of stone, beneath the moon in shadow. And clasped her fast, both flesh and bone; and they were clad in shadow.
There never more she walks her ways by sun or moon or star; she dwells below where neither days nor any nights there are. But once a year when caverns yawn and hidden things awake, they dance together then till dawn and a single shadow make.	And never more she walked in light, or over moonlit mountain, But dwelt within the hill, where night is lit but with a fountain— Save once a year when caverns yawn, and hills are clad in shadow, They dance together then till dawn and cast a single shadow.

Both variants show a man and woman who are lovers of a sort. Especially given their associations with death, I think it plausible to take as one of their significations that they represent the dead parents.

The man is flagged with images of death: "still as carven stone," "no shadow cast" (like a living-dead vampire, or a ghost), the owls "thought him dead." When he does come to life, it is to seize a lady and take her to an Underworld from which they emerge only once per year; this echoes the myth of Persephone abducted by Hades, god of the underworld, where the dead dwell.

The lady's state of life or death is more ambiguous. Although she has flesh and bone, indicating living corporeality, and flowers entwining her hair, she is clad in gray and comes in twilight or moonlight that would hide the living colors of the flowers. More tellingly, unlike Persephone, she does not obviously object to her endless fate with the deathlike man.

The man's central motivation in "Shadow-Bride," and his final achievement, is that he "wrapped her shadow round him" so that they "a single shadow make." Paradoxically, the only way he can create an image demonstrating that he has substantial existence is by hiding within and showing himself through the lady's shadow. In "The Shadow Man" it is not specified that it is the woman's shadow that he wraps around him, but nevertheless after he captures her, they both dance within a single shadow. I propose that this a picture both of Tolkien's desire to memorialize his father along with his mother, and of his difficulty doing so—and that this is exactly how we perceive masculine attributes within the Galadriel/Shelob symbol.

I began by stating that the Galadriel/Shelob symbol not only memorializes Tolkien's lost parents, but also represents his effort to process these losses. This effort is seen in the split between Galadriel and Shelob. Splitting the conjoined parental image into good, idealized Galadriel and bad, devalued Shelob may be understood as an effort to maintain an image of goodness in the face of threatening experiences of badness. This is a specific example of the dynamic I described in the previous chapter, whereby Tolkien appears to have split off negative aspects of his mother in order to maintain an idealized image of her.

Psychologists such as Freud, Jung, and Klein have described the difficulty we have forming unified images of people so that we see both their good and bad qualities. Psychologically splitting off bad qualities from ourselves and/or our loved ones, often accompanied by projecting these qualities onto others, protects our sense that we are good and that our loved ones are good. This psychological mechanism is very common in mild forms, such as shifting levels of self-esteem wherein we have trouble believing in our good points when we feel bad, or vice versa; similar fluctuations in our esteem of others; blaming others for our own mistakes; seeing our children as better than other children; or seeing people who anger us as out to get us when "we would never act like that." In stronger forms, splitting contributes to personal and social pathologies such as racism, sexism, and homophobia, wherein we preserve our sense of goodness at the expense of seeing others as monsters.

The dynamism of splitting appears in Tolkien's text when Frodo and Sam encounter Shelob. Although their battle is put into external action via the phial of Galadriel, the primary battle is interior, between the hobbits' despair on the one hand and their memories of Galadriel on the other. As Shelob first approaches in the dark tunnel, Sam is nearly overcome by "darkness about him and a blackness of despair and anger in his heart" but he remembers Galadriel in light and then reminds Frodo of the phial.[34] Frodo's first use of the phial is minimally effective, the light broken on Shelob's eyes; it is only when Frodo interrupts his terror by calling the name of Galadriel and his "heart flamed within him" that the phial blazes enough to drive Shelob back.[35] Similarly, in Sam's final confrontation with Shelob, it is only when he counters his horror with memories of Galadriel, Elrond, and Gildor's company that the phial shines with brightness unbearable to Shelob. In all this we see that the phial is a tool, but what actually beats back despair and threat is Frodo and Sam's recovery of the sense of goodness and hope in the moment by accessing memories of goodness completely untouched by despair and threat.

From this perspective, Galadriel is like the good mother in fairy tales, and Shelob like the wicked stepmother. Bruno Bettelheim has discussed how in fairy tales with wicked stepmothers replacing beloved mothers, the stepmother is a split-off "bad mother" that facilitates children recognizing and working through their anger and disappointment in their mothers while not threatening their loving feelings for her.[36] Jack Zipes has pointed out that fairy tales may represent real problems as well as fantasy;[37] especially during the times that many fairy tales were passed along in folk traditions, but also today, exploitation and powerlessness may create actual traumas lying behind some of these "bad mother" images. As discussed in the previous chapter, the record of Tolkien's life shows no overt evidence of anger at his mother, but it is commonplace for orphaned children to experience intense anger and disappointment at the loss of their parents, and to repress or split off these feelings in order to remain secure in the remembered love of the parent. Tolkien's memories of his mother as expressed in his letters show a high degree of idealization, and although she in reality does appear to have been a remarkable and admirable person, high degrees of conscious idealization often screen anger that is kept from consciousness.

In summary, the Galadriel/Shelob symbol can be understood both as memorializing Tolkien's lost parents, and as protecting memories of his lost parents as good and loving by splitting off bad, dangerous, hostile feelings. Most of us are lucky enough not to be orphaned, but losing one's parents, psychologically as well as literally, is a universal experience. One part of maturing is accepting the loss of our parents in their role as caretakers, even though if things go well, we will still have them in other loving roles and may eventually ourselves become their caretakers prior to the final separation in death. In creating Galadriel and Shelob, Tolkien transformed the trauma of losing his parents into densely packed symbols that will touch different readers in different ways, depending on their own personal histories.

CHAPTER 7

Seeing the Self in the Mirror of Galadriel

In the previous chapter we looked at the two-faceted symbol of Galadriel/ Shelob, exploring ways that it can be understood as memorializing both of Tolkien's lost parents as well as processing their loss. In this chapter we will turn our gaze to Galadriel's Mirror, considering ways that it both reflects the lost parents and strengthens the self in times of crisis.

There is much to unpack in the scene of Galadriel's Mirror; almost every aspect that might seem to be there only to create an ambiance of Elvish beauty has in fact specific emotional connections and resonance in Tolkien's world. Let us start with Galadriel's own description, ambiguous as it is, of her Mirror: It shows "things that are, things that were, and things that yet may be . . . which it is, even the wisest cannot tell."[1] Later she says, "the Mirror is dangerous as a guide of deeds."[2]

We might wonder, given all this risky uncertainty, what is even the point of looking in Galadriel's Mirror? Although Galadriel's use of the word *things* has made it sound as though the Mirror will give information about the external world, and although what the hobbits actually see are external events, the value of looking in the Mirror turns out to be that it deepens self-knowledge.

Although neither Sam nor Frodo sees his actual image in the Mirror, the Mirror metonymically reflects who the characters really are. For Sam, the simpler homebody, the Mirror starts out showing "'only stars, as [he] thought,'" briefly confirming his expectation to see nothing meaningful. Then it shows "trees waving and tossing . . . Frodo with a pale face lying fast asleep under a great dark cliff . . . himself going along a dim passage and climbing an endless winding stair . . . [and then that the trees] were not waving in the wind, they were falling, crashing to the ground."[3] These are straightforward visions of the future (although the reader does not yet know it is the future, Sam, in a trusting way, assumes so). And it is the future of Sam with Frodo and then of the Shire, home, showing people Sam grew up with, including his father.

For Frodo, the more complex and worldly character, the Mirror clears at once and he sees many scenes that are harder to identify, and rather than being focused on loved and familiar people (with the exception of someone who may have been Gandalf, and a brief glimpse of Bilbo), it shows "parts of a great history in which he had become involved."[4] Sam of course is right there with Frodo living in the same history, so having only Frodo see it in the Mirror signifies his greater insight. Then, abruptly, Frodo is face to face with his deadly quest in the form of Sauron in the present.

On another level, the Mirror shows both Sam and Frodo a possible alternate self. Sam considers abandoning Frodo and the quest and returning to the Shire to set things right: "'I can't stay here,' he said wildly, 'I must go home.'"[5] Frodo considers abandoning the quest by giving the Ring to Galadriel. Both of them, with Galadriel's help, set aside these alternate selves, which together with Galadriel's own decision is what she means when she says they must leave tomorrow "for we have chosen."[6] So Tolkien is indicating that reflections can show us truer or falser versions of ourselves.

Some of what Frodo and Sam view in the Mirror hints that to fully understand what they are seeing, we need to consider why they undertake this increased self-exploration at this point in their journey; why does the Mirror of Galadriel scene occur at this point in the book? The hints to which I refer are the glimpses of father figures: Sam sees his actual father in trouble. Frodo sees not his actual father but his aging adoptive father Bilbo, as well as a father substitute, someone who he thinks might be Gandalf, on a lonely journey in the past. In Jungian terms, Gandalf is a manifestation of the archetype of the Wise Old Man, which in more Freudian language would be described as an idealized elderly father figure. Gandalf has been leader, guide, and in his crotchety way the main emotional support on the expedition so far—but he has just died. Much of the hobbits' stay in Lothlórien prior to gazing into Galadriel's Mirror has been taken up with mourning Gandalf's death, composing elegiac songs about him, and wondering how to go on without him. So perhaps the self-reflection in Galadriel's Mirror is a way of dealing with this dreadful loss.

This supposition becomes more compelling when we realize that another mirror, the only other mirror developed at any length in *The Lord of the Rings,* was invoked between the moment of Gandalf's death and the encounter with Galadriel's Mirror. Just outside the tunnels of Moria lies the Mirrormere, legendary among dwarves as the place where their forefather Durin was crowned king. Tolkien introduces the emotional significance of the Mirrormere and its link with grieving for Gandalf in steps. First, as the Fellowship contemplates ascending Caradhras, Gandalf says, "'we shall come down by the Dimrill Stair into the deep vale of the Dwarves. There lies the Mirrormere' . . . 'Dark is the water of Kheled-zâram,' said Gimli, 'and cold are the springs of Kibil-nâla. My heart trembles at the thought that I may see them soon.' 'May you have joy of the sight, my good dwarf!' said Gandalf."[7] Days later, as the Fellowship prepares for a night in Moria, Gimli tries to convey the grandeur of the former dwarf kingdom by chanting:

The world was young, the mountains green,
No stain yet on the Moon was seen,
No words were laid on stream or stone
When Durin woke and walked alone.

He named the nameless hills and dells;
He drank from yet untasted wells;
He stooped and looked in Mirrormere,
And saw a crown of stars appear,
As gems upon a silver thread,
Above the shadow of his head . . . [8]

As Frodo and the Fellowship flee from Moria and their grief after Gandalf has fallen with the balrog, Gimli insists that Frodo share the experience of Mirrormere with him. They hurry aside, followed by Sam. "They stooped over the dark water. At first they could see nothing. Then slowly they saw the forms of the encircling mountains mirrored in a profound blue, and the peaks were like plumes of white flame above them; beyond there was a space of sky. There like jewels sunk in the deep shone glinting stars, though sunlight was in the sky above. Of their own stooping forms no shadow could be seen.

"'O Kheled-zâram fair and wonderful!' said Gimli. 'There lies the Crown of Durin till he wakes. Farewell!' He bowed, and turned away."[9]

But in what way does looking in these mirrors help the hobbits process the loss of Gandalf? In writing these passages I believe that Tolkien intuited a fundamental psychological truth (although I do not think that he had this consciously in mind): Seeing yourself reflected, literally or metaphorically, is a building block of identity. This idea is widespread in current psychoanalysis, growing out of contributions by Winnicott and Jacques Lacan.

For Winnicott, the mother's face was the paradigmatic mirror. He believed that the infant finding herself in the mother's face—nowadays we recognize that this can also be the father's face—was a normal part of healthy development, leading to a gradual differentiation of the self from the merged mother-infant matrix, and to a creative relationship with external reality. If the mother was not responsive to the infant's actuality, so that he found in her face only the mother herself, or the mother's desires for him, development would be derailed with the formation of a false self dedicated to pleasing the mother, and an uncomfortable relationship with reality. Here are these ideas in Winnicott's own words, taken from *Playing and Reality:*

> What does the baby see when he or she looks at the mother's face? I am suggesting that, ordinarily, what the baby sees is himself or herself. In other words the mother is looking at the baby and *what she looks like is related to what she sees there*. . . . Many babies, however, do have to have a long experience of not getting back what they are giving. They look and they do not see themselves. There are consequences. First, their own creative capacity begins to atrophy. . . . Second, the baby gets settled in to the idea that when he or she looks, what is seen is the mother's face. The mother's face is not then a mirror. So perception takes the place of apperception, perception takes the place of that which might have been the beginning of a significant exchange with the world, a two-way process in which self-enrichment alternates with the discovery of meaning in the world of seen things.[10]

Where Winnicott focused on the growth-promoting effect of accurate emotional mirroring, Lacan focused on the illusory comfort that can be derived from mirroring. For Lacan, what the child saw in the mirror was always a false image that alienated him from the truth. According to Lacan, the truth for a six-to-eighteen-month-old infant is the experience of being unintegrated and lacking either a smoothly functioning body or a coherent sense of self, and therefore the infant is excited and relieved to see in a looking glass an image of himself or herself as whole. The child seizes upon and identifies with this idealized image, and this becomes the kernel of the ego. Lacan did not think of the mirror stage as a developmental step that could be successfully resolved with good-enough parenting; rather, it was the first manifestation of an ongoing experience of identifications that form the ego. Lacan named this register of experience the Imaginary, and believed that the ego's function was always to protectively alienate the subject from the truth of his or her life.

Here are these ideas in Lacan's own words (Lacan's writing is fabulously hard to understand, and this is not only a matter of translation, as he was renowned as a difficult-to-parse writer even in France. Readers not interested in the subtleties of Lacan can skip these quotations without loss): "the mirror stage is a drama whose internal pressure pushes precipitously from insufficiency to anticipation—and, for the subject caught up in the lure of spatial identification, turns out fantasies that proceed from a fragmented image of the body to what I will call an 'orthopedic' form of its totality—and to the finally donned armor of an alienating identity that will mark his entire mental development with its rigid structure."[11] And "the whole of analytic experience . . . teaches us not to regard the ego as centered on the *perception-consciousness system* or as organized by the 'reality principle' . . . but, rather, to take as our point of departure the *function of misrecognition* that characterizes the ego in all the defensive structures."[12]

In light of these ideas, we can see that Galadriel's Mirror shows qualities of both Winnicott's true mirroring and Lacan's false mirroring. It may, like the mother's mirroring face, show true reflections—things that are, things that were, and things that will happen. But it may, like Lacan's alienating mirror, show false reflections—"things that yet *may* be" implies that they may *not* be; and falsification is also introduced because whether past, present, future, true, or false, even the wise cannot tell. (This ambiguity, of course, is typical of Tolkien and is one of his strengths as a writer, as he often presents both sides of a conflict without easy or fixed resolution.) When Sam contemplates leaving for the Shire versus continuing with Frodo, when Frodo contemplates giving the Ring to Galadriel versus continuing on his task, they are choosing between false comfort and strengthening their true selves.

At the surface level, the reflection in the Mirrormere appears to be a Lacanian-style disavowal of the impact of Gandalf's death: Frodo, Sam, and especially Gimli turn from their grief to a reassurance that another lost father figure will someday reawaken. For the reader, the scene provides a brief moment of comfort, even if it is somewhat chilly comfort, in the midst of grief over the death of one of the most beloved characters. While maybe it is true that Durin will someday reawaken, that ideal hope is false to the broken feeling of the moment. Gimli later expresses the disappointment that often results from such illusory comfort as he laments leaving Lothlórien and Galadriel and states, "Memory is not what the heart desires. That is only a mirror, be it clear as Kheled-zâram."[13]

But there are other levels to the Mirrormere, and to Galadriel's Mirror as well. These mirrors share two significant features in common, and by better understanding these features, we can better understand how the mirrors strengthen Frodo's and Sam's selves in the midst of their grief over Gandalf's death.

Their first significant shared feature is that they are neither looking glasses, like Lacan's mirror, nor faces, like Winnicott's mirror. Galadriel's Mirror and the Mirrormere are both still water. This serves first of all as one of the many ways that Tolkien creates a natural, nonconstructed, nonmechanical, premodern world. But *The Lord of the Rings* and Tolkien's other writings contain many other examples of waters that we can think of as associations that lead to deeper meanings.

To begin with, another body of water, the stream called Nimrodel, lies on their journey between Mirrormere and the Mirror of Galadriel. As Frodo waded across, "he felt that the stain of travel and all weariness was washed from his limbs,"[14] and upon reaching the other shore the Fellowship entered the Elven sanctuary of Lothlórien. In this aspect, Nimrodel fills a common fairy-tale trope, that fairyland is reached by crossing water; escaping in water is also a common element in the myth of the birth of the hero.[15] The stream Nimrodel is literally a transitional space.

As the Fellowship rests beside a waterfall, "Almost Frodo fancied that he could hear a voice singing, mingled with the sound of the water." Legolas explains that it is the voice of Nimrodel, an Elf maiden who dwelt beside the stream long ago and who gave the stream its name. So Nimrodel the stream is also Nimrodel the maiden, making her reminiscent of water nymphs and fairies from traditional tales. Much earlier in his journey Frodo had met a still-living water spirit: Goldberry, the wife of Tom Bombadil, who is called River-Daughter or sometimes River-Woman's daughter. Tom Bombadil first encountered her bathing in a river pool, and when the hobbits first meet Tom, he is carrying water lilies to give to Goldberry. When the hobbits reach Tom and Goldberry's house, they see her seated and "About her feet in wide vessels of green and brown earthenware, white water-lilies were floating, so that she seemed to be enthroned in the midst of a pool."[16]

So far these associations have linked water with feminine power, beauty, and healing. But if we return to the banks of the Nimrodel, we will hear darker associations. Legolas tells Nimrodel's "long and sad" story about "how sorrow came upon Lothlórien."[17] Long ago the same balrog that pulled Gandalf into the abyss awoke and brought evil to the area, and many Elves, including Nimrodel and her lover Amroth, fled to the seacoast to take ship to safety. Nimrodel was lost on the journey to the coast and never seen again; when Amroth realized that she was not on the ship he had boarded, he dove into the sea to go after her but drowned before he could swim to shore.

As we have seen in chapter 5, the sea for Tolkien is a source of mingled fascination, attraction, and grief. Remember Galadriel's later message to Legolas:

> "Legolas Greenleaf, long under tree
> In joy thou hast lived. Beware of the sea!
> If thou hearest the cry of the gull on the shore,
> Thy heart shall then rest in the forest no more."[18]

Remember also Frodo's ominous dream about the sea that I quoted in the introduction. And remember Tolkien's description in *The Silmarillion* of how water embodies the mixture of joy and sorrow: "In the deep places [Ulmo, Vala of the sea] gives thought to music great and terrible; and the echo of that music runs through all the veins of the world in sorrow and in joy; for if joyful is the fountain that rises in the sun, its springs are in the wells of sorrow unfathomed at the foundations of the Earth. The [Sea-elves] learned much of Ulmo, and for this reason their music has both sadness and enchantment."[19]

In addition to the emotional quality of these associations, we should note one more thing: they link to fantasies about both the feminine (Nimrodel, Goldberry) and the masculine (Ulmo). Although the feminine seems to be linked to the potential for joy in streams and pools, and the masculine to sorrow in the depths, these linkages will be scrambled in the next set of associations.

I mentioned above that water was the first of two significant features we should notice that Galadriel's Mirror shares with the Mirrormere. The second feature is that both are focal points for stars. The most important vision in Mirrormere is that "like jewels sunk in the deep shone glinting stars"[20] that comprise the Crown of Durin. At first glance the stars that the hobbits see in the Mirror of Galadriel seem trivial, although the possibility that starlight may in fact be important is signified by the fact that stars bound the viewing experience: the first thing Sam sees in the Mirror is stars, and stars are the last things Frodo sees. The significance of stars becomes clearer when one notices that stars bound not only the Mirror-viewing but the entire scene. As Galadriel leads Frodo and Sam to her Mirror, "they came into an enclosed garden. No trees grew there, and it lay open to the sky. The evening star had risen and was shining with white fire above the western woods."[21] After Frodo has seen the Eye of Sauron and pulled back from the starry mirror, Galadriel "lifted up her white arms, and spread out her hands towards the East in a gesture of rejection and denial. Eärendil, the Evening Star, most beloved of the Elves, shone clear above. So bright was it that the figure of the Elven-lady cast a dim shadow on the ground. Its rays glanced upon a ring about her finger; it glittered like polished gold overlaid with silver light, and a white stone in it twinkled as if the Even-star had come down to rest upon her hand."[22] Just before they all leave the garden of the Mirror, Galadriel asks Sam if he had seen a ring upon her finger. "'No, Lady,' he answered. 'To tell you the truth, I wondered what you were talking about. I saw a star through your fingers.'"[23]

Like water, stars serve on the surface as a part of Tolkien's creation of a natural, nonconstructed, nonmechanical world, but *The Lord of the Rings* and Tolkien's other writings contain many examples of stars that we can think of as associations that lead to deeper meanings of this symbol too. Two lines of associations, actually, because Eärendil the Evening (and Morning) Star leads in a different direction than generic stars. I'll begin with the latter.

Stars reflected in water is a favorite trope of Tolkien's, seen several times in addition to the Mirrormere and Galadriel's Mirror: When Goldberry sings to the hobbits, "they saw in their minds pools and waters wider than any they had known, and looking into them they saw the sky below them and the stars like jewels in the depths."[24] In *The Silmarillion,* Barahir, father of Beren, camps with his men beside a lake that is a mirror of stars. In fact, Tolkien liked the motif so much that in *The Lord of the Rings* he twice turned the sky into metaphorical pools: Legolas, as he prepares to slay the Nazgul's flying steed, is described thus: "His head was dark, crowned with sharp white stars that glittered in the black pools of the sky behind";[25] and when Treebeard carries Merry and Pippin to one of his homes, they reach an area that "was open to the sky; stars were shining already in lakes between shores of cloud."[26]

Legolas sings a song about Nimrodel that begins

An Elven-maid there was of old,
A *shining star* by day:

Her mantle white was hemmed with gold,
Her shoes of silver-grey.

A *star* was bound upon her brows . . . [27]

Since we have seen that Nimrodel is both maiden and stream, these lines provide a transition to Tolkien describing stars not linked to water but more broadly to feminine beauty and power. Strider sings a song about Lúthien Tinúviel and Beren that includes a verse associating her with stars and describing her as like a star herself—and note that her eyes are a mirror:

As Beren looked into her eyes
Within the shadows of her hair,
The trembling *starlight* of the skies
He saw there mirrored shimmering.
Tinúviel the elven-fair,
Immortal maiden elven-wise,
About him cast her shadowy hair
And arms like silver glimmering.[28]

And Strider's own affianced is the Elven maiden Arwen Undómiel, in whom the beauty of Lúthien was thought to have returned to Middle-earth, and whose second name translates as Evenstar. Late in *The Lord of the Rings,* when the Ring has been destroyed and Frodo is deeply wounded both physically and psychologically, Arwen with these words passes to him her right to travel across the sea to Elvenhome, where ordinary mortals cannot go: "If your hurts grieve you still and the memory of your burden is heavy, then you may pass into the West, until all your wounds and weariness are healed. But wear this now in memory of Elfstone and Evenstar with whom your life has been woven!" And she took a white gem like a star that lay upon her breast hanging upon a silver chain, and she set the chain about Frodo's neck."[29]

Tolkien's most fundamental linkage of stars with a woman is hinted at early in *The Lord of the Rings* when the hobbits are still in the Shire. A Black Rider approaches in the dusk, and although the hobbits do not yet know that this is a Ringwraith, enslaved by Sauron and dedicated to recovering the One Ring for him, they know they are in terrible danger. Frodo cannot resist reaching for the Ring to put it on, which would have fatally signaled his presence to the Black Rider. He is saved by approaching Elves; the Black Rider flees from their song, which ends with these verses:

O stars that in the Sunless Year
With shining hand by her were sown,
In windy fields now bright and clear
We see your silver blossom blown!

O Elbereth! Gilthoniel!
We still remember, we who dwell
In this far land beneath the trees,
Thy starlight on the Western Seas.[30]

Neither hobbits nor readers at this point have any clear idea who Elbereth is; to learn this one must turn to the creation stories in *The Silmarillion*. Elbereth is another name for Varda, the Vala who is wife of Manwë, the Vala of sky and winds, considered the most powerful with the exception of the evil Melkor. Varda is also known as Lady of the Stars or the Kindler because she created the stars.

As Verlyn Flieger has explicated, the history of Tolkien's cosmos can be seen as a progressive splintering and diminishment of the original divine light.[31] The sun and moon were not primordial; when the Valar entered the newly formed earth, Varda illuminated it by creating two lamps that were set atop mighty pillars in Middle-earth. Melkor destroyed the lamps, after which the Valar retreated to the western land of Valinor, which they illuminated with the light of two trees created by Yavanna. The light of these trees did not reach Middle-earth so it was lit only by dim stars that Varda had created. Up to this point there were no Elves or men, although the Valar knew that they would eventually awaken, the Elves first. After eons, the Valar felt that the awakening of the Elves was imminent, and Varda determined to create brighter stars for them. "It is told that even as Varda ended her labours, and they were long, when first Menelmacar strode up the sky . . . in that hour the [Elves] awoke . . . *by the starlit mere* . . . they rose from the sleep . . . and . . . their eyes beheld first of all things the *stars of heaven*. Therefore they have ever loved the starlight, and have revered Varda Elentári above all the Valar."[32]

So we see that the primal pool lit by stars, the prototype so to speak of the Mirrormere and the Mirror of Galadriel, was the pool by which the Elves first came to life. And we see that stars create greatly loved beauty but at the same time encapsulate loss, as they are enormously diminished compared to the light of the Lamps or the Trees.

To summarize this line of associations, it has circled around a complex composed of beauty, power, hope, and loss, and feminine love and healing culminating in a mother goddess archetype, all of this embedded in deep history and extending over eons. To return to Galadriel, she can be seen as representing the same complex on a slightly less exalted level. Galadriel is not a mother goddess, but as we saw in the previous chapter, she has a number of qualities that emphasize her maternal nature. And although Galadriel does not create stars, she does give a star to Frodo—a star enclosed with waters from her mirror. As the Fellowship departs, she speaks her last words to Frodo: "She held up a small crystal phial: it glittered as she moved it, and rays of white light sprang from her hand. 'In this phial,' she said, 'is caught the light of Eärendil's star, set amid the waters of my fountain. It will shine still brighter when night is about you. May it be a light to you in dark places, when all other lights go out. Remember Galadriel and her Mirror!'" (376).

With Galadriel's gift we have returned to Eärendil's star, which as I said above leads to a second line of associations. Let's follow them now.

Eärendil is a powerful hero whose exploits the hobbits have heard glossed by Bilbo in a song in Rivendell, exploits that are more clearly explicated in *The Silmarillion.* He it is whose embassy to the Valar is accepted because he bears the Silmaril wrested from Morgoth's crown by Beren and Lúthien, and the Valar responding to his plea return to Middle-earth and defeat Morgoth, casting him into the Void. However, since Eärendil has walked in Valinor, the Valar do not allow him to return to Middle-earth. Instead, they place him to sail forever in the sky bearing the Silmaril as the Morning and Evening Star, a beacon of hope. And thus it is the light of the Silmaril that brought hope and salvation to the world, which is captured in the phial that Galadriel gives to Frodo. Yet at the same time that he is a symbol of hope and power, Eärendil embodies loss: two of the three Silmarils that hold the last light of the Two Trees are lost to the world, and the third is a remote star; in becoming this star, Eärendil himself has lost both Middle-earth and Valinor as other than a distant vision.

Thus, this line of associations also circles around a complex of beauty, power, hope, and loss. The main difference from the other line of associations to stars is that this one has to do with masculine healing and a powerful father figure: Eärendil is father to both Elrond and Elros, the first king of the Númenoreans and ancestor to Aragorn. In the depths of Galadriel's Mirror and the Mirrormere we can thus see both of Tolkien's dead parents, as well as hope for the ease of pain. This star-hope is described most clearly in Sam's experience as he and Frodo struggle, starving and exhausted, through the blasted land of Mordor: "peeping among the cloud-wrack above a dark tor high up in the mountains, Sam saw a white star twinkle for a while. The beauty of it smote his heart, as he looked up out of the forsaken land, and hope returned to him. For like a shaft, clear and cold, the thought pierced him that in the end the Shadow was only a small and passing thing: there was light and high beauty for ever beyond its reach."[33]

There is another set of associations to Eärendil that may come as close as possible to a nexus for the entire complex we have been discovering: The name Eärendil lies at the origin of Tolkien's creation of his imaginary world. In 1913 he encountered the Old English poem "Crist I," which begins "Éala Éarendel engla beorhtast" ("Hail Éarendel, brightest of angels") and "I was struck by the great beauty of this word (or name), entirely coherent with the normal style of A-S [Anglo-Saxon], but euphonic to a peculiar degree in that pleasing but not 'delectable' language."[34] By comparing it with cognates in related languages, Tolkien recognized that Éarendel was a name for Venus, which of course is both the morning and evening star depending on its position relative to the earth. In 1914 Tolkien wrote a poem titled "The Voyage of Éarendel the Evening Star," which is the first piece of writing unmistakably part of his legendarium. And the importance to Tolkien of this origin is emphasized when we realize that in the book, when Frodo wields the star-glass against Shelob, he cries out in Quenya the words "Hail Earendel, brightest of stars," almost identical to the words of the Old English poem.

In two fictions written late in his life, Tolkien depicted a star as the badge of entry to a Faerie that must be lost. The poem "The Sea-Bell" (from *The Adventures of Tom Bombadil*) begins:[35]

I walked by the sea, and there came to me,
as a *star-beam* on the wet sand,
a white shell like a sea-bell;
trembling it lay in my hand.
In my fingers shaken I heard waken
a ding within, by a harbor bar
a bouy swinging, a call ringing
over endless seas, faint now and far.[36]

The narrator boards a boat that carries him to Faërie, but no one will acknowledge him there and when he tries to claim its beauty, he is struck down and returns to the regular world, old and ailing, only to find that no one will speak to him there either. The signification of the loss of Faërie in this poem is emphasized by the editor's preface, in which he states that in the Red Book "a hand has scrawled at its head *Frodos Dreme*. That is remarkable, and though the piece is most unlikely to have been written by Frodo himself, the title shows that it was associated with the dark and despairing dreams which visited him in March and October during his last three years."[37] March and October were the anniversaries of Frodo's poisoning by Shelob and wounding on Weathertop.

In the short story "Smith of Wootton Major," the Elf king places a star in a cake, and when Smith eats the piece containing it, the star appears on his forehead. For years this star is his badge of entry to Faërie as well as protection against its perils. He has many wondrous experiences there, but eventually is told that he does not belong. Soon the king and queen of the Elves tell him it is time to pass the star on to another child. Smith lives on with his memories but can never return to Faërie.

Both the poem and story are generally considered to be semiautobiographical depictions of Tolkien's feeling that as an older man, his imaginative ability and time remaining for entering Faërie were fading. And so at both the beginning and the end of his imaginative career, Tolkien experienced a star as the portal to Faërie and imagination. Personally as well as in his legendarium, the star was a symbol of both hope and loss, with hope emphasized when Tolkien was young, when Éarendel beckoned him into years of exploring Faërie (with its mixture of hope and loss); and with loss emphasized as an older man, when he felt that his creative badge of entry to Faërie was losing its power.

To close this chapter, I will draw together these intricate lines of association: In his scenes of Galadriel's Mirror and the Mirrormere, Tolkien has intuitively given life to the ideas of Winnicott and Lacan that seeing oneself reflected structures identity, and that this structuring can either bring one closer to truth (Winnicott) or alienate one from truth (Lacan). Frodo and Sam look in the mirrors when they have been destabilized by Gandalf's death, and in the Mirror of Galadriel they both see alternate versions of themselves and have to choose which version to actualize.

These mirror scenes and their associations that we have followed are replete with images of profound depths, ranging from Frodo's vision of a great history in which he has become involved, to the history of Varda creating the stars and Eärendil becoming the Evening Star; and from the depths of pools that reflect stars, to Ulmo's waters in the deep places of the earth. In these depths are seen images of loss and tremendous darkness: the destruction of the Shire; Sauron's Eye searching for Frodo; the ongoing diminishment of the original divine light with the destruction of the Lamps, then the Two Trees, then the theft of the Silmarils ending in the loss of two out of three; Morgoth's near total conquest of Middle-earth. At the same time in these depths are seen images of beauty, healing, and hope: Varda creating the stars; Beren and Lúthien recovering a Silmaril from Morgoth; Eärendil carrying the Silmaril to Valinor, resulting in the Valar finally defeating Morgoth; Eärendil in the sky as a beacon of hope; Galadriel giving Eärendil's light to Frodo to give hope in dark places.

Are these visions hopeful or despairing? If the self-knowledge gained from gazing in Galadriel's Mirror leads the hobbits to despair, are they denying their power to change things? After all, Eärendil summoned the help that defeated Morgoth, and now Frodo has the light of Eärendil in his hands. But if self-knowledge gained from the Mirror makes the hobbits hopeful of victory, are they denying their predicament? After all, Morgoth's defeat was followed by the rise of Sauron.

This interplay of loss and hope grew out of the interplay of loss and hope in Tolkien's life; the Mirror of Galadriel reflects Tolkien's struggle to cope with and grow from his multiple traumas. And so we see the same unresolved tension between hope and despair in Tolkien's personal metaphors of stars as entry badges to Faërie. As a youth he was thrilled by the name Éarendel, and from it found his first path toward Galadriel's Mirror with its blended hope and despair. As an older man he wrote "The Sea-Bell," in which a star leads to a Faërie land of despair and then back to a normal world of despair with no more chance to enter Faërie. Also as an old man he wrote "Smith of Wootton Major," in which a star leads to a Faërie land of wondrous experiences followed by a fulfilling normal life—but here too there is no longer a chance to reenter Faërie. So what was Faërie for Tolkien? The hope of Eärendil? The despair of "The Sea-Bell?" Or something in between, like "Smith of Wootton Major"?

"Something in between" is a tempting answer, but it would be false, a lapse into Lacan's Imaginary to comfort ourselves in the face of the complexity Tolkien presents us with. To resolve this ambiguity in favor of despair, or in favor of hope, would also be false, another lapse into Lacan's Imaginary. But if we do not resolve it in any of these three directions, we are left with living in ambiguity. The truth value of what we see reflected is likely to be indeterminate. We resolve this ambiguity when we can and tolerate it when we cannot. The deepest truth lies not in resolving the ambiguity, but in the process of looking at the ambiguity directly and honestly.

I'll close with two brief quotes that I think together capture this ambiguity. First Galadriel: "together through the ages of the world we have fought the long defeat."[38]

And finally Gandalf: "despair is only for those who see the end beyond all doubt. We do not."[39]

CHAPTER 8

From the Ineluctable Wave to the Realization of Imagined Wonder

In chapter 1 I quoted what I consider Tolkien's pithiest description of enchantment: "the primal desire at the heart of Faërie [is] the realization, independent of the conceiving mind, of imagined wonder."[1] With these psychologically sophisticated words, Tolkien not only named a desire, but also depicted a state of consciousness in which this desire can come to fruition. For these words capture a paradox: the desire at the heart of Faërie is to have an experience that is both subjective—*imagined* wonder—and objective—*realized independent* of the conceiving mind. Tolkien is saying that to enter Faërie, it is necessary to have one foot in subjectivity and the other foot in objectivity.

As noted in chapter 1, this vision of Tolkien's bears a striking similarity to the British psychoanalyst D. W. Winnicott's description of *transitional objects* and *transitional phenomena*. In this chapter, I intend to explore how Tolkien's personal experience of transitionality affected his own creativity.

With his conceptualization of transitional phenomena, Winnicott gave us a tool both to understand how people can develop to live a richly experienced life, and what happens when this development is derailed. Even the luckiest of us have times when we find it difficult to integrate inner and outer reality comfortably. The risk of not being able to imbue external reality with enough inner meaning is alienation, the experience of aloneness in a cold, uncaring world; the risk of not being able to imbue inner reality with enough external meaning is madness, the insistence that the world is as one wants it to be.

Artistic creativity is one of the activities of adults that Winnicott saw as occurring in transitional space. "Art" that is dominated by the way other people see things with no transformation by the artist would simply be an object; "art" that is dominated by the artist's vision with no connection to the world of other people would be crazy. Tolkien addressed the transitionality of art in his own terms when he repudiated the concept of the willing suspension of disbelief: "this [the willing suspension of disbelief] does not seem to me a good description of what happens . . . the 'sub-creator' . . . makes a Secondary World that your mind can enter . . . inside it, what he relates is true . . . you therefore believe it while you are, as it were, inside."[2] Thus, successful storytelling requires successful integration of the storyteller's mind with the minds of the audience. Tolkien captured both sides of this with another statement about the essence of Faërie: "Fantasy, the *making or glimpsing* of Other-worlds, was the heart of the desire of Faërie."[3]

In Winnicottian terms, Tolkien's statement about the realization of imagined wonder means that Faërie exists in potential space. But what about Tolkien's statement that one of the three great benefits provided by fairy stories is recovery, which he defines as "'seeing things as we are (or were) meant to see them'—as things *apart from ourselves*"?[4] At first glance he seems to be describing something different here from his description of the primal desire at the heart of Faërie, and something opposite to transitional phenomena: a clarification of and emphasis on separateness: "We should meet the centaur and the dragon, and then perhaps suddenly behold, like the ancient shepherds, sheep, and dogs, and horses—and wolves."[5]

In fact, though, I think that Tolkien's concept of recovery is also a description of a transitional phenomenon, but at an adult level that shows greater differentiation and integration than the transitional object of infancy. The clear-seeing of recovery is an experience of separation and simultaneously of closeness because the separate object is loved. Let me clarify this by a look at the Valar.

From the perspective of the Valar, the creation of Arda is a beautiful example of "the realization, independent of the conceiving mind, of imagined wonder." At the invitation of Ilúvatar, the Valar join in composing the cosmic music. When the cycles of harmony, discord, and integration are completed, the Valar behold Arda as an immaterial vision—imagined wonder. Then Ilúvatar says "*Eä!* Let these things Be!" and Arda takes on physical form; here we have realization independent of the Valar's conceiving minds.

Only the Elves and Men, the Children of Ilúvatar, are created with no input from the Valar, and so unlike the rest of creation, they exist for the Valar as "things apart from [them]selves." This apartness is emphasized by the story of Aulë's creation of the dwarves, which in Winnicottian terms we can understand as an effort to too greatly impose internal wishes on the external world. Ilúvatar demonstrates to Aulë that the dwarves he created can have life only when Aulë is directly concentrating on giving it to them, and they can only do as he thinks; they have no independence. Then, in another moment of realization independent of the conceiving mind, Ilúvatar grants the dwarves independent life.

Aulë had created the dwarves because he couldn't stand to wait any longer for the Firstborn; like all the "good" Valar, he was deeply and affectionately involved with the Children of Ilúvatar even before they appeared. Although they did not know in advance the time of the Firstborn's appearance, they already considered their welfare and debated whether to alleviate Melkor's marring of the world in preparation for their coming. Varda created brighter stars to illuminate the darkness in which they would awaken. And when Oromë finally encountered the Elves, he "was filled with wonder, as though they were beings sudden and marvelous and unforeseen; for so it shall ever be with the Valar. From without the World, though all things may be forethought in music or foreshown in vision from afar, to those who enter verily into Eä each in its time shall be met at unawares as something new and unforetold."[6] This is a clear description of the sense of wonder and love that for Tolkien is a crucial aspect of seeing things "as we are meant to see them." The Valar further show their love and care by inviting the Elves to dwell with them and be taught by them in Valinor. In fact, the Valar love the Children so much that they clothe themselves in their form.[7]

So when Tolkien talks about "seeing things . . . as things apart from ourselves" he is not implying anything like separation or alienation. Feeling separate would mean "seeing things" as only a sense perception. For Tolkien, "seeing" is seeing with love. Feeling completely separate can only happen if one does not put enough of oneself into the world.

Melkor's relationship with the Children of Ilúvatar illustrates more sharply than Aulë's creation of the dwarves the danger of putting too much of oneself into the world because with Melkor, this grandiosity ran amok. Melkor's desire was to enslave, corrupt, and control Elves and Men. Although for theological reasons it was important to Tolkien to stress that Melkor (evil) could not create but only corrupt,[8] Melkor was able to produce an entire race, the orcs. Tolkien never settled on exactly how the orcs were brought into being, or exactly how much independence of mind they had. Frodo tells Sam, "The Shadow that bred them can only mock, it cannot make real new things of its own. I don't think it gave life to the Orcs, it only ruined them and twisted them."[9] As to what the Shadow had ruined or twisted, Tolkien early on suggested Elves, and in late writings variously suggested that orcs included strains of Elves, men, and even beasts while also denying the likelihood of Elvish origin.[10] As for their independence of mind, Tolkien's contradictory statements included among others that they had both independent wills and reasoning power, and that they showed "servitude to a central will that reduced the Orcs almost to an ant-like life."[11] In *The Lord of the Rings* the orcs that capture Merry and Pippin, and those of the Tower of Cirith Ungol, behave with considerable independence, whereas when the Ring is destroyed and Sauron is diminished, his creatures, including orcs, run about witlessly. But even with all these varying particulars, it is clear that Melkor intended, and largely succeeded in, the formation of a race after his own desire.

What Melkor did with the orcs he did to an extent with the entire world, imbuing it with his evil so that all of Arda is Morgoth's Ring. "Thus, outside the Blessed Realm, all 'matter' was likely to have a 'Melkor ingredient,' and those who had bodies . . . had as it were a tendency, small or great, towards Melkor: they were none of them wholly free of him in their incarnate form, and their bodies had an effect upon their spirits."[12] In all these examples—imbuing Arda with his evil, forming the orcs, enslaving the Children—we see that a crucial aspect of Melkor's evil was that he strove to impose himself so that the Other would no longer be truly Other.

"Seeing things as apart from ourselves," then, does not mean relating to the Other on one extreme as separate and disinterested, or on another extreme by controlling it. It means relating to the Other with love, which includes love of its otherness. Tolkien sums all this up as follows: "The uncorrupted Valar, therefore, yearned for the Children before they came and loved them afterwards, as creatures 'other' than themselves, independent of them and their artistry."[13] In Winnicottian terms, this is relating to the Other in transitional space, where the external world and the internal world are both separate and integrated. Unlike the baby's transitional object, this is transitional space appropriate to adulthood, when separate internal and external worlds are clearly recognized.

A hallmark of transitional experience and transitional space is the recognition that things can have multiple meanings and that different people can have different but equally valid points of view; this is why Winnicott also called transitional space "potential space." The opposite of transitional/potential experiencing is to experience things as solid, unchanging facts. If one is exclusively invested in the external world, one disregards feeling and fantasy in favor of rational facts; if one is exclusively invested in the internal world, one experiences one's feelings and fantasies as themselves being rational facts.

Both internal conflict and psychic trauma produce thought and experience that feel like concrete fact in this way. Intractable conflicts center around thoughts/emotions/fantasies that are too frightening to face openly and directly, and instead manifest themselves in repetitive maladaptive symptoms or patterns of behavior. Psychic trauma can result in unchanging reexperiencing of the trauma in the repetitive failed attempt to master it.[14] Part of the process of resolving conflicts or healing from trauma is to move these experiences into potential space where one can discover new ways of understanding and handling them.

Winnicott's ideas apply to creativity broadly conceived—to the potential in all of us to live rich, creative lives—but they also apply to artistic creativity per se. In the case of artists, areas of the mind that are difficult to experience in potential space can result in blocked or unsatisfying artistic production. Even artists who are often comfortable with transitional experiencing can have times, or areas of their mind, where transitional experiencing is blocked due to internal conflict or experiences of trauma. In these areas, rather than creating symbols that have multiple meanings, they may create "frozen symbols" that have fact-like immutability.[15] Such symbols unfreeze only when they can be brought into potential space and used creatively.

Tolkien's dream of the ineluctable wave was such a frozen symbol. In Tolkien's fullest descriptions of the dream, he also tells how he unfroze the symbol. In a letter dated June 7, 1955, he wrote: "I have what some might call an Atlantis complex . . . I mean the terrible recurrent dream (beginning with memory) of the Great Wave, towering up, and coming in ineluctably over the trees and green fields. (I bequeathed it to Faramir.) I don't think I have had it since I wrote the 'Downfall of Númenor' as the last of the legends of the First and Second Age."[16] In a letter dated July 16, 1964, he wrote: "What I might call my Atlantis-haunting. This legend or myth or dim memory of some ancient history has always troubled me. In sleep I had the dreadful dream of the ineluctable Wave, either coming out of the quiet sea, or coming in towering over the green inlands. It still occurs occasionally, though now exorcized by writing about it. It always ends by surrender, and I awake gasping out of deep water."[17] Tolkien elaborated on the meaning of "Atlantis-haunting" in a letter of September 25, 1954: "the Atlantis tradition . . . seems to me so fundamental to 'mythical history'—whether it has any kind of basis in real history . . . is not relevant—that some version of it would have to come in," meaning come in to Tolkien's mythology.[18]

We can glean several psychologically important meanings from these descriptions:

1. The Atlantis/Wave symbol complex was important to Tolkien from a very early age.
2. The symbol recurrently troubled his dreams without changing.
3. The Atlantis/Wave complex symbolized Tolkien's experience of passive surrender to overwhelming impersonal force.
4. The symbol was so fundamental to him that he knew he would have to put it into his mythology.
5. Putting the symbol complex into his mythology by writing the "Downfall of Númenor" (which henceforth I will call "Downfall") was psychologically healing for Tolkien. In the 1955 letter he reported that he no longer had the dream at all. In the later letter of 1964, he reported that the dream did still occasionally recur, but it was clearly less frequent and less troubling; he had "exorcised" it. Indeed, after this time the image of a great wave became flexibly available for Tolkien to use as a metaphor: In a letter from the autumn of 1970 he described the house in which he was living as "contented and quiet but at the same time a bit surprised, as if it had been dumped here by a wave while asleep, and did not feel sure where it was," and in a letter of January 24, 1972, after the death of his wife, Tolkien wrote, "suddenly I feel like a castaway on a barren island under a heedless sky after the loss of a great ship."[19]

Tolkien wrote versions of the "Downfall" in several works: "The Fall of Númenor," "The Lost Road," "The Notion Club Papers," "The Drowning of Anadûnê," "The Akallabêth," and the appendices to *The Lord of the Rings*. Although some versions are more complete than others, all are basically consistent. Boiled down to its essence, the key elements are the following: The Valar reward a group of humans for their services against Morgoth by granting them long life and the island of Númenor to live on within sight of Eressëa in the Undying Lands; the Valar forbid the Númenóreans to sail west out of sight of their own shores or set foot in the Undying Lands; under the influence of Sauron, the Númenórean king hubristically invades Valinor in the vain hope of attaining immortality; Ilúvatar responds by sending a great wave that destroys their armada and sinks Númenor; prior to this calamity, Elendil's father Amandil tried to sail to Valinor to prevent it but failed and was never seen again; a small group of men under the leadership of Elendil, who were faithful to the Valar, escapes to Middle-earth.

What was it about writing the "Downfall" that was psychologically healing for Tolkien? First of all, the story of the "Downfall" is much more complex than Tolkien's recurrent dream, and by thus enriching and elaborating the Atlantis/Wave symbol, Tolkien was moving into transitional space where the symbol was less rigid and fact-like. Similarly, writing the dream into forms intended for an audience was a move into transitional space, where the symbol was no longer Tolkien's alone but was intended to be integrated with the larger community of minds.

Additionally, the particular ways that Tolkien elaborated on his dream show him struggling to transcend and understand his Atlantis/Wave complex. The element of a small group of Númenóreans surviving introduces hope where the dream presented only hopeless surrender. Furthermore, since those who survived were the "Faithful" who both enjoyed a relationship with the Elves and Valar and accepted that the Undying Lands were eternally separate, the survival of this small group shows that hope arises for people whose love for the Other includes love of its otherness, as discussed above.[20]

Most importantly, Tolkien shows that hubris was the cause of the "Downfall." On one level, this is simply good storytelling. But on another level, it raises the possibility that conflict over hubris was an important unconscious meaning of Tolkien's Atlantis/Wave complex, and therefore that the "Downfall" was psychologically healing because in the process of writing it, Tolkien gained insight into his conflict over hubris.[21] As a first step in further developing this idea, let us take a closer look at how writing the "Downfall" unfroze Tolkien's creativity.

By moving his dream of the ineluctable wave into transitional space, Tolkien freed himself of an anxiety and made an important addition to the history of Middle-earth. But he also did much, much more. The dream appears to have been only the consciously visible aspect of a conflict over hubris that was inhibiting Tolkien in writing and publishing from his legendarium, in particular *The Lord of the Rings.*

In a letter of January 14, 1956, Tolkien described how he got to the point that he could write *The Lord of the Rings:* "And I saw that I was *meant* to do it (as Gandalf would say), since without thought, in a 'blurb' I wrote for *The Hobbit,* I spoke of the time between the Elder Days and the Dominion of Men. Out of that came the 'missing link': the 'Downfall of Númenor,' releasing some hidden 'complex.'"[22] If we take a close look at the history of writing the "Downfall," we can see how Tolkien used it to release his complex: Tolkien wrote versions of the "Downfall" during periods when he was either making his legendarium public or felt blocked in doing so, which are times when we can infer that any feelings of hubris about his creation would be especially prominent for him: times of publication are when an author feels most exposed; times of creative inhibition occur when an author feels most conflicted about creating.

The following table shows the correspondences in time between Tolkien's writing of versions of the "Downfall," the public status of other parts of Tolkien's legendarium (*The Hobbit, The Lord of the Rings,* and *The Silmarillion*), and Tolkien's health.

Table 8.1 The "Downfall of Númenor" Was Midwife to *The Lord of the Rings**

Date	"Downfall"	Public Status of *The Hobbit*/*The Lord of the Rings*/The Silmarillion	Health
1936/1937	"Fall of Númenor" written	*The Hobbit* going public	
Nov. 1937	"The Lost Road" submitted to publisher	The Silmarillion papers also submitted; begins writing *The Lord of the Rings*	
1945–46	"Notion Club Papers" written Dec. 1945–first half of 1946; "Drowning of Anadûnë written early 1946	Stuck writing *The Lord of the Rings* early 1945–Sept. 1946	Feb.–Mar. 1946 ill from worry; Mar.–Apr. 1946 "near to a real nervous breakdown"
Autumn 1948	Writing "Akallabêth"	Writing appendices to *The Lord of the Rings*	

*Dates taken from Cristina Scull and Wayne Hammond, *The J. R. R. Tolkien Companion and Guide: Chronology*, rev. ed. (Boston: Houghton-Mifflin, 2017), and Cristina Scull and Wayne Hammond, *The J. R. R. Tolkien Companion and Guide: Reader's Guide*, rev. ed. (Boston: Houghton Mifflin, 2017).

Scull and Hammond tell us that the first version, "The Fall of Númenor," can be roughly dated to 1936 or possibly 1937.[23] This is about the time when *The Hobbit,* originally composed for private pleasure and the enjoyment of Tolkien's children, was going public. Although it was not actually published until September 1937, Susan Dagnall read it in early 1936, it was submitted for publication in October 1936, and it was accepted in December.[24] Thus, "The Fall of Númenor" coincided with Tolkien's first major public exposure of legendarium-related materials.

The Hobbit had rapid success and Tolkien's publishers quickly called for a sequel. Tolkien submitted "The Lost Road," the next version of "Downfall," in November 1937 for consideration as a possible follow-up to *The Hobbit,* so he must have been writing it in 1937.[25] Tolkien submitted a version of the Silmarillion at the same time, and actually began writing *The Lord of the Rings* in December 1937.[26] Thus, "The Lost Road" coincided with considerable exposure and anticipated exposure of the legendarium.

The writing of the next versions, "The Notion Club Papers" and "The Drowning of Anadûnê," overlapped: Tolkien wrote the former between December 1945 and the first half of 1946, and the latter in early 1946.[27] This coincided with the long hiatus from early 1945 until September 1946 during which Tolkien was stuck in writing *The Lord of the Rings,* making no progress on it. (The correspondence in time may have been even tighter: on December 18, 1944, which is immediately subsequent to Tolkien's last progress on *The Lord of the Rings* until after the hiatus, he seems to refer to "The Notion Club Papers" as "my dimly projected third [novel]," although it is unclear how much thought he was putting into it at the time.)[28] Tolkien read "The Drowning of Anâdunê" to the Inklings in August 1946, and had apparently read them "The Notion Club Papers" previously.[29] He then finally resumed writing *The Lord of the Rings* in late September.[30] "The Notion Club Papers" is written about a club much like the Inklings, including characters partially based on specific Inklings, including Tolkien himself, and it likely that Tolkien found it particularly freeing to thus write about the ineluctable wave in a context so closely connected to himself. Tolkien appears to have been inhibited in writing *The Lord of the Rings* by internal factors during this period, and these versions of the "Downfall" appear to have been the crucial ones for "releasing [Tolkien's] hidden 'complex'" about writing *The Lord of the Rings.*

Tolkien wrote the final version of the "Downfall," "The Akallabêth," in the autumn of 1948, at the same time that he was working on the appendices to *The Lord of the Rings.* By this time, he appears to have worked through his complex: *The Lord of the Rings* was largely complete, and "The Akallabêth" was in sufficiently final form that Christopher included it in the published *Silmarillion.*

I have included in table 8.1 a note on Tolkien's mental and physical health during the period when he was blocked writing *The Lord of the Rings.* It is risky to make too much about the timing of Tolkien's ailments, since he was afflicted on so many occasions during his life (see chapter 9). Nevertheless, it is worth noting in particular that during the period when *The Lord of the Rings* lay fallow and Tolkien was working on "The Notion Club Papers," he had an episode when he was "ill from worry" and another when he was "near a real nervous breakdown."[31] These episodes are certainly consistent with the idea that Tolkien's complex behind the ineluctable wave was seriously debilitating.

Writing the "Downfall" may not have been the only time that Tolkien freed himself from a frozen symbol. John Garth has argued that a similar process of transforming traumatic memory by incorporating it into his writing enabled Tolkien to overcome a block in writing *The Lord of the Rings* from December 1943 to April 1944. World War II, and in particular the involvement of Tolkien's sons Christopher and Michael in the war, stirred up Tolkien's memories of his own war experience to an extent that inhibited his creativity. He was finally able to resume writing *The Lord of the Rings* by integrating these memories into the chapters about Frodo and Sam's approach to Mordor. Tolkien sent these chapters to Christopher as he completed them, and this immediate sharing was likely a part of his process of shifting from isolated traumatic memory to shared transitional experience.[32]

The chronology demonstrates the truth of Tolkien's statement that writing the "Downfall" freed him from a complex, and indicates that the complex centered around a conflict over hubris. To further develop this idea, we need additional evidence that Tolkien struggled with a sense of hubris. And indeed, Tolkien appears to have struggled mightily with a feeling that writing and publishing his legendarium and *The Lord of the Rings* was hubristic.

Tolkien's concept of subcreation may be understood as a defense against any possibility that in his creativity he was overreaching, as an assurance that rather than usurping any power from God the Father, he was honoring God by using skills that God had given him and emulating God's creative acts. Tolkien first wrote of subcreation in his poem "Mythopoiea," the relevant lines of which he quoted in "On Fairy-Stories":

> Although now long estranged,
> Man is not wholly lost nor wholly changed.
> Dis-graced he may be, yet is not dethroned,
> and keeps the rags of lordship once he owned,
> Man, Sub-creator, the refracted Light
> through whom is splintered from a single White
> to many hues, and endlessly combined
> in living shapes that move from mind to mind.
> Though all the crannies of the world we filled
> with Elves and Goblins, though we dared to build
> Gods and their houses out of dark and light,
> and sowed the seed of dragons, 'twas our right

(used or misused). The right has not decayed.
We make still by the law in which we're made.

So Tolkien's beloved Elves, goblins, dragons, even the Gods (Valar) that he wrote about, were not his self-determined creations—that would have meant Tolkien was like Aulë creating the dwarves—but splinters of God's single light. Tolkien had the right to make them because his making them was mimetic of God making all Creation. Tolkien made these points more prosaically in "On Fairy-Stories": "Fantasy remains a human right: we make in our measure and in our derivative mode, because we are made: and not only made, but made in the image and likeness of a Maker."[33]

Tolkien's theory of subcreation was enormously important to him, so much so that he stated, "the whole matter [his legendarium] from beginning to end is mainly concerned with the relation of Creation to making and sub-creation."[34] (Tolkien claimed at different times in different contexts that different things were central to his creation—I cited him referring in this way to death in chapter 1—so the statement I just quoted is not definitive that subcreation was the main concern of his legendarium, but it does make the case that subcreation was very important.) And Tolkien was also concerned that the relation of subcreation to Creation be understood correctly, as he defended it strongly in the same letter, written to a reader who thought that Tolkien had overreached by writing about reincarnation (in the case of Elves), something that God had not already put into the world: "We differ entirely about the relation of sub-creation to Creation. I should have said that liberation 'from the channels the creator is known to have used already' is the fundamental function of 'sub-creation,' a tribute to the infinity of His potential variety, one of the ways in which it is exhibited." Tolkien is reasserting here that when he writes about something fantastical, he is not in conflict with God but is honoring God.

It should be clear that in positioning himself as a subcreator, Tolkien was not expressing a sense of abjection or impotence. Rather, he was declaring the relationship with God the Father in which he could comfortably work, a relationship in which no iota of hubris could be found: in no sense a challenger, in no sense creating something independently from the father figure but rather showing his connection to the father figure by creating as he was created.

Although Tolkien was expressing his Catholic faith in his formulation of subcreation, he was expressing his faith in a manner unique to him. Clearly it was not mandatory in Catholicism to come up with such a formulation or to invest it with such importance, or every Catholic would have done so already. By creating this expression of faith, Tolkien demonstrated the importance to him in particular of avoiding any semblance of hubris.

Tolkien's letters contain a number of descriptions of how moments of creation felt to him. As befits his ideas about subcreation, Tolkien often disavowed personal responsibility for what he wrote. We already saw this in the letter of January 14, 1956, quoted above, where Tolkien said he was "meant" to write *The Lord of the Rings.* Here are other examples: "It would be idle to pretend . . . that I have not a pleasure in praise, with as little vanity as fallen man can manage (he has not much more share in his writings than in his children of the body, but it is something to have a function)";[35] "The mere stories . . . arose in my mind as 'given' things . . . always I had the sense of recording what was already 'there,' somewhere: not of 'inventing'";[36] "parts seem (to me) rather revealed through me than by me";[37] "I have long ceased to *invent* . . . I wait till I seem to know what really happened. Or till it writes itself";[38] "[the appendices] will be a big volume, even if I only attend to the things revealed to my limited understanding!";[39] and describing his response to a man who said, "'Of course you don't suppose, do you, that you wrote all that book by yourself?'": "Pure Gandalf! . . . I think I said: 'No, I don't suppose so any longer.' I have never since been able to suppose so."[40] To these statements we must add Tolkien's famous claim about how he began *The Hobbit* while grading exams: "On a blank leaf I scrawled: 'In a hole in the ground there lived a hobbit.' I did not and do not know why,"[41] as well as his reply to G. B. Smith, who had asked what Tolkien's Éarendel verses were about: "I don't know. I'll try to find out."[42]

As the apogee of this attitude to his writing, consider Tolkien's comment about his creation of the Ents: "Take the Ents, for instance. I did not consciously invent them at all. The chapter on Treebeard . . . stands with an effect on myself (except for labor pains) almost like reading someone else's work. And I like Ents now because they do not seem to have anything to do with me."[43] Here Tolkien not only disavows responsibility for creating the Ents, but expresses his pleasure in "seeing [them] . . . as things apart from [him]self." This is a beautiful example of transitional experiencing, where "the making *or* glimpsing of Other-worlds" becomes the making *and* glimpsing of Other-worlds.

All the above passages are descriptions of artistic inspiration—literally "being breathed into" with the implication that all the artist is doing is setting forth something that was put into him; Tolkien's metaphor of giving birth in the last passage is a direct expression of this (and I borrowed the metaphor for the title of table 8.1). In many religions, inspiration is understood as coming from the gods; in Christianity, inspiration comes from the Holy Spirit. Tolkien's repeated descriptions of inspiration are thus congruent with his concept of subcreation. One of the psychological functions of experiencing one's creations as inspired is to protect oneself from the terrors of claiming the work as one's own. And despite Tolkien's efforts to position himself without hubris, he knew these terrors. After receiving qualified appreciation of the Silmarillion from Stanley Unwin, Tolkien wrote, "I have suffered a sense of fear and bereavement, quite ridiculous, since I let this private and beloved nonsense out; and I think if it had seemed to you to be nonsense I should have felt really crushed."[44] And shortly before publication of *The Lord of the Rings* he wrote, "I am dreading the publication, for it will be impossible not to mind what is said. I have exposed my heart to be shot at."[45]

Heretofore I have been demonstrating one side of Tolkien's conflict over hubris: his defense against hubris with his theory of subcreation and his experience of inspiration. Tolkien also showed us the other side of this conflict, open hubris and its consequences, which he described in the letter to Waldman in late 1951: "sub-creative desire . . . may become possessive, clinging to the things made as 'its own,' the sub-creator wishes to be the Lord and God of his private creation. He will rebel against the laws of the Creator."[46] Tolkien of course illustrated this in the character of Melkor, but the character who really brings it alive because we know him before he is overcome with hubris, and we see the moments that hubris overtakes him, is Fëanor.

Fëanor was "of all the Noldor . . . the most subtle of mind and the most skilled in hand."[47] His mother was so exhausted by giving birth to him that her spirit left her body and, most unusually, chose not to return. His father, Finwë, later remarries; significantly, *The Silmarillion* does not speak of Fëanor's grief about losing his mother, but emphasizes his displeasure at his father for remarrying, and it is the latter that other observers focused on: "In those unhappy things which later came to pass, and in which Fëanor was the leader, many saw the effect of this breach within the house of Finwë."[48] This emphasis on Fëanor's emotional rebellion against his father draws our attention to it as a sign of his developing hubris.

Fëanor's skill was such that he devised an improved writing system, learned how to make gems more beautiful than those naturally occurring, and eventually, of course, created the Silmarils that preserved the light of the Two Trees. After creating them, Fëanor fell in love with them: "The heart of Fëanor was fast bound to these things that he himself had made."[49] With the emphasis provided by "he himself," Tolkien makes sure we notice that now Fëanor's pride and hubris begin to overmatch him. Soon "Fëanor began to love the Silmarils with a greedy love . . . he seldom remembered now that the light within them was not his own."[50]

When Melkor and Ungoliant destroy the Two Trees, Yavanna pleads that it is beyond her power to remake them, but that with their light from the Silmarils she could recall them to life. Fëanor responds that he could never again make the like of the Silmarils, "and if I must break them, I shall break my heart, and I shall be slain . . . this thing I will not do of free will."[51] It is then discovered that Melkor and Ungoliant have already stolen the Silmarils, slaying Finwë in the process. The narrator states that therefore "all one it may seem whether Fëanor had said yea or nay to Yavanna; yet had he said yea at the first . . . it may be that his after deeds would have been other than they were."[52] His after deeds were, of course, the oath that he and his sons took "to pursue with vengeance and hatred to the ends of the World Vala, Demon, Elf or Man . . . whoso should . . . keep a Silmaril from their possession," as well as the entire resulting tragedy of the Elves.[53] By swearing their oath, Fëanor and his sons lock themselves into a repetitive, unchangeable pattern of conflict. They have destroyed potential space.

It is not Melkor's killing of the Two Trees and theft of the Silmarils that causes disaster; rather, disaster results from Fëanor's response, his pride and hubris. Could Tolkien have asserted any more strongly the dangers of artistic hubris than by thus placing it at the core of his legendarium?

So Tolkien's concept of subcreation was an effort to position his creativity properly vis-à-vis the creativity of God the Father, and a first sign of Fëanor's hubris was his emotional rebellion against his father for remarrying. What about Tolkien's relationship with his actual father?

Tolkien dated his dream of the ineluctable wave to the earliest days he could remember, suggesting that a childhood experience of hubris was already part of his personality. Because we have only fragmentary information about Tolkien's early childhood, what follows is necessarily tentative; however, both biographical and textual data are consistent with the idea that the young Tolkien had anxieties about overreaching, linked to the death of his father.

Tolkien's earliest memories date from late in his third year and early in his fourth, about the age when he experienced the first of a series of dramatic traumas: separation from his father and his father's subsequent death before they ever saw each other again. For my purposes, what is important about these memories is not their historical, factual truth but what they tell us about Tolkien's emotional life. Like many people's earliest memories,

Tolkien's record seemingly trivial events; such memories appear to be retained because they symbolize emotionally significant life themes.[54] Memory is malleable and can be affected by suggestion,[55] although at least one study has demonstrated continuity in earliest reported memories from age twenty-one to forty-three.[56] Therefore, although we cannot be certain that Tolkien's earliest recorded memories represent historical truth, and we do not know if they became important to him at precisely the ages he remembers, it is reasonable to assume that they represent emotionally significant themes from his early life.

Tolkien's earliest memories that we know of include two where the exact date is uncertain: he remembered running in fear through long, dead grass after a tarantula bit him, although he did not remember the tarantula;[57] and he remembered being horrified to see an archdeacon eat corn in native fashion.[58] He ascribed a memory of bathing in the Indian Ocean to his second year, although memories from such an early age are rare and are likely to be misdated or partly constructed later in life. Tolkien's earliest memories that can be dated with more certainty come from when he was about three years old. He had a faint memory of a long train journey in November 1894, and of running back from the sea to a bathing hut.[59] He recalled a clearer image from Christmas 1894: "My first Christmas memory is of blazing sun, drawn curtains, and a drooping Eucalyptus."[60] His other earliest memories are from just before and during his trip to England, when he was a young three-year-old: in late March or early April 1895 he watched his father paint "A. R. Tolkien" on the lid of a cabin trunk,[61] and from the voyage itself that same April, he remembered dark people diving into the water to collect coins thrown from the ship, and a city on a hill, which later in life he realized must have been Lisbon.[62]

Several emotionally significant things are notable about these memories. First, none of them involve direct interaction with people; this suggests that already at an early age Tolkien was prone to feelings of aloneness/loneliness/loss. Second, the only person important in Tolkien's life to appear in these memories was his father; and third, the memories of his father and of the voyage all concern the time of separation from his father. This cluster of memories indicates that Tolkien's loss of his father was a major organizer of his emotions. Finally, we may wonder if memory of the sea voyage that carried Tolkien away from his father is one of the roots of his dream of the ineluctable wave.[63]

Textual evidence indicates that the "Downfall" was in part a working-through of Tolkien's feelings about his father. In the basic elements of the story, we see four father figures: The king of Númenor, the father of his people, who in the wish to avoid death commits an act of fatal hubris; Ilúvatar, God the Father, who punishes this hubris; Elendil, the father of the subsequent line of Númenórean royalty on Middle-earth, who is allowed to escape; and Amandil, Elendil's father, who out of good motives also commits an act of hubris and is lost. Taken together, these elements represent a complex of feelings linking father, death, and punishment for hubris.

And as I noted in chapter 6, one version of the "Downfall," "The Lost Road," was primarily a work about father-son relationships. As Tolkien described it, "the thread was to be the occurrence time and again in human families . . . of a father and son called by names that could be interpreted as Bliss-friend and Elf-friend." The autobiographical similarity is overt, with Alboin, the son in the first pair, having language interests, school career, and professional interests very like Tolkien's.

To repeat, these inferences about early childhood are tentative. However, Tolkien's biography, his earliest reported memories, and textual evidence from the "Downfall" all converge in indicating that Tolkien responded to separation from his father when he was three and to his father's subsequent death when he was four by developing anxiety about overreaching.

We can speculate about the more precise form of Tolkien's reaction to his father's death by considering typical developmental issues for children around the age Tolkien was at that time. Erik Erikson considered these to be the stages when development of autonomy and initiative are central;[64] a boy's loss of his father at this age deprives him of a strong figure with whom to identify and can thus interfere with his sense of autonomy and initiative. The transition from the third to the fourth year is also typically when the child is in the early Oedipal phase, when cognitive and emotional maturation are such that children begin to feel rivalry with each parent for the love of the other. If a boy's father dies at this age, the boy's experience may be that he now has the mother mostly to himself, with consequent pleasure at the exclusivity, guilt at this pleasure resulting from the father's death, and anxiety about imagined responsibilities. It is common for young children to unrealistically blame themselves for calamities that befall them, so a boy in this situation may guiltily imagine that his rivalrous feelings had contributed to his father's death. Along these lines, we may speculate that Tolkien responded to the death of his father by developing inhibition, shame, and/or guilt about age-appropriate feelings of rivalry, competition, autonomy, and initiative, and that this conflict was the origin of his complex around hubris.

Of course, we do not have Tolkien's own associations to confirm, disprove, or clarify this reconstruction. But even if we set it aside as too speculative, Tolkien's "associations" in the form of his memories and writings do support the interpretation that his complex around hubris was focused on worries about overreaching in relation to father figures more generally. Writing the "Downfall" released his complex because it enabled Tolkien to play in transitional space with his concerns that hubris would be punished by father figures, and lack of hubris rewarded.

To briefly sum up: In his elucidation of the psychological foundations of Faërie, Tolkien described the process of entering what Winnicott named *transitional space,* the foundation of creative living in general, and artistic creativity specifically. The opposite of transitional space—and therefore the opposite of Faërie—is a space of concrete, material fact. Intrapsychic conflict and/or experiences of trauma situate a person in this kind of factual space where creative living and artistic creativity cannot occur. Tolkien's dream of the ineluctable wave appears to have symbolized an intrapsychic conflict over hubris that he developed in response to the trauma of his father's death, such that he unconsciously inhibited his creativity so as not to threaten his relationship with father figures. By writing the "Downfall"—putting it into transitional space—Tolkien "exorcised" the dream so that it no longer troubled him and, more importantly, "released [the] hidden complex" so that he could complete *The Lord of the Rings.*

This understanding of Tolkien's creativity leads to a subtler understanding of what he meant by "Escape." In Tolkien's justification of "Escape" as one of the main benefits of fairy stories, he focuses on the value of escaping from unpleasant material realities of the modern world.[65] This has left him open to charges of anachronism and avoidance of modern realities. But I think these charges are invalidated, and Tolkien's concept of Escape made more profound, if we see it as a metaphor for "escaping" a concrete, material state of mind—in other words, for finding or refinding transitional space. Tolkien went through this process in his own artistic creation, and all of his oeuvre that is set in Faërie or at its boundaries draws his readers into this process. Perhaps part of his appeal is that he helps people move from their own ineluctable waves to the realization of imagined wonder.

CHAPTER 9

Something Has Gone Crack

It is widely understood that World War I had a major impact on Tolkien's writing. From the more general to the more particular, we have studies exploring how Tolkien shared the modernist concern with trying to find a way to express the culture-changing horror of the war, however different from the modernists his solution was;[1] Janet Croft's exploration of themes in Tolkien's work that are congruent with themes of the war;[2] studies of traumatic reactions experienced by Frodo and Túrin;[3] and manifest one-to-one similarities, such as the tank-like mechanical dragons in "The Fall of Gondolin," or the similarity acknowledged by Tolkien between the Dead Marshes and the Somme battlefield.[4]

On one level, these effects of the war can be understood as Tolkien using his monumental creative talent to integrate and find meaning in his war experiences. I wish to explore the effects of the war on a more personal level by examining Tolkien's prewar suffering from emotional loss, and his susceptibility to physical ailments particularly at times of stress, and then examining how the traumatic exacerbation of these vulnerabilities by World War I shaped Tolkien's later life and writings.

To begin, it will be illuminating to unpack Tolkien's well-known statement in his letter of August 12, 1916, to G. B. Smith about his reaction to the battlefield death of fellow TCBS member Rob Gilson: "So far my chief impression is that something has gone crack. I feel just the same to both of you [Smith and the other surviving TCBS member, Christopher Wiseman]—nearer if anything and very much in need of you—I am hungry and lonely of course—

but I don't feel a member of a little complete body now. I honestly feel that the TCBS has ended."[5]

This is a very powerful statement of distress—but distress at what, exactly? By writing "*something* has gone crack" (italics added), Tolkien, an extremely skilled wordsmith not prone to vagueness, indicated uncertainty about just what was troubling him. Judging from the end of the quoted passage, the "something" surely includes the TCBS, but if that were all it included, then why did Tolkien not express himself along the lines of, "The TCBS has gone crack," or why did he not employ a word like *coterie,* which Wiseman found fitting in his response quoted below?

A crack in the TCBS is apparently the meaning Smith and Wiseman responded to in Tolkien's statement. An incensed Smith wrote that when he and Tolkien next met, "I am not quite sure whether I shall shake you by the hand or take you by the throat" and "'As to the winnowing of the TCBS,' he said, 'I really do not care two straws. It only refers to its executive capacity. . . .' The group was spiritual in character, 'an influence on the state of being,' and as such it transcended mortality; it was 'as permanently inseparable as Thor and his hammer.' The influence, he said, was 'a tradition, which forty years from now will still be as strong to us (if we are alive, and if we are not) as it is today.'"[6] And Wiseman "was baffled by Tolkien's assertion that he no longer felt part of a 'little complete body,' and went on, 'Speaking for myself I know that I belong to a coterie of three. . . . Now this coterie is for me quite sufficient. It is the TCBS . . . I as yet see no reason to doubt that there is an achievement for our striving and a prize for our winning provided we are willing to pay the price. I cannot see that the TCBS is altered.'"[7]

Another meaning of Tolkien's "something" can be gleaned by considering other words in his statement and seeing how they contrast with Smith and Wiseman's language. Tolkien refers to the TCBS not as a coterie, or any similar word such as *club, set,* or *circle,* but as "a little complete body." Tolkien implicates his own body with his statement that he is hungry as well as lonely. And the word *crack* conjures a physical break in something, as well as an immediate auditory experience such as the sound of gunfire. Perhaps without consciously intending it, Tolkien has associated his feelings about the death of his friend to the bodily insults of war. This vivid, immediate, body-oriented language is quite different from the abstract language of Smith and Wiseman quoted above, utilizing words such as "executive capacity," "spiritual," "state of being," "tradition," "achievement," and "prize." Smith's metaphor of the inseparability of Thor and his hammer makes the point even clearer because it insists not on the intactness of an actual body but of a relationship between body and object. I propose that Tolkien wrote "*something* has gone crack" because he experienced Gilson's death not only in terms of the interpersonal loss of a beloved member of an intense social group, with all the creative and spiritual implications focused on by Smith and Wiseman, but also as a blow to his body-self.

In this chapter I intend to develop these thoughts in two interrelated directions. First, although it is clear that the trauma of World War I affected Tolkien strongly, these effects can be understood fully only if we take into consideration the psychological vulnerabilities that Tolkien brought into the war. As the reactions of the remaining TCBS members to Gilson's death indicate, trauma affects different people in different ways: unlike Tolkien, Smith and Wiseman did not invoke the body and they vehemently denied as well that any crack had taken place in the social, creative, and spiritual realms. Second, the most important specific vulnerabilities that Tolkien brought into the war were those I have indicated above as forming his reaction to Gilson's death: vulnerabilities to emotional loss and physical ailment. The crack of World War I exacerbated preexisting fault lines in Tolkien's interpersonal relationship schemas and his body-self.

A brief discussion of the general psychological effects of trauma will be helpful before exploring Tolkien's personal reaction to the trauma of World War I.

Traumatic events overwhelm the victim's ability to cope with them and assimilate them into his or her ongoing sense of self. This happens because the quantity of aversive stimulation is too much to handle and/or because the victim must totally devote himself or herself to managing and surviving the external event.[8] In either of these situations, self-continuity is disrupted. Traumatic events include *shock trauma,* such as abrupt exposure to death, physical injury, or sexual violence,[9] and *cumulative* or *strain trauma,* in which repeated experiences of less shocking stressors cumulatively have traumatic effect.[10] An example would be responding to a baby's or toddler's distress with scolding; if this happens on rare occasion, it is unlikely to have significant impact, but if it happens regularly, the child learns that the world is critical and rejecting of his or her needs.

Certain reactions are common after experiencing traumatic events.[11] These include repetitive reexperiencing of the event in thought, fantasy, dream, or action; avoidance of reminders of the event; somatic symptoms, including illness, irritability, and sleep disturbance; affective states such as rage, terror, shame, or emotional numbing; and cognitive symptoms such as constant rumination about the event or, in an opposite manner, being unable to remember or think about the event.[12]

All of these reactions are manifestations of the victim's ongoing but failing effort to heal from the trauma and find meaning in it by integrating it with the preexisting self.[13] This effort to process the trauma continually fails because the trauma is too painful to think about and feel at a tolerable level of arousal, so it is *desymbolized*—rendered unavailable for conscious verbal reflection.[14] As a result, the trauma either is repeatedly reexperienced without becoming more tolerable (such as in flashbacks or traumatic dreams), or is split off from verbal and affective processing and therefore expressed in ways that are hidden from conscious awareness (such as in somatic symptoms, emotional numbing, and dissociation). These dynamic processes do not necessarily, or even usually, mean that the trauma is absent from conscious memory, although that can occur. Rather, desymbolization means that even if consciously remembered and spoken about, the full horror of the trauma is not tolerable in conscious thought and feeling and so cannot be put into words.

As I describe at length below, somatization appears to have been a major avenue for Tolkien to express traumatic experience, so I will briefly elaborate here on why the body is a common location for trauma symptoms. Infants primarily relate to the world via their bodies. They explore by touching things and putting them into their mouths, they express distress by crying and wriggling or thrashing their bodies, and they are comforted by being held. They of course do not yet have words, and their feelings are inchoate states of arousal rather than clearly delineated emotions. With appropriate caretaking, infants and toddlers gradually learn language and develop the ability to recognize and name specific emotions, but these higher-order symbol systems do not eliminate the body as a locus of self-expression, and it remains available as an avenue to express emotions too painful to put into words.[15] When experience is of traumatic intensity so that words cannot effectively symbolize it, a psychic message of warning bypasses language and goes instead straight to the body.[16]

The typical traumatic reactions described above build upon, and are intertwined with, the pretraumatic personality. Whether one is traumatized by a particular event, and how severe the trauma is if it occurs, depend on the preexisting strengths and vulnerabilities of the experiencing person.[17] This is apparent, for example, from the fact that some, but not all, soldiers experience trauma symptoms after battle, and from the fact that those who are traumatized may experience different specific symptoms at different intensities. More importantly for the understanding of Tolkien that I am developing here, post-traumatic symptoms may not only result from the trauma but also express individual personal meanings resulting from earlier life history.[18] Rafael Moses gives examples of a soldier who repetitively relived his killing of an enemy soldier and eventually recognized that this repetition was partly motivated by childhood guilt over angry feelings, and another soldier whose guilt about the battlefield deaths of his buddies was linked to his guilt about the earlier deaths of family members.[19] From my own practice I mention the not uncommon examples of young women and men who find their first sexual experiences traumatic, even if consensually desired, because they stir up childhood memories of parental misattunement and abuse.

The young Tolkien's most obvious emotional losses, of course, were due to his orphaning. Tolkien's mother Mabel died of diabetes on November 14, 1904, when he was twelve years and ten months old. It is clear from Tolkien's letters that he was intensely grieved by her death ("I remember . . . when I was not yet thirteen after the death of my mother, and vainly waving a hand at the sky saying 'it is so empty and so cold'"; "When I think of my mother's death . . . worn out with persecution, poverty, and, largely consequent, disease, in the effort to hand on to us small boys the Faith . . . I find it very hard and bitter, when my children stray away").[20] Humphrey Carpenter reports that Tolkien's personality changed after his mother's death so that from then on, he was subject to dark, despairing moods.[21]

Tolkien's reaction to his father's death is less apparent from available records. His father had died on February 15, 1896, when Tolkien was four years and one month old, and it is likely that the conscious impact of this death on Tolkien was ameliorated by his young age and by the fact that he, with his mother and brother, had already traveled away from his father ten months earlier. Conscious thoughts, feelings, and needs for his father at this age were probably much less than for his mother at age twelve.

However, it is important here to take note of Tolkien's Atlantis dream, which I discussed in chapter 8. Several aspects of Tolkien's descriptions of it show that this was a traumatic dream: it was "terrible" and "dreadful," it consisted of feeling inexorably overwhelmed and appears to have involved actual motoric gasping for breath during awakening, and it was repetitive and unchanging until Tolkien was able to creatively transform it in his legendarium. Tolkien also noted that the Atlantis dream had been part of his life "beginning with memory." This indicates that Tolkien had traumatic experience long before the death of his mother, and thus suggests that his father's death had a greater impact than was consciously apparent.

Could the Atlantis dream also signify other early relational trauma in addition to the death of his father? Nancy Bunting has hypothesized that Tolkien's mother was physically and emotionally abusive, even attacking him and his brother murderously in the year before her death, and that the resulting insecurity in their relationship intensified the trauma of her death so that Tolkien had ten- and twenty-year anniversary reactions.[22] Although Bunting's focus on the psychological significance of Tolkien's prewar life is valuable, I think her conclusions extend beyond what is tenable, and currently available records do not support the view of Tolkien's mother as abusive.[23] However, as discussed in chapter 5, examination of a number of songs in Tolkien's legendarium indicates that he had unusual sensitivity to themes of early mother-child separation and reunion, and this may indicate that he experienced "strain trauma"—repeated small painful separation experiences that have a powerful cumulative effect—in relation to his mother.

Tolkien's vulnerability to physical ailments, particularly correlated with times of stress, began very early. The infant Tolkien is reported (without specifics) to have suffered from the heat, so much so that it was bad for his health and was a prominent reason given for his being taken back to England when he was three years old.[24] After what appears to have been an idyllic period living in the small village of Sarehole and being taught at home by his mother, Tolkien at age eight began attending the autumn term at King Edward's School, and in September his family moved to the city, which Tolkien remembered as "dreadful."[25] In his first term he frequently missed school due to illness;[26] the timing of these illnesses suggests that they were influenced by the stress of new school and new home.

When Tolkien was twelve, both he and his brother were seriously ill with measles and whooping cough at a time that corresponded with the beginning of their mother's fatal illness. Mabel reported in a letter of Christmas 1903 that she felt like staying in bed, and she was formally diagnosed with diabetes in April 1904. The boys became sick in January 1904, and appear to have been affected until at least late May, since Mabel commented in a late June letter that the boys now looked very much healthier than they had a month previously.[27] Although it is unremarkable that the Tolkien boys contracted these diseases, which were common in children in the early twentieth century, the duration of their illnesses was unusually long; measles typically lasts one week or less, and whooping cough typically about seven weeks, with cases lasting three months or more being at the extreme of the range.[28] The unusually long duration of these illnesses, together with their co-occurrence with Mabel's sickness, suggests that they were influenced by the stress of his mother's illness.

Tolkien had numerous milder ailments prior to the war: When he was seventeen, he decided to be "ferocious" on the school rugby team, and during games he badly damaged his tongue and nose.[29] During the summer of that year he accidentally cut his hand on a knife.[30] At age twenty-one Tolkien injured his foot (it is unclear how this happened or how severe it was).[31] Later that year, and again just after turning twenty-two, Tolkien was briefly ill.[32]

To summarize our knowledge of Tolkien's prewar sensitivity, he entered the war with two prominent areas of psychological vulnerability developed in his earlier life. First, he was highly sensitized to the pain of emotional loss, certainly from the deaths of his parents, and possibly from strain trauma in his early relationship with his mother. Second, Tolkien was vulnerable to physical ailments, and this vulnerability was probably exacerbated by experiences of stress.

Tolkien's war experience landed blows precisely on the two areas of sensitivity I have described: he was struck hard with interpersonal loss and physical sickness. That Tolkien suffered greatly from interpersonal loss is obvious from his reactions to the deaths of his friends described above; this was central to his feeling that "something has gone crack," and see also his statement in the prologue to *The Lord of the Rings:* "One has indeed personally to come under the shadow of war to feel fully its oppression; but as the years go by it seems now often forgotten that to be caught in youth by 1914 was no less hideous an experience than to be involved in 1939 and the following years. By 1918 all but one of my close friends were dead."[33] There is no need to belabor the point.

Tolkien's physical illness incurred during the war merits more examination. On October 27, 1916, about six weeks after writing that "something has gone crack"—six weeks filled with military operations documented by John Garth and by Scull and Hammond—Tolkien reported sick with a fever of 103 degrees. He was diagnosed with trench fever and sent back to England. I have summarized his subsequent career as a patient in table 9.1. All information is drawn from Scull and Hammond, with the exception of the asterisked entry drawn from Carpenter and Garth.[34] Although it is always risky to give a diagnosis more than one hundred years after the fact, the pattern of illness documented by these sources strongly indicates that Tolkien's physical suffering was in part caused by traumatic emotions expressed via the body.

Table 9.1 Tolkien's World War I Illnesses

Date	Medical Status	Military Status
Oct. 27, 1916	103-degree fever; diagnosed with trench fever	Hospitalized, arrives in England Nov. 9
Dec. 2, 1916	Fever abated one week previously, but still has pain and weakness	Unfit for service for six more weeks
Jan. 23, 1917	Improved, but had two slight returns of fever and still has pain and weakness	Unfit for general service for two more months
Mar. 28, 1917	Improving but still has pains	Unfit for general service for one more month
June 1, 1917		Declared fit for general duty; posted in England
July 1917*		Fails examination that would have qualified him for noncombat posting in England*
Mid-August, 1917	Hospitalized for fever	
Oct. 16, 1917	Discharged from hospital, still weak and in pain	Unfit for general duty for one month
Nov. 16, 1917	Slowly recovering; has had one slight bout of fever	Unfit for general duty for two months
Jan. 19. 2018	Slowly recovering; has had two slight attacks of fever	Unfit for general duty for one month
Feb. 19, 2018	Slowly improving; weak and needs hardening	Unfit for general duty
Late Feb.–early Mar. 2018	Five days influenza	
Mar. 19, 2018	Improving but still needs hardening	Unfit for general duty
Apr. 10, 2018		Declared fit for general duty; posted in England
June 29, 2018	Contracts gastritis	
By July 12, 2018	Hospitalized	

Date	Medical Status	Military Status
July 17, 2018		Unfit to serve in any capacity for one month
Late July–Aug. 2018	Loses nearly twenty-eight pounds in hospital	
Sept. 4, 2018		Unfit in any category for two months
Sept. 11, 2018	Transferred to convalescent hospital	
Oct. 1, 2018		Authorized for sedentary employment only
Oct. 14, 2018		Unfit for any duty other than sedentary employment for six months
Nov. 11, 1918		Armistice signed
Feb. 14, 1919		Fit only for sedentary employment
June 7, 1919		Unfit for general service for six months
July 8, 1919		Discharged from military service
Sept. 4, 1919		Awarded temporary retired pay until Dec. 6; can then reapply
Nov. 11, 1919	Still has some disability	Awarded maximum disabled pay and directed to hostel for treatment; does not seek said treatment

*Carpenter, *Biography*, 103; Garth, *Tolkien and the Great War*, 239.

After November 11, 1919, Scull and Hammond document no physical ailments until March 1922—twenty-eight months later—when Tolkien suffered from influenza.[35]

Several items in table 9.1 are particularly worth highlighting because they indicate the probable contribution of unverbalizable emotional trauma to Tolkien's ailments. First is the sheer length of his suffering from trench fever and its sequelae, for a total of nearly eighteen months from October 27, 1916, to April 10, 1918. Due to imprecise record keeping, only estimates are available for the typical duration of incapacity from trench fever during World War I, but these estimates converge on the figure of three months being average or expectable. One estimate holds that 4.4 percent of sufferers were incapacitated for longer than six months, and another estimate holds that 1.3 percent were incapacitated after two to four years. The current *Merck Manual,* which is presumably based on more accurate records but might underestimate the duration of the disease during the war due to improved modern sanitary conditions and treatments, suggests three months or less as average.[36] Tolkien's case was an outlier by any of these standards.

A second particularly noteworthy item is the occurrence after the sequelae of trench fever had abated of a new severe symptom, gastritis, resulting in the overall duration of Tolkien's disability being long enough to prevent his return to combat. Third is the fact that symptoms continued long enough for Tolkien to be awarded full disability pay, after which he apparently returned to health quickly enough that he did not undergo the treatment recommended when disability pay was awarded. It is also important to note that Tolkien had two additional hospitalizations after the initial one, indicating renewed severity of symptoms, and that both rehospitalizations occurred when he was at increased risk of being sent back into combat: The first rehospitalization, lasting about two months, began in August 2017 after Tolkien had been declared fit for general duty in June and then in July had failed an examination that would have qualified him for noncombat duty in England. The second rehospitalization, from mid-July to mid-September 1918, occurred after Tolkien had been declared fit for general duty on April 10.

The above data make a strong case that Tolkien's illness during World War I in part resulted from the emotional trauma of his service on the Somme, and from anxiety about the possibility of return to combat, which were expressed through his body because they could not be otherwise symbolized.[37]

If war trauma exacerbated psychological vulnerabilities to emotional loss and physical illness that Tolkien had developed in earlier life, we would expect these areas of vulnerability to remain powerful for him in later life. A first indication that this was so is the lifelong sadness that Tolkien felt about the wartime deaths of his friends.[38] In this section I examine evidence of ongoing vulnerability to loss and illness in Tolkien's life, and in the subsequent section I examine ways that he expressed this vulnerability in his fiction.

As Tolkien himself commented in the first of the following excerpts from his letters, records often do not record deeply personal and private emotions. This limitation in understanding Tolkien's emotional life is compounded by the fact that a portion of his letters and personal papers remains unavailable to the public. Nevertheless, what is available gives a picture of Tolkien as a man deeply sensitive to loss.

In a letter of July 11, 1972, to his son Christopher about Tolkien's wife Edith, who had died on November 29,1971, Tolkien wrote, "someone close in heart to me should know something about what records do not record: the dreadful sufferings of our childhoods, from which we rescued one another, but could not wholly heal the wounds that later proved disabling; the sufferings that we endured after our love began—all of which (over and above our personal weaknesses) might help to make pardonable, or understandable, the lapses and darknesses which at times marred our lives—and to explain how these never touched our depths nor dimmed our memories of our youthful love."[39]

And in a letter of January 24, 1972, to his son Michael, Tolkien wrote, "I still often find myself thinking 'I must tell E about this'—and then suddenly I feel like a castaway left on a barren island under a heedless sky after the loss of a great ship. I remember trying to tell Marjorie Incledon this feeling when I was not yet thirteen after the death of my mother (November 9, 1904), and vainly waving a hand at the sky saying 'it is so empty and cold.' And again I remember after the death of Fr Francis my 'second father' (at 77 in 1934), saying to C. S. Lewis: 'I feel like a lost survivor into a new alien world after the real world has passed away.' But of course these griefs however poignant (especially the first) came in youth with life and work still unfolding. In 1904 we (H[ilary] & I) had the sudden miraculous appearance of Fr Francis' love and care and humor—and only 5 years later . . . I met the Lúthien Tinúviel of my own personal romance . . . and in 1934 she was still with me. . . . But now she has gone before Beren, leaving him indeed one-handed."[40]

These letters are replete with the pain of loss of love, pain so intense that Tolkien experienced derealization ("a lost survivor into a new alien world after the real world has passed away") and alienation from all relationships, both with people ("a castaway," "a lost survivor") and with the world as a whole ("on a barren island under a heedless sky," "it is so empty and so cold"). It seems clear that whether or not the "dreadful sufferings of our childhoods" included other things, primary in Tolkien's mind as he wrote those words were his and Edith's orphaning. This is shown not only by the fact that Tolkien is writing directly about the pain caused by loss, but also because only a new deep primary love relationship had been able to partly heal the pain: "trying to tell Marjorie Incledon" seems not to have been enough; the love of "second father" Father Francis, and then the Lúthien of his own personal romance, were much more soothing.

But even Lúthien's (Edith's) love "could not wholly heal the wounds that later proved disabling," or prevent "the lapses and darknesses that at times marred [their] lives." So in these letters Tolkien was describing intense suffering from emotional loss beginning well before the war and continuing throughout his life after the war, only partially smoothed over by love relationships.

A final point I wish to make about these letters is that Tolkien metaphorically described his pain at emotional loss as bodily impairment. He and Edith "could not wholly heal the *wounds* that later proved disabling," and "now she has gone before Beren, leaving him indeed *one-handed*" (italics added).

Tolkien again used a metaphor of bodily impairment to describe his pain at the death of C. S. Lewis. Tolkien's deep friendship with Lewis is attested in a variety of sources,[41] and Tolkien himself wrote "C. S. L. was my closest friend from about 1927 to about 1940, and remained very dear to me."[42] Despite their later partial estrangement, Tolkien wrote on November 26, 1963, four days after Lewis's death, "So far I have felt the normal feelings of a man my age—like an old tree that is losing all its leaves one by one: this feels like *an axe-blow near the roots*."[43]

Therefore, although bodily metaphors for emotional suffering at times of loss are far from unique to Tolkien, they appear to have had a special valence for him. He employed such metaphors in response to both Edith's and Lewis's death, and whereas "wounds" is a conventional metaphor, "one-handed" and "an axe-blow near the roots" are personal coinings. It is likely that somatic metaphors were charged with personal meaning for Tolkien because of his regular acquaintance with physical suffering.

The best summary of Tolkien's ongoing physical sufferings after the war is Scull and Hammond's entry under "Health."[44] As they report, "A remarkable number of the letters Tolkien wrote contain comments on his [poor] health," and "Tolkien used a variety of names to describe the physical pains he suffered as he advanced in years, and it is not always clear how he applied them." Such names included fibrositis, lumbago, arthritis, rheumatism, and simply "pain." Doctors could not always identify causes for his complaints; for example, gastric pains that Tolkien began to suffer in 1969 were never medically explained. Scull and Hammond tellingly quote Rayner Unwin's thoughts on Tolkien's health as follows:

> It is difficult to judge . . . to what extent his unspecific complaints . . . disguised some specific illness or were, at least in part, a defence against his failure to achieve some rashly promised goal . . . he did suffer a great number of much more specific illnesses and accidents . . . his catalogue of physical woes grew year by year. . . . There was no particular pattern to these ailments. Sometimes the less specific complaints seem to have been associated with worry, but for

> the most part they were far from psychosomatic. . . . I might have suspected that he was protesting too much to be taken entirely seriously. . . . I now believe that . . . he was more liable than most men to minor ailments *and less able to cope with the distractions they caused.* [Italics added]

The takeaway from all this seems to be that after the war, Tolkien was plagued both by more specific, diagnosable physical ailments and by more nonspecific, vague physical ailments than most people, and that furthermore, he was less able to cope with these ailments when they did occur. Although sometimes the ailments were associated with specific stressors, and Unwin respectfully and tentatively hazarded the term *psychosomatic,* more often there were no obvious stressors.

This pattern of symptoms is consistent with the idea that Tolkien had difficulty symbolizing painful feelings, and that his body had become readily available for expressing these desymbolized emotions. In combination with his history of physical suffering discussed above, this suggests that early in life, probably in response to orphaning, Tolkien developed a propensity to express trauma through his body; that this propensity was kindled to much greater strength by war trauma; and that for the remainder of his life Tolkien suffered in his body unprocessed psychological pain.

Tolkien's sensitivity to loss during his adult life is at least as clear in his fiction as it is in the biographical detail available to us. It is widely understood that loss is a major theme in Tolkien's writings. It is worth repeating here quotes from chapter 1: "the sustained and grieved sense of loss, of which death is but one form . . . floods through the history of Middle-earth";[45] "the many quick-moving scenes . . . are secondary to the sense the book conveys of things slipping into—or already become part of—an irrecoverable past";[46] "Tolkien's whole marvelous, intricate structure has been reared to be destroyed, that we may regret it."[47] This pervasive sense of loss in his writings may be understood as a way to express and integrate the trauma of the war intertwined with the earlier trauma of Tolkien's life. As Brogan states about Tolkien's legendarium, "It was therapy for a mind wounded in war, and before that by deep sorrow in childhood and young manhood."[48] That is not all that it was, as Brogan also acknowledges, but it was an important part.

The connection between Tolkien's personal trauma and his fiction will become clearer by moving from his general fictional theme of loss to focus specifically on depictions of physical debility and loss of love as they are affected by and affect war and battle. Physical debility does not have a general presence in Tolkien's writings equivalent to that of loss, but it does play a significant role in Tolkien's depiction of war and battle, not only in the obvious form of a result of fighting, but also as something that precedes and helps to explain the course of battle. Tolkien explored the interweaving of war with loss of love and physical disability in his depiction of several characters that I now examine.

KULLERVO/TÚRIN

Although Tolkien elaborated much of his legendarium over a long period of time during and after the war, the story of Kullervo/Turin is unique in that he produced a version prior to the war as well as after, allowing us to see how he expressed in his prewar years themes that he continued to develop after the war.

"The Story of Kullervo," which Tolkien based on the *Kalevala* (Finnish traditional tales assembled by Lönnrot in the mid-nineteenth century), is rife with separation and loss beginning on the very first page, when a swan is deprived of two of her younglings (who become two important men) by an eagle and a hawk. Kullervo is born after his father is killed, so that his "mother's heart is dead within"—so one parent was actually dead and the other emotionally dead.[49] Kullervo is emotionally abused ("for lack of their mother's care the children were reared in crooked fashion, for ill cradle-rocking meted to infants by fosterers in thralldom: and bitterness do they suck from breasts of those that bore them not"[50]) and physically abused as his stepfather tries to kill him by drowning, burning, and hanging. Although Tolkien did not finish the story, his notes show that he intended to end with the melodramatically heightened episode of love that is lost because the love itself was illicit: Kullervo learns that his lover was his unknown sister and that she has killed herself upon discovering the incest; he proceeds to commit suicide.

The *Kalevala* and "The Story of Kullervo" had great personal significance for Tolkien.[51] He was infatuated with the *Kalevala* when he encountered it, and more particularly by the tale of Kullervo since this small section of the *Kalevala* is the part from which he developed his own story. Tolkien's "The Story of Kullervo" describes the character's childhood abuse more sensitively and with more detail than the original *Kalevala,* and Bunting concluded that this indicated Tolkien had been abused himself. Flieger avoided such literal extrapolation and proposed that Tolkien's fascination with the story and with Kullervo's emotional pain resulted from Tolkien's orphaning, pointing out that he first included and then deleted these lines from the original Kalevala:

> "I was small and lost my [mother-deleted] father
> I was young (weak) and lost my mother"[52]

Flieger additionally pointed out that Tolkien altered the original *Kalevala* material by changing the originally handsome central character into a person "Ill-favoured and crooked, broad and illknit and knotty."[53] The word *crooked* had already appeared in the description of the loveless fashion of Kullervo's upbringing (quoted above); Tolkien's remaking of Kullervo as physically crooked thus creates a match with his upbringing, suggesting that Tolkien was using physical debility to symbolize the consequences of loveless upbringing.

Tolkien continued to rework this story after the war, with Kullervo becoming the character Túrin Turambar. Although the final version of this story is much more literarily sophisticated and novelistic, and drops most of the wild fantasy, it too culminates in the tragedy of incestuous love resulting in suicide. Physical debility also remains central in the later story and even though it results realistically from war rather than metaphorically from lack of love in childhood,[54] the themes of physical debility and loss of love are tragically wound together in the triangles of Gwindor, Finduilas, and Túrin, and Brandir, Níniel/Nienor, and Túrin. The Elf maiden Finduilas loved the Elf Gwindor, but when Gwindor returned from years of enslavement under Morgoth after being captured in battle as "a bent and fearful shadow of his former shape and mood"[55]—an echo of "crooked" Kullervo as well as a description of damage both physical and emotional—and Túrin arrived, healthy, beautiful, and commanding, "the heart of Finduilas was turned from Gwindor and against her will her love was given to Túrin."[56] Túrin, however, was never aware that she loved him other than as a sister would. Gwindor died brokenhearted in battle, asking Túrin to protect Finduilas, but after orcs bore her away, Túrin failed to rescue her because the dragon Glaurung had bewildered him.

The triangle of Brandir, Níniel/Nienor, and Túrin presents the themes of physical disability and loss of love with acute dramatic intensity. When Túrin meets dragon-bewildered Níniel and carries her to where he dwells with lame Brandir and his people, Brandir cures Níniel of her physical ailments but not her mental confusion. Brandir falls in love with Níniel, but she gives her heart to Túrin and they wed. Years later, when Túrin goes to confront the dragon Glaurung and Níniel goes after him, Brandir is scorned and shamed for holding back. Eventually he follows Níniel, but lags far behind because of his lameness. Then comes the final tragedy of the tale: Túrin gives Glaurung a fatal blow but falls unconscious, the dying dragon informs the pregnant Níniel that she is really Túrin's sister Nienor; Nienor jumps to her death in horror at her incest; Brandir, who has observed this, informs Túrin, who in rage slays him; and after learning that Brandir spoke the truth, Túrin asks his sword to kill him, which it willingly does.

Taken together, the stories of Kullervo and Túrin demonstrate the consistent importance for Tolkien of themes of loss of love and of physical debility, originating before the war and continuing after. After the war Tolkien worked these themes into scenes of war and its effects, but he did not essentially alter them. This is consistent with the idea that Tolkien's war trauma built upon and integrated preexisting childhood trauma.

FARAMIR AND ÉOWYN

Tolkien once stated that Faramir was the character in *The Lord of the Rings* most like himself.[57] The genuineness and depth of this identification allowed Tolkien to take one step in the process of healing himself of his traumatic dream of the Great Wave by bequeathing it to Faramir.[58] Because of this identification, we can expect Tolkien to have attributed to Faramir trauma reactions especially similar to his own, and indeed we see in the story of Faramir and Éowyn that battle wounds were compounded by loss of love that was experienced as bodily ailment, and that final healing required new love.

Both Faramir and Éowyn were borne to the Houses of Healing after the Battle of the Pelennor Fields, afflicted near to death with ailments that were compounded of the physical and the emotional: battle wounds and loss of love. When Aragorn ministers to Faramir, he comments, "'He is nearly spent. . . . But this comes not from the [physical] wound. See! That is healing.'" Imrahil's subsequent comment emphasizes that the physical wound was relatively unimportant: "'the wound was not deep or vital. How then do you read the matter?'" And Aragorn replies, "'Weariness, grief for his father's mood, a wound, and over all the Black Breath.'"[59]

Although Aragorn places less etiological importance on grief than on the Black Breath, the grief he alludes to is Faramir's distress over being so far below his brother in his father's esteem that his father appeared willing for him to die, distress so acute that Gandalf had feared it would make Faramir suicidal. Denethor had bemoaned not having a captain of Boromir's quality in the thick of battle, and Faramir said, "'Since you are robbed of Boromir, I will go and do what I can in his stead—if you command it.' 'I do so,' said Denethor . . . Gandalf it was that last spoke to Faramir ere he rode east. 'Do not throw your life away rashly or in bitterness,' he said. . . . 'Your father loves you, Faramir, and will remember it ere the end.'"[60]

As Aragorn ministers to Éowyn, it becomes clear that her wounds too were more emotional than physical, that she was primarily wounded by loss of love. After commenting that her physical wounds were well tended, Aragorn wonders out loud about her emotional state. Beginning with, "'I know not how I should speak of her,'" he compares her as he first encountered her to a shapely lily that is hard as steel or perhaps turned to ice, about to die, and then says, "'Her malady begins far back before this day, does it not, Éomer?'" Aragorn, Éomer, and Gandalf then discuss Éowyn's hopeless love for Aragorn, and Gandalf elaborates that even before she met Aragorn, "'she was doomed to wait upon an old man [Theoden], whom she loved as a father, and watch him falling into a mean dishonoured dotage.'" Aragorn concludes with, "'I have power, maybe, to heal her body. . . . But to what she will awake: hope, or forgetfulness, or despair, I do not know. And if to despair, then she will die, unless other healing comes which I cannot bring.'"[61]

The other healing to which Aragorn refers is love, and it comes in the form of Faramir. Faramir does not go to the Field of Cormallen to celebrate the destruction of the Ring because as Steward, his job is to remain in Minas Tirith. Éowyn does not go because although healed of her physical wounds, she still is burdened with grief. Aware that she loved and may still love Aragorn, Faramir declares his love for her. Éowyn replies, "'I wished to be loved by another . . . but I desire no man's pity.'" Faramir explains that his feeling for her is not pity and again declares his love. "Then the heart of Éowyn changed, or else at last she understood it. And suddenly her winter passed, and the sun shone on her."[62]

GORLIM AND MAEGLIN

In Gorlim, from the story of Beren and Lúthien, and Maeglin, from "The Fall of Gondolin," Tolkien depicted loss of love leading to betrayal, battle trauma, and death. In a sense this is the opposite of the relationship between love and loss depicted in the story of Faramir and Éowyn: rather than love eventually healing wartime wounds, broken love leads to wartime wounds. But in both these forms, positive and negative, these stories manifest Tolkien's entanglement between love, its loss, and physical suffering.

Early in the tale of Beren and Lúthien we learn that Gorlim was one of a small band of warriors led by Beren's father Barahir fighting against Morgoth's troops. Lonely and weary of battle and hiding, Gorlim sometimes steals away to his old home in search of his wife Eilinel, and Sauron, on learning of this, creates a phantom vision of her that lures Gorlim so that Sauron's hunters are able to capture him. (Although presented in the narrative as an act of wizardry, this vision can also be thought of as an interesting depiction of a hallucinatory traumatic stress reaction.) Gorlim is brought before Sauron, who promises to unite him with Eilinel if he will betray Barahir; Gorlim complies, and Sauron informs him of his trickery and that his wife has already been killed. He then reunites Gorlim with her by having him executed. Barahir and all his men then are slain with the exception of Beren, who was away when the attack took place.

In "The Fall of Gondolin" we learn that Maeglin covets the hand of Idril, daughter of Turgon King of Gondolin. Maeglin is described (in a manner that Tolkien never used for Elves as he later developed them) as follows: "Less fair was he than most of this goodly folk, swart and of none too kindly mood . . . and whispers there were that he had orc blood. . . ."[63] Tolkien thus worked physical fault into the tale, although in milder form than that suffered by Kullervo or Gwindor. Idril has no liking for Maeglin and instead weds the heroic man Tuor. Maeglin is later captured by orcs and betrays the secrets of Gondolin, with possession of Idril one of his promised rewards. Similar to what happened to Barahir and his men but on grander scale, Gondolin is then destroyed after a mighty battle. Tuor slays Maeglin and escapes together with Idril, their son Eärendil, and a few others.

FRODO

In Frodo, Tolkien gave his clearest depiction of someone suffering stress reactions subsequent to trauma. Michael Livingston diagnosed Frodo with post-traumatic stress disorder because of the following symptoms: after the Ring was destroyed, Frodo became strongly avoidant of additional violence, initially demonstrated when he did not wish to wear a sword for the feast in his honor to be held in Ithilien, and demonstrated more dramatically as he repeatedly tried to prevent violence during the Scouring of the Shire, even though Merry stated and events proved that violence was necessary to defeat Sharkey and his ruffians. Frodo even tried to restrain violence against Sharkey after Sharkey attempted to stab him (although he was unable to prevent Wormtongue's fatal attack). Additionally, Frodo manifested a series of anniversary reactions to trauma during which he was struck with mixtures of physical and emotional pain: on the homeward journey on the anniversary of being stabbed by the Nazgul, when they reached the Ford of Bruinen where he had almost succumbed to the wound; on the anniversary of being attacked by Shelob; and then again on the second anniversary of these two events.[64]

Frodo's sufferings on these anniversaries mingle physical and emotional pain that resonate with Tolkien's own mingled sufferings of physical pain and pain of loss. The site of Frodo's physical injury hurts on the anniversary of the Weathertop attack, but as he describes to Gandalf, he also knows that he has lost his home: "'There is no real going back. Though I may come to the Shire, it will not seem the same; for I shall not be the same. I am wounded with knife, sting, and tooth, and a long burden. Where shall I find rest?"[65] And when Frodo is found on the first anniversary of Shelob's attack, he is muttering, "'It is gone forever . . . and now all is dark and empty.'"[66] As Michael Livingston pointed out, although "It" is generally thought to refer to the Ring, this is not explicit; Livingston wonders if "It" might also refer to loss of innocence or hope.[67] Whether or not "It" points to loss of innocence and hope, the vagueness of "*It* is gone forever" (italics added) emphasizes loss rather than a specific thing lost.

The poem "The Sea-Bell" (discussed at greater length in chapters 7 and 11) also illustrates Frodo's trauma. Janet Brennan Croft points out that this poem can be considered a depiction of a post-traumatic dream about shell shock.[68] To this we can add that it shows mingled physical suffering and emotional loss, Tolkien's twin trauma themes, especially in the following lines:

to the ground falling, on my hands crawling
with eyes blind and my back bent . . .
My hands were torn and my knees worn,
and years were heavy upon my back . . .
Never will my ear that bell hear,
never my feet that shore tread
Never again, as in sad lane,
in blind alley and in long street
ragged I walk. To myself I talk;
for still they speak not, men that I meet.[69]

Anna Smol expounded on how Frodo's mingled bodily suffering and emotional loss are manifested not only in his specific post-traumatic reactions but in his ongoing traumas as he endures them throughout his quest. Using Julia Kristeva's concept of abjection, Smol explored how Frodo's sufferings put him on the edge of losing both his sense of self and his connection to others. As described in chapter 2, the abject is that which must be expelled from the self in order to maintain a coherent sense of self: "what is abject . . . is radically excluded and draws me toward the place where meaning collapses"; and abjection is caused by "what disturbs identity, system, order. . . . The in-between, the ambiguous, the composite."[70] Specimens include thoughts about foulness, pollution, rotting corpses, and horror. Yet even though expelled, the abject may be experienced as fascinating so that one is drawn to relate to it or even own and identify with it, in which case one becomes abject oneself and alienated from validating relationships.

Smol discussed how Frodo's response to the corpses—quintessential abjects, according to Kristeva—in the Dead Marshes shows him attracted to abjection, which begins to lead to the loss of his coherent self: whereas Sam responds to the sight of the corpses with horror, he finds Frodo "standing lost in thought, looking at the pale lights. His hands hung stiff at his sides; water and slime were dripping from them," showing that Frodo had tried to reach the corpses.[71] When Sam wonders who they were, Frodo gives his answer "in a dreamlike voice."[72] This allusion to an altered state of consciousness points to the destabilization of Frodo's identity.

Smol further explicated Frodo's mingled bodily and emotional loss by exploring his identification/disidentification with Gollum. Gollum is a figure of abjection in that he is horrible and animal-like, an eater of disgusting uncooked food, even suspected by Sam of eating corpses, and as pointed out by Gergely Nagy because his language is regressed from civilized speech—even the name Gollum is onomatopoeic with rude swallowing.[73] In trying to reconstitute Gollum as Sméagol, Frodo is trying to protect himself from the process that he is succumbing to under the influence of the Ring: becoming like Gollum an abject, cut off from all human relationships.

Frodo's final loss, of course, is of the Shire, and his friends, and especially Sam, as he sails from the Grey Havens. In his farewell he says, "I have been too deeply hurt, Sam. I tried to save the Shire, and it has been saved, but not for me. It must often be so, Sam, when things are in danger: some one has to give them up, lose them, so that others may keep them."[74] Frodo's loss of human connection is emphasized by his contrast with Sam, who marries, has many children, and as mayor plays an important role in the larger Shire community.

BEREN AND LÚTHIEN

As I discussed in chapter 1, Tolkien identified the love between himself and his wife Edith with the love between Beren and Lúthien. Because he gave such intense personal meaning to this story, it is fitting that in it he presents a complex arrangement of signifiers of love, loss of love, and physical damage. First, Beren is maimed in a way that furthers love by earning him permission to wed Lúthien; subsequently Beren's death leads not only to the loss of him that necessarily follows, but also to Lúthien and the world losing each other because of her continuing love for Beren. After Beren and Lúthien emerge from Angband, the wolf Carcharoth bites off Beren's hand, which holds the Silmaril. When Beren and Lúthien return to Doriath, Beren informs Thingol that a Silmaril is in his hand and reveals his maimed limb. "Then Thingol's mood was softened. . . . Therefore at the last he yielded his will, and Beren took the hand of Lúthien before the throne of her father."[75] Beren is slain in the ensuing successful Hunting of the Wolf, but Tolkien indicates that this tale is primarily about the complexity of love and loss with the words, "Thus ended the Quest of the Silmaril; but the Lay of Liethian, Release from Bondage, does not end."[76] Lúthien successfully sues the Valar to be reunited with Beren, and they are granted a mortal return to Middle-earth, she "forsaking the Blessed Realm." The final few words of the tale show Tolkien's entwining of love, death, and loss: "she is the forerunner of many in whom the Eldar see yet, though all the world is changed, the likeness of Lúthien the beloved, whom they have lost."[77]

Thus we see that in numerous places in his fiction, when Tolkien addressed battle trauma, he depicted it as the intermingling of his two psychological vulnerabilities that he brought to the war and which then were intensified by it: physical suffering intermingled with emotional loss. Tolkien appears to have struggled all his life to find words to symbolize his trauma. And so it is fitting to close this chapter with Frodo saying good-bye to Sam in language that could serve as almost a direct rejoinder to "something has gone crack": "Do not be too sad, Sam. You cannot always be torn in two."[78]

CHAPTER 10

The One Ring and Tom Bombadil

> One Ring to rule them all, One Ring to find them
> One Ring to bring them all and in the darkness bind them

With these well-known lines, J. R. R. Tolkien depicted the One Ring of Power, the central symbol of evil in *The Lord of the Rings*. The lines describe the Dark Lord Sauron's intent when he created the Ring to use it to establish total domination over the world.

In chapter 8 I traced a biographical episode that showed Tolkien struggling to experience the transitional space necessary for his creativity, rather than being stuck in more concrete, constricted experience. In this chapter I will argue that *The Lord of the Rings* as well as other parts of Tolkien's fictional universe can be read as an exploration of this dynamic contrast, which was so important in his life: transitionality represented by Tom Bombadil contrasted with concrete, constricted experience represented by perverse thinking and the One Ring as a fetish symbol.

Viewed from one angle, transitional objects and fetishes are opposites, but viewed from another angle they are very similar to each other. Both are things that are imbued with tremendous importance by their creator/possessors, and both create illusions to soothe anxieties—the transitional object soothes anxiety resulting from increasing recognition of the external, Not-me world;[1] the fetish soothes anxieties about self-integrity and bodily intactness during intimate relationships.[2] Yet their meaning is otherwise opposite: the transitional object opens connections to the external world, other people, and imagination, and eventually develops into the wider transitional space of play, art, and culture;[3] the fetish locks its creator into a repetitive scenario and disavows the external world and other people. Transitional phenomena integrate and share aspects of the internal and external world; the fetish splits the ego so that reality is simultaneously known and disavowed.[4]

Winnicott's original paper discussed transitional phenomena mainly in their adaptive aspects, but when he expanded the paper for a chapter in *Playing and Reality,* he added a section on "psychopathology manifested in the area of transitional phenomena." Here he described a boy whom he first saw at age seven who was preoccupied with string. The boy often tied objects together, and Winnicott understood this to be a denial of many separations he had experienced from his depressed mother. Winnicott saw potential for the string to develop into a fetish, and in fact the potential sadomasochistic meanings of the boy's first drawings (lasso, whip, crop, a yo-yo string, a string in a knot, another crop, another whip) suggest perverse inclinations even more strongly than Winnicott noted. Phyllis Greenacre also emphasized that the fetish differs from the transitional object in being used to handle early loss of loved ones, deprivation, and aggression. She pointed out that sexual fetishes typically originate at puberty but also cited Wulff and Sterba on infantile fetishes.[5] She thought that transitional objects and fetishes were opposite ends of a continuum with intermediate steps.[6]

As originally formulated by psychoanalysis, *fetish* referred to a sexual fetish, an object used to achieve sexual potency, and *perverse* referred to nonnormative sexual practices,[7] and thus both terms connoted the imposition of heteronormative standards. I will be following a second line of psychoanalytic thought in which the terms refer not to specific acts or behaviors but to underlying attitudes and experiences that may or may not motivate a nonnormative sexual act, and that may or may not motivate a normative sexual act.[8] Tolkien's work, notoriously lacking in overt sexuality, does not lend itself to exploration of sexual perversion but provides insight into relational perversity more broadly defined. For my purposes, *perversion* refers to a relationship in which the other person is treated as a thing rather than as a human being, in order to defend against deep fears of what a relationship with a human being would entail—including fears of castration or other loss of bodily integrity, fear of loss of reality, loss of the loved one, loss of love, and loss of the self. A *fetish* is a thing that facilitates a perverse relationship by replacing the partner as the focus of attention.

The quintessential form of perverse relating is emotional sadomasochism, whether or not it is accompanied by sadomasochistic sexual practices.

Both partners relate on the basis of power, to eliminate the possibility of separation, rather than on the basis of mutuality; it is as though the sadist is communicating, "'I can do anything I want to you and you'll still always be there,'" and the masochist is communicating, "'Do anything you want to me but don't leave me.'"[9] Splitting leads to experiencing the self as fragmented and others as part-objects. Kristeva maintained that perversion develops from a matrix of preobjectal abjection before the baby has separated enough from the mother to develop the sense of being a separate subject and a sense of the mother being a separate object. This formulation is very similar to Winnicott's idea that transitional objects first form before the child has become "a unit with a limiting membrane and an outside and an inside."[10] Kristeva stated that the child at this stage is both terrified of and longing for remerger with the mother, so that the abject is experienced with both abhorrence and fascination.

In what follows I will first discuss how all these aspects of perversion can be found in the symbol of the One Ring. I will then show how Tolkien contrasted the One Ring with transitional experience symbolized by the character of Tom Bombadil.

The Lord of the Rings tells of the quest to destroy the Dark Lord Sauron's One Ring of Power before he regains it and uses it to dominate and enslave the world. The Ring has minor powers, such as conferring invisibility on whoever wears it, but is most dangerous because whoever wields it has enormous power to impose their will on others. Because of Sauron's influence on the Ring, it will always turn to evil; good people who try to use it to do good will sooner or later be overmastered by it and become evil themselves.

The One Ring instantiates perversity by establishing sadomasochistic relationships. This was the conscious intent of its creator, Sauron, but also took place outside his awareness. Sauron's sadomasochistic intent is encapsulated in the lines quoted above: he made the Ruling Ring as a tool to control other rings of power via sympathetic magic and thus enslave their wearers. This effort can be seen as an attempt to create pseudo-Others, companions who were entirely under his control, and it succeeded completely with men, producing the evil Ringwraiths who had no will of their own and were entirely beholden to Sauron. Jennifer Culver has discussed Sauron's gifting of rings to the Ringwraiths in the context of medieval ring-giving, a customary way for lords to establish relations with their men that Tolkien was professionally knowledgeable about.[11] But Sauron took ring-giving beyond relations of loyalty to slavery.

Other people who came in possession of the Ring sooner or later found themselves also in a perverse relationship with it: it was an object that filled their minds and grew more precious to them than other people, and they could not bear to be without it. Tom Shippey has discussed this helpless desire as analogous to addiction.[12] The hobbits Bilbo and Frodo were affected this way, but it was especially clear with Gollum, who murdered to take possession of the Ring and then cast aside all relationships except his relationship with the Ring. The enthrallment that bearers develop for the Ring is not based on knowledge of its power—the Ring became precious to the hobbits and Gollum when they knew nothing of its power potential. For Frodo, the Ring was a vision of loveliness, a perfect circle of gold without flaw, and he was besotted with it simply because "It was an admirable thing and altogether precious."[13] Even the noble Faramir (a man with whom Tolkien identified), who comfortably rejects the Ring in full knowledge of its power, fears seeing the Ring lest he should start to lust after it. It is the Ring as an ideal object that he fears.

And yet, in the emotional blending typical of perversity, if someone possesses the Ring long enough, they grow to hate it as much as love it because they experience it taking possession of and eliminating their selves; Gergely Nagy considered this double border of love/hate and self/Ring to be a perfect example of abjection.[14] Bilbo Baggins was just beginning to develop this hatred at the time he passed the Ring on to Frodo: "it would be a relief in a way not to be bothered with it any more. It has been so growing on my mind lately."[15] Frodo finds the Ring a worse and worse burden as he approaches Sauron's stronghold to destroy it. For example, after his companion Sam asks Frodo if he recalls some pleasant events, Frodo replies, "No taste of food, no feel of water, no sound of wind or memory of tree or grass or flower, no image of moon or star are left to me. I am naked in the dark, Sam, and there is no veil between me and the wheel of fire."[16] This process reaches its maximum in the character of Gollum, a hobbit-like creature who possessed the Ring longest before he lost it to Bilbo and who now loves and hates it, identifies with it, and thus loves and hates himself.

Although Tolkien does not say this explicitly—it was not Sauron's conscious intent—by creating the Ring, Sauron also created a perverse relationship with it for himself. In the moment of creating the One, Sauron placed a substantial part of himself in it, so he himself now existed in the world external to him, a pseudo-companion that was totally in his control because it was a part of him. At the same time, by placing himself into a thing, Sauron created the possibility of losing himself—as happened in the battle of the Last Alliance in which Sauron was defeated and his ring cut from his hand.[17] Yet even then Sauron and the Ring remained in a perverse relationship, Sauron constantly seeking the Ring, and the Ring seeming to have a will of its own and seeking Sauron.

Sauron's creation of the One Ring by placing himself in it is a literal depiction of splitting. The effect of this action—to both deny and create the possibility of loss for Sauron—is another example of splitting. Several scenes in which characters imagine taking possession of the Ring gain part of their power by showing splits in action, so that normally decent people act or imagine themselves as drastically different. Galadriel, a noble and powerful Elf, shifts so that she appears as an imperious Queen before rejecting the Ring and then seeming a slender Elf-maiden with less than her usual charisma. Boromir is overcome with madness and tries to take the Ring, then regretfully returns to his normal self. Humble Sam imagines himself as Samwise the Strong, leading conquering armies. Even pathetic Gollum imagines himself as Gollum the Great.

On a more imagistic level, the split in the self is illustrated by the hobbits' changed perceptions of reality when they wear the Ring. Vision is obscured so that they perceive a shadowy world, although wraiths can be seen with clarity. Hearing is sharpened. Sam perceives himself surrounded by a huge shadow of himself.[18] Similarly, although a wearer of the Ring becomes invisible, a bearer of the Ring, at least near Sauron's dominion where it was forged, does the opposite when behaving commandingly, growing large and threatening.

A ring is by its nature an apt symbol for splitting because a ring simultaneously represents opposites. On the one hand, a ring is a perfect circle, symbolizing completeness; on the other hand, a ring is empty, a zero, enclosing nothing. Frodo draws our attention to the Ring's completeness when he stares at it and "Frodo thought . . . how perfect was its roundness."[19] Tom Bombadil, a character whom I discuss in detail below, draws attention to the Ring's usual emptiness by contrasting it when he holds it to his eye and "the hobbits had a vision, both comical and alarming, of his bright blue eye gleaming through the circle of gold."[20]

Widely shared unconscious meanings of body orifices may underlie these meanings of the Ring. The mouth can open to food or close to refuse it, open to communicate or close to remain silent. Leonard Shengold discussed anal rings as signifiers of closing or opening.[21] An old folktale implicates power concerns about opening or closing of the vagina: A man tormented by worries about whether his wife is faithful dreams that a demon approaches him with a magic ring that has such power that as long as the man wears it, it will be impossible for his wife to have sex with another man without him knowing and willing it. The man puts on the ring with great relief. When he awakens, he finds that he has inserted his finger in his wife's vagina.[22]

Frodo experiences the simultaneous fascination and horror of abjection, as well as its threatened boundary loss and merger, almost every time he puts on the Ring. Tolkien leaves it ambiguous as to whether Frodo chooses to put on the Ring, or the Ring chooses for him to do so—neither Frodo nor the reader can quite tell whose will is acting, or if there is in fact any difference between Frodo's will and the Ring's in these moments. An experience in the inn at Bree can serve as an example. Early in their quest, Frodo and his hobbit companions, traveling incognito, have stopped at the Prancing Pony and do not know whether any of the assembled guests may be enemies. Pippin is talking unrestrainedly and Frodo fears that he may give away their identities. "Frodo . . . felt the Ring on its chain, and quite unaccountably the desire came over him to slip it on and vanish out of the silly situation. It seemed to him, somehow, as if the suggestion came to him from outside. . . . He resisted the temptation firmly."[23] But soon after, Frodo jumps onto a table, sings a drinking song, accidentally falls off the table, and vanishes. "Frodo felt a fool. . . . How [the Ring] came to be on his finger he could not tell. He could only suppose he had been handling it in his pocket while he sang, and that somehow it had slipped on. . . . For a moment he wondered if the Ring itself had not played him a trick."[24]

Tom Shippey discussed this ambiguity in terms of two views of the nature of evil, what he calls the Boethian view, that evil is not a thing in itself but merely the absence of good, and the Manichean view, that evil is an actual force in the world.[25] If Frodo chose to put on the Ring to escape the embarrassing situation, then the evil act was merely Frodo's weakness, an absence of good behavior. But if the Ring compelled him to put it on, then it represents an actual evil force. Tolkien never provides a clear boundary between Frodo as subject and Ring as abject by resolving this ambiguity. Shippey pointed out a subtle example of this in the language Frodo uses much later at his moment of truth when he claims the Ring for himself rather than throwing it into the volcano, which can melt it: Frodo says, "But I do not choose to do now what I came to do. I will not do this deed. The Ring is mine!"[26] Thus, at the moment of his greatest self-inflation, Frodo says not, "I choose now to do" but "I do not choose to do now." Has the Ring chosen for him?

As noted above, the Ring and Sauron are different parts of one entity, so Sauron's qualities can help us recognize the perverse status of the Ring. Sauron is a representation of thoroughgoing sadism; Gandalf says of him, "'the only measure that he knows is desire, desire for power; and so he judges all hearts.'"[27] The closest that anyone comes to encountering Sauron is to experience themselves being hunted or seen by his Eye. Limiting Sauron's appearances to this synechdoche is novelistically effective, leaving it up to the reader's imagination to put shape to this paragon of evil. But it also evokes abjection by depicting Sauron as a split-off part object toward whom Frodo experiences fascination and horror. After Boromir attempts to take the Ring by force, Frodo climbs the hill of Amon Hen to look about and decide what he should do next. "And suddenly he felt the Eye. . . . A fierce eager will was there. . . . Very soon it would nail him down . . . he threw himself from the seat, crouching, covering his head with his grey hood. . . . He heard himself crying out: *Never, never!* Or was it: *Verily I come, I come to you?* He could not tell."[28] It is unclear whether Frodo's horror or attraction will prove the stronger until Gandalf intervenes to help him free himself.

Frodo also experiences conjoined horror and desire in his encounters with the Ringwraiths, who themselves can be read to signify failed transitional space and abjection. The Ringwraiths were powerful men to whom Sauron gave rings that enabled him to control them through the One Ring. They became invisible and terrible. "They had, as it seemed, unending life, yet life became unendurable to them. . . . And they became forever invisible save to him that wore the Ruling Ring, and they entered into the realm of shadows. The Nazgûl were they, the Ringwraiths . . . the Enemy's most terrible servants; darkness went with them, and they cried with the voices of death."[29] In between life and death, invisible, dwelling in the shadows, they fit Sheldon Bach's description of dwellers in failed transitional space: "other-than-human-creatures, whether monsters, aliens, ghosts, or goblins, are an inevitable product of our ever-changing psychic boundaries, for they are the exotic inhabitants of that mental territory that stretches between the self and the other, between the past and the future, between the known and the unknown."[30]

In Frodo's first encounter with a Ringwraith the question of whether desire for the Ring is internal or external again arises. In hiding, "A sudden unreasoning fear of discovery laid hold of Frodo, and he thought of his Ring . . . the desire to get it out of his pocket became so strong that he began slowly to move his hand . . . he felt he had only to slip it on, and then he would be safe."[31] A later episode, wherein Frodo is stabbed by a Ringwraith and under the influence of a splinter of the knife that remains in his wound begins to turn into a wraith himself, can be understood as a physical representation of Frodo internalizing the Ringwraith's desire.

With their status between life and death, the Ringwraiths hint at the intense feelings of abjection, of undoing the sense of being a coherent subject, which can be brought on by encountering a corpse. Frodo has an encounter even closer to the abjection of the corpse when trapped in a burial mound. "He heard behind his head a creaking and scraping sound. . . . Round the corner a long arm was groping, walking on its fingers towards Sam, who was lying nearest, and towards the hilt of the sword. . . . At first Frodo felt as if he had indeed been turned into stone. . . . Then a wild thought of escape came to him. He wondered if he put on the Ring, whether the Barrow-wight would miss him. . . . He thought of himself running free over the grass, grieving for [his companions], but free and alive himself. Gandalf would admit there had been nothing else he could do."[32]

Frodo's shift of self-state toward abjection and perverse thinking is seen in his feeling of being turned to stone, his disavowed shame ("Gandalf would admit there had been nothing else he could do") at his uncharacteristic thought of abandoning his friends, and his desire to put on the Ring. This time Frodo finds the courage to fight the living dead arm and sing a song that summons the aid of Tom Bombadil.

From the above descriptions it is obvious that one prominent theme of *The Lord of the Rings* is the misuse of power and how to oppose this misuse. This conflict can be described as an opposition between perverse and transitional experience, with the character of Tom Bombadil an especially important representation of the latter.

Tom Bombadil's transitional quality is seen in his origin, his qualities, and the role he plays in the story. He originated as a Dutch doll named Tom Bombadil, which belonged to one of Tolkien's children before Tolkien began writing *The Lord of the Rings*. Dutch dolls were wooden, jointed figures, whereas transitional objects typically are soft and pliable, so it is unlikely that the Tolkien doll was a true transitional object. Nevertheless, Winnicott identified play as a childhood form of transitional experience, so as a favored toy from later in childhood, the doll is likely to have had transitional qualities that contributed to Tolkien developing the character of Bombadil as a transitional symbol who lives in transitional space.

Tom Bombadil in *The Lord of the Rings* is all about music, dance, and play, three qualities that grow in transitional space. Tom's nature can be illustrated by his first appearance. Frodo and his companions hear:

> Hey dol! Merry dol! Ring a dong dillo!
> Ring a dong! Hop along! Fal lal the willow!
> Tom Bom, jolly Tom, Tom Bombadillo

"There was another burst of song, and then suddenly, hopping and dancing along the path, there appeared above the reeds an old battered hat with a tall crown and a long blue feather stuck in the band. With another hop and a bound there came into view a man, or so it seemed . . . his eyes were blue and bright, and his face was red as a ripe apple, but creased into a hundred wrinkles of laughter."[33] Throughout their time with Tom he continues capering and singing, and even his prose is usually spoken with poetic cadence and sometimes rhymes as, for example, "'Some things are ill to hear when the world's in shadow. Sleep till the morning-light, rest on the pillow! Heed no nightly noise! Fear no grey willow!"[34]

Tolkien did not fit Tom Bombadil into any of his clearly defined fictional races, frustrating some of his readers who have tried to pin his identity down, perhaps as a Maia, a minor godlike figure (see, for example, Foster). Tolkien responded to queries by stating that Bombadil might be thought of as the spirit of the vanishing Oxford and Berkshire countryside, but that every work of imagination should include some things that are unexplained.[35] To thus leave Bombadil unexplained is an act of freedom and ambiguity allowing for multiple meanings, which again are qualities of transitional space and are opposite both to the One Ring and to fetishism.

Tom's domain plays the role of a literal transitional space for the hobbits. It lies between their familiar home base of the Shire and the road they must take to get on with the adventure of the Ring, and it is the first place they enter after leaving the Shire. What happens there is not relevant to the greater plot of the Ring, as though the hobbits had taken a time-out from their main task. This transitional meaning of Tom's domain for the hobbits is emphasized by its absence on their return trip; Tom and his domain cannot be transitional for the hobbits as they approach the Shire because the Shire has been ruined by interlopers so transition back to comfortable home life cannot take place until the hobbits have rectified the situation. Gandalf tells them that they still have a job to do, but that he does not, and so it is for Gandalf that Tom provides a transitional space upon return. The hobbits bypass Tom, but Gandalf visits him to have "such a talk as I have not had in all my time," before sailing to his own home in the Undying Lands.[36]

And finally, it is for Frodo's own trip to the Undying Lands that Tom provides transitional space. Because of multiple spiritual and physical wounds sustained on his quest, Frodo finds transition back to a comfortable Shire life impossible, and eventually travels to Elvenhome, where his Middle-earth injuries may be healed. Upon his first glimpse of Elvenhome from his ship, he recalls that he had dreamt of it in Tom's house: "a pale light behind a grey rain-curtain . . . until at last it was rolled back, and a far green country opened before him under a swift sunrise."[37]

In his actions, Tom directly opposes perversity and the Ring. After Frodo summons him from the barrow as described above, Tom sings to defeat the wight and rescue the hobbits from their abject state, culminating with

> Wake now my merry lads! Wake and hear me calling!
> Warm now be heart and limb! The cold stone is fallen;
> Dark door is standing wide; dead hand is broken.
> Night under Night is flown, and the Gate is open![38]

This chant is replete with images contrary to rigid, perverse experience: waking from near-death, static stone fallen, and doors and gates opening.

Most importantly, Tom Bombadil is directly contrasted with the One Ring. He is the only character unaffected by the Ring; not merely able to resist its pull, he is not tempted at all, can wear it without becoming invisible, can see Frodo while the latter wears it, and even briefly makes the Ring itself invisible. This is demonstrated in a scene when Tom requests to see the Ring and Frodo hands it to him: "he put it to his eye and laughed. For a second the hobbits had a vision, both comical and alarming, of his bright blue eye gleaming through a circle of gold. Then Tom put the Ring round the end of his little finger and held it up to the candlelight. . . . There was no sign of Tom disappearing! Tom . . . spun the ring in the air—and it vanished with a flash. Frodo gave a cry—and Tom leaned forward and handed it back to him with a smile."[39] Frodo puts the Ring on in annoyance, but Tom can still see him. Among all these ways that Tom is shown to be opposite to the Ring, perhaps the most telling is when his comical blue eye shines through the Ring because it provides a direct contrast with Sauron's perverse eye.

But readers may be wondering how Tom can be the opposite of Sauron since Tom, despite his comical capering, song, and dance, also displays considerable power. As has already been noted, he is immune to the Ring and he saves the hobbits from the barrow-wight. At their first encounter, he saved them from Old Man Willow. He is able to wave his arms over his head in a rainstorm and keep the rain off himself. Frodo asks Bombadil's wife Goldberry who Bombadil is, and she responds, "'He is the Master of wood, water, and hill.'" Frodo asks, "'Then all this strange land belongs to him?'"[40] With this phrasing Tolkien has likened Tom to Sauron, who by wielding the Ring desires to become the great Master of everything. This commonality is in accord with the developmental similarity of fetish and transitional object.

But Goldberry's response to Frodo differentiates Tom's power from that of Sauron. "'No indeed,' she answered. . . . That would indeed be a burden. . . . The trees and grasses and all things growing or living in the land belong each to themselves. Tom Bombadil is the Master. No one has ever caught old Tom. . . . He has no fear. Tom Bombadil is master.'"[41] So Tom's power is of a form that does not control or diminish others. In the same manner, Tom's relationship with the Ring is not a matter of him defeating the Ring, power versus power; rather, it is a matter of Tom existing in a state wherein the Ring has no relevance. As the Council of Elrond tries to decide what to do with the Ring, the Elf Erestor proposes giving it to Tom to keep it safe because he appears to have power over it. Gandalf replies, "'Say rather that the Ring has no power over him. He is his own master. . . . And if he were given the Ring, he would soon forget it, or most likely throw it away. Such things have no hold on his mind."[42]

So rather than showing a congruence with Sauron, Tom's power illustrates something about the subtleties of power in human relationships. Since there is no relationship that does not involve issues of power and narcissism, avoiding perverse relating does not mean avoiding power, but managing power in a system of mutuality that balances assertion and recognition of self and other.[43]

Tom's mastery is fleshed out in the poems "The Adventures of Tom Bombadil" and "Bombadil Goes Boating," the first published before Tolkien began writing *The Lord of the Rings* and the second after, which show Bombadil engaged in a series of adventures in which various creatures try to overpower him only to have him overpower them instead. Making engagement with power so central to Tom's story once again creates a seeming similarity between him and Sauron, for whom power is central, like the seeming similarity between a transitional object and a fetish. The difference lies in the quality of their engagement with power: unlike an encounter with Sauron, which would be deadly serious, Bombadil's encounters are playful and comical, and no one gets hurt. When Tom wins, he simply releases his opponents with the insistence that they not continue their attacks—with one exception (discussed below).

Tom's playfulness is conveyed not only by the content of these poems but by their lighthearted form as well. This can be seen in the lines describing Tom's first encounter with Goldberry in "The Adventures of Tom Bombadil":

> Old Tom in summertime walked about the meadows
> gathering the buttercups, running after shadows,
> tickling the bumblebees that buzzed among the flowers,
> sitting by the waterside for hours upon hours.
>
> There his beard dangled long down into the water:
> up came Goldberry, the River-woman's daughter;
> pulled Tom's dangling hair, in he went a-wallowing
> under the water-lilies, bubbling and swallowing.[44]

Tom easily escapes, and after his other adventures returns to capture Goldberry and take her for his wife, making her the only exception to his policy of releasing his attackers. Since Goldberry had initially captured him, this whole sequence appears to be a playful flirtation, in which both Tom and Goldberry show a balance of assertion and recognition.

Nevertheless, there are aspects of Tom's and Goldberry's relationship that to the modern eye suggest a lack of mutuality. When the hobbits first encounter Tom, he is returning from a hike to gather the last waterlilies of the season to place in bowls around Goldberry's feet to last her through the winter. Then when the hobbits meet Goldberry, she is depicted as quite static among the lilies Tom gathered: "In a chair . . . sat a woman. . . . About her feet in wide vessels of green and brown earthenware, white water-lilies were floating, so that she seemed to be enthroned in the midst of a pool."[45] Goldberry soon springs up, and later is depicted dancing and running, but always close to the home. Why doesn't Goldberry go to the river herself to collect lilies? She is well acquainted with where they grow; after all, that is where she first dunked Tom. Do Tom or Goldberry or both of them want her to avoid her mother, River-woman?

But such speculations are anachronistic—at the time Tolkien was writing, it was the expected role of a wife that she stay at home more than the husband—and unanswerable within the text, and this unanswerability itself contributes to the transitional, open-ended meaning of Tom Bombadil. Not only Tom's identity but the characters and space around him are, as Tolkien intended, unexplained. As for the handling of power between Tom and Goldberry, they later set the table, "and the hobbits sat half in wonder and half in laughter: so fair was the grace of Goldberry and so merry and odd the caperings of Tom. Yet in some fashion they seemed to weave a single dance, neither hindering the other, in and out of the room, and round about the table."[46] This is a description of the mutuality that can grow when couples are able to share transitional space.

In these ways *The Lord of the Rings* contrasts the One Ring as a fetish symbol with Tom Bombadil as a symbol of transitional experience. *The Lord of the Rings* demonstrates the horrifying yet fascinating danger of falling into perverse experience, and shows that this danger can be countered by transitional experience. In chapter 8 I traced in Tolkien's biography a period of personal struggle to create in transitional space, during which he overcame constriction and was freed to write *The Lord of the Rings*. In chapter 11 I will depict how in later life Tolkien's sense of freedom decreased and his writing became more constricted. It is likely that the theme of fetishism and transitionality in *The Lord of the Rings* grew out of Tolkien's sensitivity to this issue in his own life. This is not to say, nor is there any evidence, that Tolkien was significantly perverse. Rather, he was able to create in transitional space the One Ring as a symbol of the threat to transitional space, which he knew from personal experience.

Winnicott and Greenacre noted that transitional objects and fetishes resemble each other in that both are things imbued with great importance that create illusions to soothe anxiety about the boundary between self and other. The difference appears to be that the transitional object, and transitional space more broadly, provide a way to meet the other in a state of relative openness and mutuality, whereas the fetish defends against aggression and fear of losing the self in the object or the object in the self by relating to the other in constricted and controlling ways. Tolkien made both this similarity and this difference between transitionality and perversion come to life by depicting the different meanings of power for Tom Bombadil and Sauron.

Tolkien did not have a comic or sanguine vision that transitional forms of relating would prove more lasting or widespread than perversity. As Elrond recounts the history of the Ring, he says, "'I have seen three ages in the West of the world, and many defeats, and many fruitless victories.'"[47] And as I will discuss in the next chapter, Tolkien stated that through the actions of Morgoth, all the world became Morgoth's Ring. This meant that "all 'matter' was likely to have a '[Morgoth]' ingredient" and "the final eradication of Sauron . . . was achievable by the destruction of the Ring. No such eradication of Morgoth was possible, since this required the complete disintegration of the 'matter' of [earth]."[48] Yet neither was Tolkien entirely pessimistic. Elrond soon amends his comment as follows: "Fruitless did I call the victory of the Last Alliance? Not wholly so."[49] The Silmarils are lost to earth, but Eärendil still carries one as a beacon of hope to all who see it. Innumerable other examples could be drawn from the legendarium. Tolkien's vision is better described as one of ongoing tension between transitionality and perverse uses of power. After all, it is part of the human condition throughout life to negotiate the boundaries between self and other.[50]

CHAPTER 11

Late Life Loss of Transitionality

Although the final volume of *The Lord of the Rings* was published in 1955 and Tolkien lived until 1973 while his audience eagerly awaited more, Tolkien published very little after *The Lord of the Rings*. The only fiction was a short story (*Smith of Wootton Major*), and a book of poems (*The Adventures of Tom Bombadil*), most of which were revisions of poems written long before; only one appears to have been mostly new.[1] He was engrossed in revising the stories that were later posthumously edited and published by his son Christopher as *The Silmarillion*, but Tolkien himself never managed to bring these stories to final form.

Although Tolkien had lifelong difficulty completing projects, his lack of production in later life is even more notable and suggests that something additional was holding him back. The drop-off has been attributed to general vicissitudes of old age, such as his and his wife's illnesses, and adjusting to the death of his wife in 1971.[2] Tolkien himself wrote in 1965, "I find it difficult to work—beginning to feel old and the fire dying down."[3] But Tolkien was only sixty-three when *The Return of the King* was published. In this chapter I will adduce evidence that indicates a more specific answer as to what fire was dying down: Tolkien's access to creative transitional experience.

Tolkien's progressing difficulty in maintaining transitionality can be recognized by comparing *Leaf by Niggle*, published in 1945 while the fifty-three-year-old Tolkien was working on *The Lord of the Rings*, with later works. *Leaf by Niggle* directly depicts a conflict between engaging in creative transitionality on the one hand and attending to real-world responsibilities and moral obligations on the other. The main character is an artist whose name, Niggle, already serves as an accusation that his attention to the details of his art is excessive, and whose consequent neglect of his garden allegorizes Tolkien's feeling that he was neglecting professorial duties in favor of his fiction.[4] His intention to paint a leaf grows into an effort to paint a complex tree and the life within it and the landscape around it, but he never completes the painting because of frequent interruptions, and especially because of the obligation to aid his lame neighbor, Parish, the representative of the mundane world. Niggle is required to go on a journey (an allegory for death) and spends time in a Workhouse (an allegory for purgatory).[5] Eventually Niggle is allowed to travel to a land where his Tree is real. There he meets Parish, and the two of them work together to improve the land. Significantly, "As they worked together, it became plain that Niggle was now the better of the two at ordering his time and getting things done. Oddly enough, it was Niggle who became most absorbed in building and gardening, while Parish often wandered about looking at trees, and especially at the Tree."[6] The edges have been worn off the conflict between transitionality and mundane obligations, and Niggle travels higher into the beautiful landscape (heaven) while Parish waits for his wife.

So at the age of fifty-three, while engaged in creating his greatest work, Tolkien was able to imagine a peaceful resolution to his conflict between transitionality and everyday life—although even here he hints at underlying melancholy in his description of the fate of Niggle's painting back in the everyday world: "Most of it [the last corner of the painting] crumbled; but one beautiful leaf remained intact. Atkins had it framed. Later he left it to the Town Museum, and for a long while 'Leaf: by Niggle' hung there in a recess, and was noticed by a few eyes. But eventually the Museum was burnt down, and the leaf, and Niggle, were entirely forgotten in his old country."[7]

Tolkien's writings later in life suggest that it became more difficult for him to comfortably enter transitional space. Sometime between 1962 and 1965,[8] Tolkien wrote the poem "Once Upon a Time" about Tom Bombadil. As I discussed at length in the previous chapter, Tom Bombadil is a symbol of transitional space both because of the role he plays in the hobbits' journey and because of his qualities. In brief, Bombadil provides literally transitional space for the hobbits in their journey from home to the wider world, and he himself is lovingly related with the area in which he dwells; as Tolkien stated, he can be thought of as "the spirit of the vanishing Oxford and Berkshire countryside." Tom knows endless stories about the weather, the land, and the creatures that live there, understands them all, and is their "master," although he never controls them except to stop harm from happening. He is typically seen singing, laughing, and dancing, clad in colorful clothes.

But things have changed in "Once Upon a Time." Tom encounters diminutive creatures called lintips:

> Once upon a moon on the brink of June
> a-dewing the lintips went too soon.
> Tom stopped and listened, and down he knelt:
> "Ha! Little lads! So it was you I smelt?
> What a mousy smell! Well the dew is sweet,
> So drink it up but mind my feet!"
> The lintips laughed and stole away,
> But old Tom said: "I wish they'd stay!
> The only things that won't talk to me,
> Say what they do or what they be.
> I wonder what they have got to hide?"[9]

Tom, formerly the joyful symbol of transitional space who used to see and understand everything therein, now sorrows that he has trouble "seeing things as they were meant to be seen." Color, one of the symbols of his previous transitional status, has been leached from the scene in this poem.[10] It is the mysterious lintips themselves who exist in transitional space. Swank considers various possibilities for what they might be and concludes that the answer is unknowable. Scull and Hammond write, "the lintips cannot be defined or, beyond a point, described, and absent any further explanation by Tolkien, no one can say 'what they do or what they be.'"[11] So when the lintips laugh and steal away from Tom, it is transitional space that is leaving him. Tolkien is depicting the melancholy loss of transitionality.

The late-life *Smith of Wootton Major* can be read as a charming fairy tale, but looked at more closely conveys deep sadness and loss. Smith is given a star that grants him entry to Faërie, where he has many adventures. But "Defeat hangs heavy in *Smith of Wootton Major*. Smith has to hand over his star, and enter Faërie no more . . . these points are hard to read except as a kind of valedictory, an admission of retirement."[12] But *eviction* is a better word than *retirement*, since during one of Smith's trips to Faërie he steps onto a lake that is magically harder and sleeker than glass, falls, and sets off an echoing boom. A wild destructive wind springs up and Smith saves himself by clinging to a birch tree, but the tree loses all its leaves. When Smith asks what he can do to make amends, the tree replies, "Nothing. Go away. The Wind is hunting you. You do not belong here. Go away and never return!"[13] If we remember the equivalence between Tolkien's concept of Faërie and transitional space, it appears that Smith finds himself cruelly evicted from transitionality.

The way the Wind springs up after Smith falls on the lake indicates that he has somehow transgressed, suggesting that Tolkien's old conflict over hubris was again interfering with his creativity. The sense of hubris is even stronger on Smith's next journey, which takes him to a dell, where Elven maidens dance. One of them approaches and says, "'You are becoming bold, Starbrow, are you not? Have you no fear of what the Queen might say, if she knew of this? Unless you have her leave.' He was abashed, for he became aware of his own thought and knew that she read it: that the star on his forehead was a passport to go wherever he wished; and now he knew that it was not."[14] Smith later learns that this maiden was the Queen herself, underlining the hubris of dancing with her.

Hubris causing the loss of Faërie/transitionality is clearer yet in "The Sea Bell," a 1962 revision of the poem "Looney," originally published in 1934. Once again the theme is a man finding Faërie and then losing it, but this time the reason for the loss is clearly spelled out. Frustrated by the evanescence of the Faërie folk, the traveler reports:

> proudly I cried: 'Why do you hide?
> Why do none speak, wherever I go?
> Here now I stand, king of this land,
> with gladden-sword and reed-mace.
> Answer my call! Come forth all!
> Speak to me words! Show me a face!'
>
> Black came a cloud as a night-shroud.
> Like a dark mole groping I went,
> to the ground falling, on my hands crawling
> with eyes blind and my back bent.[15]

Shippey has elucidated how although both "Looney" and "The Sea-Bell" "are poems of 'disenchantment' . . . and in both the speaker, who has been in a magic boat to a far land, finds himself hunted out of it by a 'dark cloud,' and returned to lonely and ragged craziness, scorned by others," the late-life "The Sea-Bell" is considerably darker than "Looney," which was published when Tolkien was forty-two.[16] In the later poem the far land is more menacing; the traveler returns clutching "a sea-shell silent and dead," whereas in the earlier poem he "bore . . . a single shell, where I hear still the spell / Echoing far"; and while after his return people "seldom" speak to him in the first poem, in the later poem "still they speak not, men that I meet." And I agree with Shippey that the most important difference is the role of the black cloud. The relevant section of "Looney," to compare with the parallel section of "The Sea-Bell" quoted above, goes as follows:

> There was dancing there, wings in the air,
> Feet going quick on the green floors.
>
> There came a dark cloud. I shouted aloud;
> Answer was none, as onward I went.
> In my ears dinned a hurrying wind;
> My hair was a-blowing, my back was bent.[17]

As Shippey states, this change indicates "that in the later version the speaker seems in a way guilty, as 'Looney' did not. In both poems the 'black cloud' comes, but in the earlier it is for no reason, while in the later it appears to be called, or provoked, by the speaker presumptuously naming himself 'king.'"[18]

We saw in chapter 8 that one way Tolkien dealt with the possibility of hubris toward God's creation was with the concept of subcreation, justifying his own creations as honoring God the creator by in his own image acting as a creator. Tolkien considered it crucial for a good story to avoid direct representations of religion, criticizing the overt Christianity in Arthurian legends by saying, "that seems to me fatal. Myth and fairy-story must, as all art, reflect and contain in solution elements of moral and religious truth (or error), but not explicit."[19] But in his late revisions of the Silmarillion he showed increasing concern that his creations be consonant with Christianity,[20] suggesting increased worry about hubris; subcreation now needed to be very close to God's creation.

This effort to fit his writings to Christianity can be seen in Tolkien's development of the character of Galadriel, and in the late story called "Athrabeth Finrod ah Andreth." I discussed Galadriel in detail in chapters 6 and 7. For now, I merely want to make the point that although she always showed a mixture of characteristics of dark Celtic sorceresses like the Corrigan,[21] with characteristics of the Virgin Mary,[22] the trend over time was to decrease her Corrigan qualities and make her more like Mary. For example, in *The Lord of the Rings* Galadriel is struggling with the possibility that she will be punished for her past participation in a rebellion against the Valar, but in Tolkien's final writings about her, he decides she was never part of the rebellion; she was without sin.

The "Athrabeth" presents a conversation about what happens after death between Finrod, an Elf lord, and Andreth, a wise human woman. As they discuss various griefs, Andreth reveals and also conceals human beliefs that humans were originally made not to die, but suffered a Fall in their beginning, and that Eru (another name for Ilúvatar, God the Father) will send to earth a redeemer, and that this redeemer will himself partake of the nature of Eru. This clearly introduces speculation about something very close to the Christian Fall and of Christ himself into Middle-earth, and is a far cry from "that seems to me fatal."

Posthumous publications allow us to see Tolkien's thought processes becoming cramped and concrete—losing transitionality—as he tried to fit *The Hobbit* into the more precise world-building of *The Lord of the Rings,* and as he tried to fit his mythology overall into conventional understandings of the world. John Rateliff has documented Tolkien's 1960 attempt to rewrite *The Hobbit* so as to reconcile it with his larger work.[23] In this rewrite, "all first person references by the narrator are excised from the text, along with all direct (second person) addresses by the narrator to the reader," eliminating the sense of a storyteller addressing an audience of children.[24] Tolkien also squeezed out playful, comedic qualities, as can be seen by comparing Bilbo's initial interchange with Gandalf in the two versions. In the published *The Hobbit* we have:

> "Good Morning!" said Bilbo, and he meant it. . . . But Gandalf looked at him from under long bushy eyebrows that stuck out further than the brim of his shady hat.
>
> "What do you mean?" he said. "Do you wish me a good morning, or mean that it is a good morning whether I want it or not; or that you feel good this morning; or that it is a morning to be good on?"
>
> "All of them at once," said Bilbo . . .
>
> "Good morning!" [Bilbo] said at last. . . . By this he meant that the conversation was at an end.
>
> "What a lot of things you do use *Good morning* for!" said Gandalf. "Now you mean that you want to get rid of me, and that it won't be good till I move off."
>
> "Not at all, not at all, my dear sir! Let me see, I don't think I know your name?"
>
> " . . . you do know my name, though you don't remember that I belong to it. I am Gandalf, and Gandalf means me!"[25]

In the 1960 revision, this becomes:

> "Good morning!" said Bilbo cheerily. . . . But Gandalf looked at him from under his bushy eyebrows that bristled beneath the brim of his hat.
>
> "What do you mean?" he said. "That it is a fine morning, and you feel pleased with yourself? Perhaps you wish me to feel pleased too. I may. We'll see."
>
> "Indeed I hope you will," said Bilbo . . .
>
> "Good morning!" [Bilbo] said at last . . .
>
> "Now I understand what you mean by *Good morning*," said Gandalf. "You mean that you want to get rid of me, and that it won't be good till I move off."
>
> "Not at all, not at all, my dear sir! Let me see, I don't think I know your name?"
>
> " . . . you knew my name once, when you were younger and brighter. It is Gandalf, in this part of the world. Gandalf! Do you hear?"[26]

No more comical exaggerations, like eyebrows that stick out beyond the brim of a hat, or wordplay like "you do know my name, though you don't remember I belong to it." Gandalf has become grouchy and humorless.

Unexplained magic too was at risk in Tolkien's rewrite, as he jotted the note to himself, "What happened to the musical instruments used by the dwarves at Bag-End?," suggesting that he was going to make these instruments conform to reality.[27] Tolkien also strove to fit precise dates and distances into the text, and Rateliff's observation about these changes actually applies well to the rewrite as a whole: "we see Tolkien attempting to take *The Hobbit*, a story written out of one storytelling tradition of long ago and far away, where details are only included when dramatically relevant or aesthetically effective and things work according to their own narrative logic, and make it into a story like *The Lord of the Rings* which is written in a very different tradition, where each mile of each day of each character's journey can be followed on a map and plotted on a timetable."[28]

These proposed alterations would not have taken *The Hobbit* out of transitional space; rather, it was a matter of Tolkien taking *The Hobbit* out of childlike transitional space and moving it into the more mature transitional space of *The Lord of the Rings*. But by thus invalidating childlike experience for his oeuvre, Tolkien was limiting the mental space wherein he felt it was legitimate to play, and in trying to make everything conform, he was moving toward the disenchanted experience that "we can in principle control everything by means of calculation," as I quoted Weber in the introduction. In the event, Tolkien thought better of this effort and dropped it upon the recommendation of a friend.[29]

It was in his cosmological speculations that Tolkien tried to fit his mythology into conventional understandings of the world. In early conceptualizations that survived into the published *Silmarillion,* Tolkien created a flat-earth cosmology: the sun and moon were latecomers; light was first provided by two lamps, and after their destruction by Melkor, light was provided by two trees, and finally after Melkor in turn destroyed them, the sun and moon were created from the last fruits of the trees. But Christopher Tolkien reported that in the late 1950s, after publication of *The Lord of the Rings,* his father became seriously engaged with the idea of revising this cosmology in a more realistic direction. In unpublished writings Tolkien stipulated that his cosmology needed to become the realistic one of a round earth with its moon, rotating around the sun as part of a solar system, from the beginning, and Tolkien struggled to work out all the changes that this would entail in his legendarium. Christopher stated, "In these writings can be read the record of a long interior debate."[30]

That Tolkien felt newly constrained in his writing can be seen when he stated, "You can make up stories of that kind [his flat-earth cosmology] when you live among people who have the same general background of imagination, when the Sun 'really' rises in the east and goes down in the west, etc. When however (no matter how little most people know or think about astronomy) it is a general belief that we live on a 'spherical' Island in 'Space' *you cannot do this any more.*"[31] Here Tolkien has given up the free play of ideas, the creative right to play with different thoughts and see what fits. Instead, it is as though he is standing in shame before an inner board of examiners who demand the realistic choice.

Tolkien's corresponding reconceptualization of the knowledge of the Valar and the loremasters of the Elves shows similar constriction. He decided that the flat-earth cosmology could have been a Mannish misunderstanding, but that the "High [Elves] living and being tutored by the demiurgic beings *must have known,* or at least their writers and loremasters *must have known, the 'truth'*"[32] Again, "the Valar *must be supposed to know the truth* about the structure of Eä (and not make mythological guesses like Men) and to have communicated this to the [Elves]."[33] And again we see constriction of Tolkien's thoughts when he states that to make his chronology work, "The making of the Sun and Moon *must* occur long before the coming of the Elves; and *cannot* be made to be after the death of the Two Trees."[34]

The simple response to all Tolkien's assertions of necessity is: "Why?" It was his chronology, so he could adjust it however he wanted, and he previously thought that unreal elements were fine in a fantasy world as long as that world obeyed its own rules faithfully.

Tolkien contemptuously referred to his flat-earth cosmology as "astronomically absurd."[35] Christopher retorted that it was not absurd but beautiful (although "primitive"), and questioned how the rest of the myth of the Two Trees, which Tolkien retained, is any less acceptable than the myth that the sun and moon were created from its fruits.[36] This perceptive question needs to be extended: If we are shifting into a mindset that will not tolerate fantastic ideas because they are absurd, then what should we do with magic rings, talking trees, hobbits, and all the rest of Middle-earth? As Christopher stated with great insight, "It seems to me that he was devising—from within it—a fearful weapon against his own creation."[37]

Associated with Tolkien's cosmological struggle was his new idea that "the whole of 'Middle-earth' was Morgoth's Ring."[38] In this way Tolkien was linking all of earth to the One Ring of Power from *The Lord of the Rings*. As I discussed in the previous chapter, the One Ring is a fetish symbol, the opposite of transitionality. The Dark Lord Sauron put a part of himself into the One Ring in order to gain power over other magic rings and thus the world, and by calling earth "Morgoth's Ring," Tolkien meant that Morgoth put much of his power into Middle-earth itself for the same purpose: "in this way Morgoth lost (or exchanged, or transmuted) the greater part of his original 'angelic' powers, of mind and spirit, while gaining a terrible grip upon the physical world."[39]

With this reconceptualization, Tolkien was saying that all of our earth was like the One Ring—a fetish—to be used as an object in the assertion of individual power, rather than to be loved in all its diversity. What he embedded in this way in his story appears to have been his own feeling at the time about the world he lived in: Tolkien now experienced the world as perversely objectified to such an extent that he was no longer able to play with ideas of a flat earth and a sun and moon created from the fruits of trees. This hypothesis accords with Tolkien's well-known distress about modernity: he repudiated mechanization, motorcars, the cutting of trees, and the destruction of pastoral England, and he referred to perpetrators of war and political control as "orcs."

So we see several ways in which Tolkien in later life felt obligated to rein in his creativity, associated with a need to avoid hubris. The conflict that he had overcome in order to free himself to complete *The Lord of the Rings* appears to have regained power. In the publications he did complete during this period, Tolkien depicted his tragic sense of being evicted from Faërie and losing access to transitionality.

Epilogue

The Road Goes Ever On and On

"'It's a dangerous business, Frodo, going out of your door,' [Bilbo] used to say. 'You step into the Road, and if you don't keep your feet, there is no knowing where you might be swept off to. Do you realize that this is the very path that goes through Mirkwood, and that if you let it, it might take you to the Lonely Mountain or even further and to worse places?' He used to say that on the path outside the front door at Bag End, especially after he had been out for a long walk."[1]

"Dangerous," "you might be swept off," "Mirkwood, the Lonely Mountain, or even worse places." The overt message is to stay safe at home. Yet I have no doubt that Tolkien knew most readers would react to those lines with a thrill of desire to hit the road. Bilbo, too, must have known that he was encouraging Frodo to walk, especially since he was most likely to speak thus at the end of one of the walks that he loved. Yet all the references to danger are not merely ironic rhetorical devices. The danger is part of what makes the journey exciting—and that is a good thing because danger will be there whether we like it or not.

Tolkien's own life journey, as we have seen, was filled with the dangerous loss of loved ones: poignant experiences of emotional separation from his beloved mother, his father's death when he was four, his mother's death when he was twelve, and the death of close friends in World War I. On one level his legendarium, with its pervasive theme of loss, may be understood as Tolkien's creative attempt to work through the tragedies of his life and stay in touch with hope and meaning.

But obviously Tolkien's legendarium is not just some idiosyncratic record of private grief—it is felt intensely by a great number of people. As with any great work of art, this is partly due to Tolkien's esthetic skill in putting his personal issues into a form that is pleasing to a wide audience. But more importantly, the personal issues that Tolkien was dealing with were issues that everyone deals with: the loss of love is one of the great dangers of life. (Freud identified this, although common sense recognizes it too.[2]) Early life, even in intact, loving families, often includes emotional separations that strike deeper or longer than is ideal. Even those of us who are lucky enough not to be orphaned eventually lose our parents to death (unless we die first, thus both losing them and causing them grief) and other loved ones as well. And of course we all die, and even the Valar do not know what lies beyond this "gift of men."

Loss of loved ones could have been written about effectively in many literary genres, but Tolkien wrote fantasy. This "choice"—although I'm sure he did not consciously choose it, he could do no other—enabled Tolkien to directly manifest in the form of his writing the working through of another, closely related loss that is at the core of both his life and his legendarium: the disenchantment of the world. As Weber identified, in modern society everyone is born into a world that is disenchanted compared to premodern societies. However, this disenchantment is not complete even for people who no longer believe in the actuality of magic. I have traced a developmental path in which people are born into a state of consciousness in which they are relatively undifferentiated and enchanted, and then must give up early forms of enchantment as they mature and find new enchantments appropriate to maturity or else live bleak, sterile adulthoods. This is why the dangers of Mirkwood and the Lonely Mountain make the road more appealing, not less: they are enchanting. By writing an enchanting story about the dialogue between enchantment and disenchantment, Tolkien gave us "product and vision in unflawed correspondence."

"The road goes ever on and on" "even further and to worse places." It is central to Tolkien's work that he never resolves whether life is basically enchanted or basically disenchanted. Living in modernity means living in ongoing tension between enchantment and loss. Think about Tolkien's statement, "If they [fairy stories] awakened *desire,* satisfying it while often whetting it unbearably, they succeeded."[3] If Tolkien had written "If they awakened *desire,* often whetting it unbearably, then satisfied it, they succeeded," the statement would make simpler sense: first comes heightened desire, then comes its satisfaction. But Tolkien joined the phrases not with "then" but with "while," indicating simultaneity. And by placing "often whetting it unbearably" after "satisfying it," he made sure we would not make the mistake of thinking that the unbearable desire had been taken care of. Our desire continues even while it is satisfied. It is because of Tolkien's absorption in the simultaneity of enchantment and disenchantment that he gave us writings both bitter and inspirational, both hopeful and despairing.

Notes

ABBREVIATIONS

ATB	*The Adventures of Tom Bombadil*. Edited by Cristina Scull and Wayne Hammond. London: George Allen & Unwin, 2014.
Beowulf T&C	*Beowulf: A Translation and Commentary*. Edited by Christopher Tolkien. New York: Houghton Mifflin, 2014.
B&L	*Beren and Lúthien*. Edited by Christopher Tolkien. New York: Houghton Mifflin, 2017.
H	*The Hobbit:50th Anniversary Edition*. New York: Houghton Mifflin. Originally published 1937.
Kullervo	*The Story of Kullervo*. Edited by Verlyn Flieger. Boston: Mariner Books, 2017.
Leaf	"Leaf by Niggle." In *The Tolkien Reader*, 100–120. New York: Ballantine, 1966.
Letters	*The Letters of J. R. R. Tolkien*. Edited by Humphrey Carpenter. New York: Houghton Mifflin, 2000.
Lost Road	"The Lost Road." In *The Lost Road and Other Writings*. Edited by Christopher Tolkien, 39–116. New York: Ballantine, 1987.
LT I	*The Book of Lost Tales, Part One*. Edited by Christopher Tolkien. New York: Ballantine, 1983.
LT II	*The Book of Lost Tales, Part Two*. Edited by Christopher Tolkien. New York: Ballantine, 1984.
LotR	*The Lord of the Rings*. New York: Houghton Mifflin, 2004.
MC	*The Monsters and the Critics and Other Essays*. Edited by Christopher Tolkien, 6–48. London: George Allen and Unwin, 1983. 5–48.
Morgoth	*Morgoth's Ring*. Edited by Christopher Tolkien. London: Harper Collins, 2002.

NCP	"The Notion Club Papers." In *Sauron Defeated.* Edited by Christopher Tolkien. 143–327. London: HarperCollins, 1993.
OFS	"On Fairy-Stories." In *The Tolkien Reader,* 33–99. New York: Ballantine, 1966.
Peoples	*The Peoples of Middle-earth.* Edited by Christopher Tolkien. London: Harper Collins, 2002
S	*The Silmarillion.* London: George Allen & Unwin, 1977.
Smith	*Smith of Wootton Major.* London: George Allen & Unwin, 1967.
Treason	*The Treason of Isengard.* Edited by Christopher Tolkien. New York: Houghton Mifflin, 1989.
UT	*Unfinished Tales.* Edited by Christopher Tolkien. New York: Houghton Mifflin, 1980.

INTRODUCTION

1. *LotR,* 108.
2. The *Oxford English Dictionary Online* traces "vague" to Latin *vagus* "wandering, inconstant, uncertain"; "vagabond" and "vagrant" to Latin *vagārī* "to wander"; from the root *vag-* "wander."
3. Weber, *Sociology of Religion,* 270.
4. Weber, "Science as a Vocation," 12–13.
5. Curry, *Defending;* Curry, "Enchantment"; Shippey, *Author,* 315.
6. *MC,* 7–8.
7. *MC,* 23.
8. Carpenter, *Biography,* 138.
9. *OFS,* 46–47.
10. *OFS,* 77.
11. *OFS,* 72–73.
12. *Letters,* 347.
13. *LotR,* 338.
14. *LT I,* xiii.
15. *Letters,* 210.
16. *Letters,* 333.
17. Pearson, "Craig Rhos-y-felin."
18. Helms, *Tolkien's World,* 44.
19. Honegger, "More Light," 1.
20. Lewis, *Pilgrim's,* 49.
21. Tolkien himself did not refer directly to Freud in any available records, but his creation of the Notion Club member Dolbear, whose interests included "philosophy, psychoanalysis, and gardening" (Tolkien, "Notion Club," 159) suggests openness to psychoanalysis. Dolbear is likable and astute; he is often quiet during meetings, even seeming to sleep, but then suddenly interjects pithy and emotionally observant comments. When we also notice the association in this character of psychoanalysis with gardening and bears, two of Tolkien's favorites, it seems likely that Tolkien was able to recognize more positive features in Freud than was Lewis.

22. Freud, "The Future of an Illusion."
23. Auden, "In Memory of Sigmund Freud."
24. Ferenczi, *First Contributions,* 293.
25. Brabant et al., *Correspondence,* 314.
26. Freud, "Creative Writers," 144.
27. *OFS,* 33.
28. Shippey, *Road,* 186–89.
29. *Letters,* 146.
30. *Letters,* 145n. At other times Tolkien stated that other aspects of his work were fundamental. Therefore, his comment here should be understood as indicating that Tolkien considered the relationship of art and Primary Reality to be extremely important in his work, but not necessarily more important than other aspects.
31. Shippey, *Author,* viii, xxix–xxxi.
32. "I am in fact a *Hobbit* (in all but size)" (*Letters,* 288).
33. Nowadays we know that "mothering" can also be done by the father. However, even in modern Western culture, it remains rare for the father to take a primary caregiving role during infancy and toddlerhood, and it seems certain that Tolkien's father would not have taken such a role, so I will be referring to *mother* and *mothering* in this context.
34. Members of the TCBS were Tolkien's closest prewar comrades.

1. TOLKIEN'S DIALOGUE BETWEEN ENCHANTMENT AND LOSS

1. *LotR,* 983.
2. Flieger, "Arch and Keystone."
3. Senior, "Loss," 173.
4. Hannon, "*The Lord of the Rings* as Elegy," 37.
5. Parker, "Hwaet," 609.
6. Curry, *Defending;* Curry, "Enchantment."
7. *OFS,* 42.
8. *OFS,* 77.
9. *OFS,* 86.
10. Smol, "Frodo's Body."
11. *Letters,* 95.
12. *Letters,* 246.
13. Flieger, *Green Suns,* 242–50.
14. Shippey, *Road,* 178–81.
15. *LotR,* 981.
16. *LotR,* 45.
17. Winnicott, *Playing,* 2.
18. Winnicott, *Playing,* 5.
19. Winnicott, *Playing,* 3.
20. Curry, "Enchantment," 101.
21. Winnicott, "Location."
22. Loewald, "Ego and Reality," 20.
23. Freud, "Formulations."

24. Winnicott, "Transitional Objects."
25. Winnicott, "Location."
26. *LT I*, 24.
27. *OFS*, 63.
28. *OFS*, 42.
29. *NCP*, 171; italics in original.
30. *H*, 38.
31. *LotR*, 2.
32. Shippey, *Road*, 118–22.
33. *LotR*, 269.
34. Carpenter, *Biography*, 237, 251.
35. Piaget, *Intelligence*.
36. Erikson, *Childhood and Society*, 261–63; Erikson, "The Problem of Ego Identity"; Levy-Warren, *Adolescent*, 9–10.
37. *Letters*, 347.
38. For example, Carpenter, *Biography*, 78.
39. *Letters*, 416.
40. *OFS*, 64.
41. *Letters*, 421.
42. Garth, *Great War*, 138.
43. *OFS*, 64.
44. *Letters*, 122.
45. *Letters*, 288, 78–79.
46. Carpenter, *Biography*, 259.
47. Curry, "Enchantment," 102.
48. *S*, 165.
49. *Letters*, 420; italics in original.
50. *Letters*, 303.
51. Croft, *Baptism;* Croft and Rottinger, *Crack;* Flieger, *Green Suns;* Garth, *Great War;* Shippey, *Author;* Smol, "Frodo's Body."
52. Shippey, *Author*, xxx.
53. Flieger, *Green Suns*, 282.

2. MY MOTHER SHE KILLED ME, MY FATHER HE ATE ME

1. *Letters*, 407.
2. Tatar, *Off with Their Heads!*, 209.
3. *OFS*, 56; italics in original.
4. Since this woman was stepmother to the boy but mother to the girl, it is convenient to refer to her as step/mother. I borrow this convention from Tatar.
5. *OFS*, 64n.
6. Ashliman, "Mother Killed Me."
7. Schutt, *Cannibalism*, 159–60.
8. Carter, "Company of Wolves"; Bettelheim, *Uses of Enchantment*, 166–83; Dundes, "Little Red Riding Hood," 44.
9. Dundes, "Little Red Riding Hood," 20–21.

10. Schutt, *Cannibalism,* 203–5; Conklin, *Consuming Grief;* Schutt, *Cannibalism,* 246.
11. *Letters,* 338.
12. Tatar, *Annotated Brothers Grimm,* 223.
13. Dundes, "Little Red Riding Hood."
14. Bettelheim, *Uses of Enchantment,* 66–73; Dundes, "Little Red Riding Hood," 44.
15. Sendak, *Where the Wild Things Are.*
16. Tatar, *Off with Their Heads!*" 216–18.
17. Freud, "Uncanny," 220.
18. Bach, *Narcissistic States,* 11–128.
19. Tatar, *Off with Their Heads!* 217.
20. Freud, "Uncanny," 250.
21. Kristeva, *Horror,* 4.
22. Kristeva, *Horror,* 4.
23. Todorov, *The Fantastic,* 25.
24. Freud, "The Uncanny," 250.
25. Tatar, *Annotated Brothers Grimm,* 223.
26. Tatar, *Off with Their Heads,* xv–xxviii; Zipes, "Dreams."

3. BILBO BAGGINS, THE MASTER OF LAKETOWN, AND THE FATE OF ENCHANTMENT

1. This journey from the mundane, to enchantment, to disenchantment, and finally to a recognition of what forms of enchantment one can continue to experience has parallels with Joseph Campbell's concept of the Hero's Journey, which progresses from the mundane, to the adventurous/supernatural/sacred world, and back (Campbell, *The Hero with a Thousand Faces*). However, where Campbell endorses a Jungian/spiritual understanding of the need to connect with universal symbols, and focuses on the similarities between stories to the extent of viewing all of them as representing a "monomyth," I am more interested in exploring varied individual psychological experiences of balancing disenchantment with enchantment.
2. *H,* 24.
3. *H,* 29, 35.
4. Lewis, "Review," 714.
5. *Letters,* 159.
6. Thomas, "Tolkien's Narrators."
7. Rateliff, *History,* 364, 496.
8. *H,* 288.
9. *H,* 228.
10. *H,* 299.
11. *H,* 210.
12. *H,* 211.
13. *H,* 261.
14. *H,* 261.
15. *H,* 264.
16. *H,* 264.

17. *H*, 317.
18. *OFS*, 73; italics in original.
19. *H*, 301.
20. *H*, 311.
21. *H*, 14.
22. *The Hobbit* was published in 1937; "The Quest of Erebor" was written from 1954 to 1955 and an abbreviated version of it was included in the appendices to *The Lord of the Rings*.
23. Winnicott, "Transitional Objects," 97.
24. Winnicott, "Transitional Objects," 91.
25. *OFS*, 42.
26. *H*, 317.
27. Curry, *Defending*, 29; italics in original.

4. IN DEEP WITH *THE HOBBIT*

1. *H*, 9.
2. Kristeva, *Horror*.
3. Rateliff, *History*, 155, 158, 161.
4. *H*, 71, 77.
5. *H*, 80–81.
6. *H*, 227.
7. Kristeva, *Horror*, 11.
8. Kristeva, *Horror*, 17, 12.
9. Kristeva, *Horror*, 17.
10. Freud, "Anal Erotism."
11. Mahler, Pine, and Bergman, *Psychological Birth*.
12. *H*, 239, 241; italics added.
13. *Letters*, 31.
14. Hooker, *Tolkien and Welsh*, 36.
15. "Geiriadur Prifysgol Cymru." http://welsh-dictionary.ac.uk/gpc/gpc.html.
16. *H*, 53.
17. *LotR*, 208.
18. Kristeva, *Horror*, 12.
19. The term *dragon sickness* in *The Hobbit* is only used to describe the death of the Master of Laketown. However, it is an apt description of Thorin's affliction by Smaug's treasure. Tolkien describes the curse of dragon treasure in his commentary on his translation of *Beowulf* (*Beowulf: A Translation and Commentary*, 351–52): "The 'treasure' is not just some lucky wealth that will enable the finder to have a good time or marry the princess. It is laden with history, leading back into the dark heathen ages beyond the memory of song, but not beyond the reach of imagination. Not till its part in the actual plot is revealed—to draw the invincible Beowulf to his death—do we learn that it is actually enchanted, *iú-monna gold galdre bewunden* *3052 ('the gold of bygone men was wound about with spells' 2564), in which the quintessence of 'buried treasure' is distilled in four words, and accursed." This conception of dragon sickness was important

to Tolkien, as can be seen in him writing a poem about accursed treasure titled with those four Old English words in 1923, and reworking the poem as "The Hoard" for *The Adventures of Tom Bombadil.*

20. *H*, 225.
21. *H*, 227–28.
22. *H*, 249.
23. *H*, 301.
24. Rateliff, *History*, 76.
25. *H*, 10.
26. *H*, 227.
27. *H*, 10.
28. *H*, 317.
29. *H*, 316.
30. *H*, 12, 312, 34.
31. *H*, 316.
32. *LotR*, 13.
33. Flieger, *Fairy Tale*, 203–12.
34. Rosegrant, "Play State," 324.
35. *H*, 105.
36. Tolkien and Tolkien, *Family Album*, 64.
37. In a note placed on a manuscript of his *Sellic Spell* (the folktale that he imagined lying behind *Beowulf*), Tolkien wrote that "Beowulf" meant "Bee-wolf to my mind the most likely etymology is a kenning—quite apart from the evident surviving 'bearish' characteristics of Beowulf" (*Beowulf: A Translation and Commentary*, 356) He described the character in *Sellic Spell* thus: "He had great liking for honey, and often sought for it in the woods, or plundered the hives of the farmers; and as he had no name of his own people called him Bee-wolf" (*Beowulf: A Translation and Commentary*, 360).
38. *H*, 126.
39. *LotR*, 228, 369.
40. For example, Foster, *Complete Guide*, 492.
41. *Letters*, 25, 174.
42. Hammond and Scull, *Artist and Illustrator*, 37.
43. Hammond and Scull, *Artist and Illustrator*, 38
44. *OFS*, 64.
45. *H*, 9.
46. *H*, 18, 27.
47. *H*, 10.
48. *H*, 211.
49. *H*, vii.
50. *H*, 127, 307.
51. *H*, 69–70.
52. *H*, 169, 272.
53. *H*, 85–86.
54. Quoted in Rateliff, *History*, xv.
55. Quoted in Rateliff, *History*, xiv.

5. MOTHER MUSIC

1. It is important to note that identifying relationship themes that have their origin in the early maternal relationship does not imply that they are childish or only important at an early age; rather, early interactions with the mother form emotional templates that influence relationships throughout life. All of us are influenced in this way; I am trying to identify something about the specific shape of this influence in Tolkien's life.

   These experiences can also take place in relationships with the father. However, even in modern Western culture, it remains rare for the father to take a primary caretaking role during infancy and toddlerhood, and it seems certain that Tolkien's father would not have taken such a role; therefore, I will continue to refer to "mother" in this chapter.
2. McIntosh, *Flame Imperishable.*
3. Beebe, Lachmann, and Jaffe, "Mother-Infant Interaction Structures."
4. Tronick, *Neurobehavioral.*
5. Bach, *Narcissistic States;* Bach, *Language of Perversion;* Kohut, *Restoration;* Winnicott, "Parent-Infant Relationship."
6. Spitz, "Hospitalism."
7. *S,* 16.
8. *S,* 110.
9. *LotR,* 908.
10. *S,* 55.
11. *S,* 165.
12. *B&L,* 56.
13. *S,* 180–81; italics added.
14. *S,* 186–87; italics added.
15. *S,* 140.
16. Freud, "Civilization," 64–73.
17. Pine, "Separation-Individuation Concept."
18. *LotR,* 191.
19. *S,* 40.
20. *S,* 238.
21. *LotR,* 503.
22. *LT I,* 116–17.
23. *LT I,* 100; italics added.
24. Donovan, "Valkyrie Reflex"; Reid, "History of Scholarship."
25. *UT,* 173–217; *Morgoth,* 301–66.
26. *Letters,* 218; see also the similar statement in *Letters,* 377.
27. *Letters,* 416.
28. *Letters,* 353–54.
29. *Letters,* 172, 340.
30. *Letters,* 44.
31. Bach, *Narcissistic States;* Bach, *Language of Perversion;* Kohut, *Restoration.*
32. *Letters,* 349.
33. *Letters,* 350.

34. *Letters*, 377.
35. Freud, "On Narcissism"; Klein, *Envy and Gratitude;* Kohut, *Restoration.*
36. *Letters*, 48–49.
37. Bunting, "1904"; Bunting, "Finding Tolkien."
38. Rosegrant, "Comment."
39. Bunting, "Reply."
40. It should be understood that as I talk about "mother" in this book, I am really talking about "mothering person," with no way to discriminate the extent to which some of Tolkien's maternal relational schemas developed in relationship to nurses.
41. Hargreaves and Lamont *The Psychology of Musical Development.*
42. Nass, "The Development of Creative Imagination in Composers."
43. Carpenter, *Biography*, 29–30.
44. *Letters*, 350.
45. *MC*, 192–93.
46. *MC*, 193–94.
47. Tolkien, *Kullervo*, 76.
48. Carpenter, *Biography*, 137.
49. *Letters*, 377, 212.
50. *MC*, 192, 191.
51. *B&L*, 75.
52. Bach, *Chimeras;* Beebe, Lachmann, and Jaffe, "Mother-Infant Interaction Structures"; Freud, "The Ego and the Id"; Stern, *Interpersonal World;* Trevarthen, "Musicality."
53. Stern, *Interpersonal World*, 47–48.
54. Carpenter, *Biography*, 29–30.
55. *LotR*, 867.
56. Kris, "Recovery," 73; Khan, "Cumulative Trauma"; Lingiardi and McWilliams, *Psychodynamic Diagnostic Manual*, 183–84.
57. I discuss the general psychological effects of trauma in more detail in chapter 9.
58. *Letters*, 100.
59. *OFS*, 86.
60. *Letters*, 221, 376.
61. *LotR*, 134.
62. *Letters*, 100.

6. The Man-Maiden and the Spider with Horns

1. Goselin, "Two Faces of Eve"; Scull and Hammond, *Reader's Guide*, 1434.
2. *LotR*, 719; italics added.
3. *LotR*, 723–24.
4. Lionarons, "Of Spiders and Elves."
5. *Letters*, 81.
6. Linley, "Tolkien and Haggard"; Rateliff, "She and Tolkien."
7. *LotR*, 375.
8. *Letters*, 288; Maher, "A Land without Stain."

9. Beebe, Lachmann, and Jaffe, "Mother-Infant Interaction Structures."
10. *LotR*, 357.
11. *LotR*, 503.
12. *LotR*, 720–21.
13. *Morgoth*, 295–97.
14. *Treason*, 249–50.
15. *Treason*, 250.
16. *LotR*, 356–57.
17. *LotR*, 374–76. Galadriel states that the gift to Aragorn is from "Celeborn and Galadriel," but Celeborn is not mentioned in connection with any of the other gifts, and in particular it is clear that the box of soil and seed for Sam, the lock of hair for Gimli, and the phial for Frodo are from Galadriel alone.
18. I do not mean to suggest anything about the extent to which Tolkien personally subscribed to these standards, a topic too broad to take on here, but see, for example, Croft and Donovan, *Perilous and Fair*, and especially Rateliff, "Missing Women."
19. *Peoples*, 337.
20. *Letters*, 428.
21. *Letters*, 217.
22. Rainer Nagel (2008, pp. 81–82) quotes an unpublished manuscript in the Bodleian Library in which Tolkien acknowledges some of Shelob's un-spider-like features.
23. *LotR*, 729.
24. *LotR*, 356.
25. Lakowski, "Fall and Repentance," 96–97.
26. Lakowski, "Fall and Repentance."
27. Parker, "Hwaet," 603.
28. *LotR*, 723.
29. *Morgoth*, 98, 190, 284.
30. *LotR*, 723, 730.
31. *Letters*, 347.
32. *Lost Road*, 57.
33. *Lost Road*, 64–65.
34. *LotR*, 719.
35. *LotR*, 721.
36. Bettelheim, *Uses of Enchantment*, 69.
37. Zipes, *Breaking*, 8–9.

7. Seeing the Self in the Mirror of Galadriel

1. *LotR*, 362.
2. *LotR*, 363.
3. *LotR*, 362.
4. *LotR*, 364.
5. *LotR*, 363.
6. *LotR*, 366.

7. *LotR*, 283.
8. *LotR*, 315–16.
9. *LotR*, 334.
10. Winnicott, *Playing and Reality*, 112–13; italics in original.
11. Lacan, “The Mirror Stage,” 78.
12. Lacan, “The Mirror Stage,” 80; italics in original.
13. *LotR*, 378.
14. *LotR*, 339.
15. Rank, *Birth of the Hero*, 47.
16. *LotR*, 123.
17. *LotR*, 341.
18. *LotR*, 503.
19. *S*, 40.
20. *LotR*, 334.
21. *LotR*, 361.
22. *LotR*, 365.
23. *LotR*, 366.
24. *LotR*, 132.
25. *LotR*, 387.
26. *LotR*, 469.
27. *LotR*, 339; italics added.
28. *LotR*, 193; italics added.
29. *LotR*, 974–75.
30. *LotR*, 79.
31. Flieger, *Splintered Light*.
32. *S*, 48; italics added.
33. *LotR*, 922.
34. *Letters*, 385.
35. I further discuss this poem and its predecessor “Looney” in chapter 11.
36. *ATB*, 103; italics added.
37. *ATB*, 33.
38. *LotR*, 357.
39. *LotR*, 269.

8. FROM THE INELUCTABLE WAVE TO THE REALIZATION OF IMAGINED WONDER

1. *OFS*, 42.
2. *OFS*, 60.
3. *OFS*, 64; italics added.
4. *OFS*, 77; italics added.
5. *OFS*, 77.
6. *S*, 49.
7. *Letters*, 260.
8. In the very early *Book of Lost Tales II*, Tolkien wrote that the orcs “were bred by Melko of the subterranean heats and slime” (159), which sounds like actual

creation rather than corruption of a preexisting race. Tolkien repudiated this possibility by the time of *The Lord of the Rings*.

9. *LotR*, 914.
10. *Letters*, 190; *Morgoth*, 411, 409.
11. *Morgoth*, 409, 419.
12. *Morgoth*, 400.
13. *Letters*, 285.
14. Freud, "Beyond the Pleasure Principle."
15. Lasky, *Symbolization and Desymbolization*, 19–20.
16. *Letters*, 213.
17. *Letters*, 347.
18. *Letters*, 154.
19. *Letters*, 405, 416.
20. *LotR*, 1036.
21. Identifying conflict over hubris as an important meaning of the dream does not rule out other meanings; dreams are multiply determined, and recurring dreams can take on new meanings over time.
22. *Letters*, 232.
23. Scull and Hammond, *Reader's Guide*, 388.
24. Scull and Hammond, *Reader's Guide*, 518–23.
25. Scull and Hammond, *Reader's Guide*, 749.
26. Scull and Hammond, *Reader's Guide*, 710.
27. Scull and Hammond, *Reader's Guide*, 870, 318.
28. *Letters*, 105.
29. Scull and Hammond, *Reader's Guide*, 870.
30. Scull and Hammond, *Reader's Guide*, 718.
31. Scull and Hammond, *Chronology*, 318–19.
32. Garth, "As Under a Green Sea."
33. *OFS*, 75.
34. *Letters*, 188.
35. *Letters*, 122.
36. *Letters*, 145.
37. *Letters*, 189.
38. *Letters*, 231.
39. *Letters*, 248.
40. *Letters*, 413.
41. *Letters*, 215.
42. Carpenter, *Biography*, 83.
43. *Letters*, 211–12.
44. *Letters*, 26.
45. *Letters*, 172.
46. *Letters*, 145.
47. *S*, 64.
48. *S*, 65.
49. *S*, 67.
50. *S*. 69.

51. *S*, 78–79.
52. *S*, 79.
53. *S*, 83.
54. Freud, "Screen Memories."
55. Loftus, *The Myth of Repressed Memory.*
56. Josselson, "Early Memories."
57. Carpenter, *Biography*, 21.
58. Grotta-Kurska, *Architect of Middle-Earth*, 15.
59. Carpenter, *Biography*, 23.
60. *Letters*, 213.
61. Scull and Hammond, *Chronology*, 3.
62. Tolkien and Tolkien, *The Tolkien Family Album*, 18.
63. Nancy Bunting has hypothesized that another memory lies behind Tolkien's dream of the ineluctable wave. She asserts that when Tolkien was seven or older, he was traumatized by witnessing the near drowning of his brother Hilary (Bunting, "'The Shadow of the Past' Part I," 6). However, the only evidence she puts forward for this is that in his *Black & White Ogre Country*, Hilary writes, "I fell in the mill's pool once, but my mother was so glad I didn't get drowned that I wasn't even scolded" (H. Tolkien, *Black & White*, 6). This statement doesn't indicate that Hilary was actually at risk or even frightened, only that his mother was glad, and it is in a whimsical book about childhood depicted like a fairy tale with ogres and witches, making no claim to realistic accuracy. Fictionalization is pointed to by the editor's subtitle, *The Lost Tales of Hilary Tolkien*, and by the title given by Hilary himself: *Black & White Ogres, Black & White Witch, & other Stories* (H. Tolkien, *Black & White*, v). For all these reasons, it is unpersuasive as evidence of trauma to Hilary, and since J. R. R. isn't even in the scene, is even less persuasive as evidence of trauma to him.
64. Erikson, *Childhood and Society*, 251–58.
65. *OFS*, 79–81.

9. Something Has Gone Crack

1. Garth, *Great War;* Hiley, *Loss and the Silence;* Honegger and Weinrich, *Modernity 2;* Shippey, *Author;* Weinrich and Honegger, *Modernity 1;* Wood, *Tolkien among the Moderns.*
2. Croft, *War.*
3. Livingston, "Shell-Shocked Hobbit"; Smol, "Frodo's Body"; Sinex, "Wounded by War."
4. *Letters*, 303.
5. *Letters*, 10.
6. Garth, *Great War*, 179–80.
7. Garth, *Great War*, 184.
8. Freud, "Beyond the Pleasure Principle"; Krystal, "Trauma"; Oliner, *Psychic Reality.*
9. American Psychiatric Association, *DSM-5*, 271; Lingiardi and McWilliams, 184.
10. Kris, "Recovery," 73; Khan, "Cumulative Trauma"; Lingiardi and McWilliams, *Psychodynamic*, 183–84.

11. American Psychiatric Association, *DSM-5*, 271–72; Lingiardi and McWilliams, *Psychodynamic*, 185–89.
12. The formal diagnosis of post-traumatic stress disorder (American Psychiatric Association, *DSM-5*, 271–80) is based on several arbitrary cutoff points in the above symptoms that actually exist on a continuum rather than categorically, so considering a trauma victim's particular stress reactions is more meaningful than trying to decide whether he or she does or does not formally have post-traumatic stress disorder.
13. Auerhahn and Laub, "Annihilation and Restoration"; Krystal, "Trauma"; Oliner, "External Reality"; Oliner, *Psychic Reality*.
14. Bucci, *Psychoanalysis and Cognitive Science;* Freedman and Lavender, "On Desymbolization"; Lasky, *Symbolization and Desymbolization*.
15. Bucci, *Psychoanalysis and Cognitive Science*.
16. McDougall, *Theaters of the Body*.
17. Lingiardi and McWilliams, *Psychodynamic*, 185.
18. Adams-Silvan and Silvan, "A Dream"; Oliner, *Psychic Reality*, 33–34; Renik, "Typical Examination Dreams"; Sugarman, "The Use of Play."
19. Moses, "Adult Psychic Trauma."
20. *Letters*, 416, 353–54.
21. Carpenter, *Biography*, 39.
22. Bunting, "Finding Tolkien"; Bunting, "1904."
23. Rosegrant, "Comment."
24. Carpenter, *Biography*, 23; Scull and Hammond, *Chronology*, 3.
25. Carpenter, *Biography*, 25.
26. Scull and Hammond, *Chronology*, 8.
27. Carpenter, *Biography*, 36; Scull and Hammond, *Chronology*, 10–11.
28. *Merck Manual*.
29. Scull and Hammond, *Chronology*, 16–17.
30. Scull and Hammond, *Chronology*, 18.
31. Scull and Hammond, *Chronology*, 49.
32. Scull and Hammond, *Chronology*, 55, 57.
33. *LotR*, xiv.
34. Scull and Hammond, *Chronology;* Carpenter, *Biography;* Garth, *Great War*.
35. Scull and Hammond, *Chronology*.
36. Atenstaedt, "Trench Fever," 566; Holmes, "Medicine"; MacPherson et al., *History of the Great War*, 360–61; Miller, "Of Lice and Men"; *Merck Manual*.

    Holmes, MacPherson et al., and Miller give the three-month figure. MacPherson estimates that in 1917, 45,000 British troops were evacuated because of trench fever, and that 2,000 of them (4.4 percent) were incapacitated for longer than six months. Atenstaedt estimates that 450,000 British troops contracted trench fever during the years 1916–18, and that 6,000 (1.3 percent) still reported trench fever as a cause of disability in 1920. *Merck* states that the typical duration of trench fever is five or six days, with one to eight recurrences of fever at five- or six-day intervals occurring in about half the cases (this would amount to ninety-six days or about three months using the higher figures), and relapses occurring up to ten years after the initial infection.

37. This is in no way to suggest that Tolkien was malingering or consciously shirking duty. Military doctors examined him regularly and documented definitely that he was suffering from genuine and severe physical ailments. The misconception that trauma symptoms expressed through the body are "all in the head" results from a false dichotomy between mind and body.
38. Tolkien and Tolkien, *Family Album*, 41.
39. *Letters*, 421.
40. *Letters*, 416–17.
41. Carpenter, *Biography;* Carpenter, *Inklings;* Kilby, *Tolkien and the Silmarillion.*
42. *Letters*, 349.
43. *Letters*, 341; italics added.
44. Scull and Hammond, *Reader's Guide*, 483–87.
45. Senior, "Loss," 173.
46. Hannon, "Elegy," 37.
47. Parker, "Hwaet," 609.
48. Brogan, "Tolkien's Great War," 358.
49. *Kullervo*, 7.
50. *Kullervo*, 7.
51. Bunting, "1904"; *Kullervo.*
52. *Kullervo*, 143.
53. *Kullervo*, 19–20.
54. Sinex, "Wounded by War."
55. *S*, 207.
56. *S*, 210.
57. *Letters*, 232.
58. *Letters*, 213; quoted in chapter 8.
59. *LotR*, 864.
60. *LotR*, 816–17.
61. *LotR*, 866–67.
62. *LotR*, 964.
63. *LT II*, 166.
64. Livingston, "The Shell-Shocked Hobbit."
65. *LotR*, 989.
66. *LotR*, 1024.
67. Livingston, "The Shell-Shocked Hobbit," 17–18.
68. Croft, *War*, 20.
69. Tolkien, *Adventures of Tom Bombadil*, 106–8.
70. Kristeva, *Horror*, 4.
71. *LotR*, 627.
72. *LotR*, 628.
73. Nagy, "The 'Lost' Subject of Middle-earth."
74. *LotR*, 1029.
75. *S*, 184–85.
76. *S*, 186.
77. *S*, 187.
78. *LotR*, 1029.

10. THE ONE RING AND TOM BOMBADIL

1. Winnicott, "Transitional Objects."
2. Bach, *Language of Perversion;* Benvenuto, *What Are Perversions?*; Freud, "Economic"; Freud, "Splitting"; Novick and Novick, "Essence of Masochism"; Stoller, "Hostility and Mystery."
3. Winnicott, "Location of Cultural Experience."
4. Freud, "Splitting."
5. Wulff, "Fetishism and Object Choice"; Sterba, "Eating Disturbances of Childhood."
6. Greenacre, "The Fetish"; Greenacre, "The Transitional Object."
7. Bak, "Fetishism"; Freud, "Three Essays."
8. Bach, *Language of Perversion;* Benvenuto, *What Are Perversions?*; Freud, "Economic"; Novick and Novick, "Essence of Masochism"; Stoller, "Hostility and Mystery."
9. Bach, "Language of Perversion," 18.
10. Winnicott, "Transitional Objects," 9.
11. Culver, "Extending the Reach."
12. Shippey, *Road,* 139–40.
13. *LotR,* 60.
14. Nagy, "'Lost' Subject of Middle-earth."
15. *LotR,* 34.
16. *LotR,* 937–38.
17. Readers of the Harry Potter series are of course familiar with these dynamics in the form of Voldemort's horcruxes. It would be interesting to know if Rowling had the One Ring in mind when she created horcruxes, or if this is an example of two storytellers independently scooping out the same ingredient from the soup of stories.
18. *LotR,* 900.
19. *LotR,* 60.
20. *LotR,* 133.
21. Shengold, "Ring."
22. Doniger, "Magic Rings," 249–50; Goldwater, "Magic," 228–29.
23. *LotR,* 157.
24. *LotR,* 160.
25. Shippey, *Author,* 135–43.
26. *LotR,* 945.
27. *LotR,* 269.
28. *LotR,* 401; italics in original.
29. *S,* 289.
30. Bach, *Language of Perversion,* 137.
31. *LotR,* 75.
32. *LotR,* 141.
33. *LotR,* 119.
34. *LotR,* 126.
35. *Letters,* 26, 174.

36. *LotR*, 996.
37. *LotR*, 135.
38. *LotR*, 143.
39. *LotR*, 132–33.
40. *LotR*, 124.
41. *LotR*, 124.
42. *LotR*, 265.
43. Aron, *Meeting of Minds;* Bach, *Language of Perversion;* Benjamin, *Bonds of Love;* Benjamin, *Beyond Doer and Done To;* Butler, *Psychic Life of Power.*
44. *ATB*, 35–36.
45. *LotR*, 123.
46. *LotR*, 131–32.
47. *LotR*, 243.
48. *Morgoth*, 400.
49. *LotR*, 244.
50. Bach, *Language of Perversion;* Winnicott, "Location of Cultural Experience."

11. LATE LIFE LOSS OF TRANSITIONALITY

1. Scull and Hammond, *Reader's Guide*, 31.
2. Edwards, *Tolkien*, 276–79.
3. Carpenter, *Biography*, 238.
4. Shippey, *Author*, 267–73.
5. Shippey, *Author*, 275.
6. *Leaf*, 115.
7. *Leaf*, 119–20.
8. Swank, "Tom Bombadil's Last Song," 187.
9. Swank, "Tom Bombadil's Last Song," 195.
10. Swank, "Tom Bombadil's Last Song," 190.
11. *ATB*, 285.
12. Shippey, *Road*, 277.
13. *Smith*, 21.
14. *Smith*, 23.
15. *ATB*, 106.
16. Shippey, *Road*, 284.
17. *ATB*, 253.
18. Shippey, *Road*, 284.
19. *Letters*, 144.
20. Agoy, "The Fall and Man's Mortality."
21. Flieger, *Fairy Tale*, 174–77.
22. Maher, "A Land without Stain."
23. Rateliff, *History*, 763–838.
24. Rateliff, *History*, 811.
25. *H*, 12–13.
26. Rateliff, *History*, 770–71.
27. Rateliff, *History*, 809, 810.

28. Rateliff, *History*, 836.
29. Rateliff, *History*, 811–12.
30. *Morgoth*, 369.
31. *Morgoth*, 370; italics added.
32. *Morgoth*, 370; italics added.
33. *Morgoth*, 389; italics added.
34. *Morgoth*, 375; italics in original.
35. *Morgoth*, 370.
36. *Morgoth*, 371.
37. *Morgoth*, 371.
38. *Morgoth*, 400.
39. *Morgoth*, 400.

EPILOGUE

1. *LotR*, 73.
2. Freud, "Inhibitions, Symptoms, and Anxiety."
3. *OFS*, 63; italics in original.

Bibliography

Adams-Silvan, Abby, and Mark Silvan. "'A Dream Is the Fulfillment of a Wish': Traumatic Dream, Repetition Compulsion, and the Pleasure Principle." *International Journal of Psychoanalysis* 71 (1990): 513–22.

Agoy, Nils I. "The Fall and Man's Mortality: An Investigation of Some Theological Themes in J. R. R. Tolkien's 'Athrabeth Finrod ah Andreth.'" In *Between Faith and Fiction: Tolkien and the Powers of His World*, edited by Nils I. Agoy, 16–27. Oslo: Arthedain, 1998.

American Psychiatric Association. *Diagnostic and Statistical Manual of Mental Disorders*. 5th ed. Washington, DC: American Psychiatric Association Publishing, 2013.

Aron, Lewis. *A Meeting of Minds: Mutuality in Psychoanalysis*. New York: Routledge, 2001.

Ashliman, D. L. "Mother Killed Me, Father Ate Me: Folktales of Type 720." https://www.pitt.edu/~dash/type0720.html.

Atenstaedt, R. L. "Trench Fever: The British Medical Response in the Great War." *Journal of the Royal Society of Medicine* 99 (2006): 564–68.

Auden, Wystan H. "In Memory of Sigmund Freud." In *W. H. Auden: Collected Poems*, edited by Edward Mendelson, 273–76. Visalia, CA: Vintage, 1991. First published 1939.

Auerhahn, Nanette, and Dori Laub. "Annihilation and Restoration: Post-Traumatic Memory as Pathway and Obstacle to Recovery." *International Review of Psychoanalysis* 11 (1984): 327–44.

Bach, Sheldon. *Chimeras and Other Writings: Selected Papers of Sheldon Bach*. New York: International Psychoanalytic Books, 2016.

———. *The Language of Perversion and the Language of Love*. Northvale, NJ: Jason Aronson, 1994.

———. *Narcissistic States and the Therapeutic Process*. Northvale, NJ: Jason Aronson, 1985.

Bak, Robert C. "Fetishism." *Journal of the American Psychoanalytic Association* 1 (1953): 285–98.

Beebe, Beatrice, Frank M. Lachmann, and Joseph Jaffe. "Mother-Infant Interaction Structures and Presymbolic Self- and Object-Representations." *Psychoanalytic Dialogues* 7 (1997): 133–82.

Benjamin, J. *Beyond Doer and Done To.* New York: Routledge, 2018.

———. *The Bonds of Love: Psychoanalysis, Feminism, and the Problem of Domination.* New York, Pantheon, 1988.

Benvenuto, Sergio. *What Are Perversions? Sexuality, Ethics, Psychoanalysis.* London: Karnac, 2016.

Bettelheim, Bruno. *The Uses of Enchantment.* New York: Random House, 1975.

Brabant, Eva, Ernst Falzeder, and Patrizia Giampieri-Deutsch, eds. *The Correspondence of Sigmund Freud and Sandor Ferenczi.* Vol. 1, *1908–1914.* Cambridge, MA: Harvard Univ. Press, 1993.

Brogan, Hugh. "Tolkien's Great War." In *Children and Their Books,* edited by Gillian Avery and Julia Briggs, 351–67. Oxford: Clarendon, 1989.

Bucci, Wilma. *Psychoanalysis and Cognitive Science.* New York: Guilford, 1997.

Bunting, Nancy A. "Finding Tolkien in His Stories." *Lembas Katern* 174 (2016): 73–86.

———. "1904: Tolkien, Trauma, and Its Anniversaries." *Mythlore* 34 (2015): 59–81.

———. "A Reply to Rosegrant." *Mythlore* 35 (2016): 133–37.

———. "The Shadow of the Past Part 1." *Beyond Bree* (May 2013): 6–8.

Butler, Judith. *The Psychic Life of Power.* Palo Alto, CA: Stanford Univ. Press, 1997.

Campbell, Joseph. *The Hero with a Thousand Faces.* Novato, CA: New World Library, 2008. First published 1949.

Carpenter, Humphrey. *The Inklings: C. S. Lewis, J. R. R. Tolkien, Charles Williams, and Their Friends.* New York: Houghton Mifflin, 1979.

———. *J. R. R. Tolkien: A Biography.* New York: Houghton Mifflin, 2000.

Carter, Angela. "The Company of Wolves." In *The Bloody Chamber,* 141–52. New York: Penguin, 1979.

Conklin, Beth. *Consuming Grief.* Austin: Univ. of Texas Press, 2001.

Croft, Janet, ed. *Baptism of Fire.* Altadena, CA: Mythopoeic Press, 2015.

———. *War and the Works of J. R. R. Tolkien.* Westport, CT: Praeger, 2004.

Croft, Janet, and Leslie Donovan, eds. *Perilous and Fair: Women in the Works and Life of J. R. R. Tolkien.* Altadena, CA: Mythopoeic Press, 2015.

Croft, Janet, and Annika Rottinger, eds. *"Something Has Gone Crack": New Perspectives on J. R. R. Tolkien in the Great War.* Zurich: Walking Tree, 2019.

Culver, Jennifer. "Extending the Reach of the Invisible Hand: A Gift Looks for Gain in the Gifting Economy of Middle-earth." In *The Body in Tolkien's Legendarium: Essays on Middle-Earth Corporeality,* edited by Christopher Vaccaro, 157–69. Jefferson: McFarland, 2013.

Curry, Patrick. *Defending Middle-Earth: Tolkien: Myth and Modernity.* Boston: Houghton Mifflin, 1997.

———. "Enchantment in Tolkien and Middle-earth." In *Tolkien's The Lord of the Rings: Sources of Inspiration,* edited by S. Caldecott and C. Honneger, 99–112. Zurich: Walking Tree Publishers, 2008.

Doniger, Wendy. "Magic Rings and the Return of the Repressed." *Annual of Psychoanalysis* 35 (2007): 243–55.

Donovan, Leslie. "The Valkyrie Reflex in J. R. R. Tolkien's *The Lord of the Rings:* Galadriel, Shelob, Eowyn, and Arwen." In Croft and Donovan, *Perilous and Fair,* 221–57.

Dundes, Alan. "Interpreting Little Red Riding Hood Psychoanalytically." In *The Brothers Grimm and Folktale,* edited by James M. McGlathery, 16–51. Urbana: Univ. of Illinois Press, 1988.

Edwards, Raymond. *Tolkien.* London: Robert Hale, 2014.

Erikson, E. H. *Childhood and Society.* New York: Norton, 1950.

———. "The Problem of Ego Identity." *Journal of the American Psychoanalytic Association* 4 (1956): 56–121.

Ferenczi, Sandor. *First Contributions to Psychoanalysis.* London: Hogarth, 1952.

Flieger, Verlyn. "The Arch and the Keystone." *Mythlore* 38, no. 1 (2019): 7–19.

———. *Green Suns and Faerie.* Kent, OH: Kent State Univ. Press, 2012.

———. *Splintered Light: Logos and Language in Tolkien's World.* Kent, OH: Kent State Univ. Press, 2002.

———. *There Would Always Be a Fairy Tale.* Kent, OH: Kent State Univ. Press, 2017.

Foster, R. *The Complete Guide to Middle-earth.* Rev. ed. New York: Ballantine, 1979.

Freedman, N., and Joan Lavender. "On Desymbolization: The Concept and Observations on Anorexia and Bulimia." *Psychoanalysis and Contemporary Thought* 25 (2002): 165–99.

Freud, S. "Beyond the Pleasure Principle." In *The Standard Edition of the Complete Psychological Works of Sigmund Freud,* edited by James Strachey, 18:1–143. London: Hogarth, 1955. First published 1920.

———. "Character and Anal Erotism." In *The Standard Edition of the Complete Psychological Works of Sigmund Freud,* edited by James Strachey, 9:167–76. London: Hogarth, 1959. First published 1908.

———. "Civilization and Its Discontents." In *The Standard Edition of the Complete Psychological Works of Sigmund Freud,* edited by James Strachey, 21:59–145. London: Hogarth, 1961. First published 1930.

———. "Creative Writers and Day-Dreaming." In *The Standard Edition of the Complete Psychological Works of Sigmund Freud,* edited by James Strachey, 9:141–53. London: Hogarth, 1959. First published 1908.

———. "The Economic Problem of Masochism." In *The Standard Edition of the Complete Psychological Works of Sigmund Freud,* edited by James Strachey, 19:157–70. London: Hogarth, 1961. First published 1924.

———. "The Ego and the Id." In *The Standard Edition of the Complete Psychological Works of Sigmund Freud,* edited by James Strachey, 19:1–66. London: Hogarth, 1961. First published 1923.

———. "Formulations on the Two Principles of Mental Functioning." In *The Standard Edition of the Complete Psychological Works of Sigmund Freud,* edited by James Strachey, 12:213–26. London: Hogarth, 1959. First published 1911.

———. "The Future of an Illusion." In *The Standard Edition of the Complete Psychological Works of Sigmund Freud,* edited by James Strachey, 21:1–56. London: Hogarth, 1955. First published 1925.

———. "Inhibitions, Symptoms, and Anxiety." In *The Standard Edition of the Complete Psychological Works of Sigmund Freud,* edited by James Strachey, 20:77–175. London: Hogarth, 1961. First published 1925.

———. "On Narcissism." In *The Standard Edition of the Complete Psychological Works of Sigmund Freud,* edited by James Strachey, 14:67–102. London: Hogarth, 1957. First published 1914.

———. "Screen Memories." In *The Standard Edition of the Complete Psychological Works of Sigmund Freud,* edited by James Strachey, 9:301–22. London: Hogarth, 1962. First published 1899.

———. "Splitting of the Ego in the Process of Defence." In *The Standard Edition of the Complete Psychological Works of Sigmund Freud,* edited by James Strachey, 23:271–78. London: Hogarth, 1964. First published 1938.

———. "Three Essays on the Theory of Sexuality." In *The Standard Edition of the Complete Psychological Works of Sigmund Freud,* edited by James Strachey, 9:125–248. London: Hogarth, 1953. First published 1905.

———. "The Uncanny." In *The Standard Edition of the Complete Psychological Works of Sigmund Freud,* edited by James Strachey, 17:217–56. London: Hogarth, 1955. First published 1919.

Garth, John. *Tolkien and the Great War.* New York: Houghton Mifflin, 2003.

———. "'As Under a Green Sea': Visions of War in the Dead Marshes." In *Myth and Magic: Art According to the Inklings,* edited by Eduardo Segura and Thomas Honegger, 285–313. Zollikofen, Switzerland: Walking Tree, 2007.

"Geiriadur Prifysgol Cymru." http://welsh-dictionary.ac.uk/gpc/gpc.html.

Goldwater, Eugene. "Magic and Psychoanalysis." *Modern Psychoanalysis* 38 (2013): 227–45.

Goselin, Peter D. "Two Faces of Eve: Galadriel and Shelob as Anima Figures." *Mythlore* 6, no. 3 (1979): 3–4, 28.

Greenacre, Phyllis. "The Fetish and the Transitional Object." *Psychoanalytic Study of the Child* 24 (1969): 144–64.

———. "The Transitional Object and the Fetish with Special Reference to the Role of Illusion." *International Journal of Psychoanalysis* 51 (1970): 447–56.

Grotta-Kurska, D. *J. R. R. Tolkien: Architect of Middle Earth.* New York: Warner Press, 1976.

Hammond, Wayne G., and Cristina Scull. *J. R. R. Tolkien: Artist and Illustrator.* London: Harper Collins, 1995.

Hannon, P. "*The Lord of the Rings* as Elegy." *Mythlore* 24, no. 2 (Summer/Fall 2004): 36–42.

Hargreaves, David, and Alexandra Lamont. *The Psychology of Musical Development.* Cambridge: Cambridge Univ. Press, 2017.

Helms, Randel. *Tolkien's World.* Boston: Houghton Mifflin, 1974.

Hiley, Margaret. *The Loss and the Silence.* Zurich: Walking Tree Press, 2011.

Holmes, Frederick. "Medicine in the First World War." https://www.kumc.edu/wwi/index-of-essays/trench-fever.html.

Honegger, Thomas. "More Light Than Shadow? Jungian Approaches to Tolkien and the Archetypal Image of the Shadow." Academia.edu, https://www.academia

.edu/12415836/_More_Light_Than_Shadow_Jungian_Approaches_to_Tolkien_and_the_Archetypal_Image_of_the_Shadow.

Honneger, Thomas, and Frank Weinreich, eds. *Tolkien and Modernity 2*. Zurich: Walking Tree, 2006.

Hooker, Mark. *Tolkien and Welsh*. N.p.: Createspace, 2012.

Josselson, R. "Stability and Change in Early Memories over 22 Years: Themes, Variations, and Cadenzas." *Bulletin of the Menninger Clinic* 64 (2000): 462–81.

Khan, M. "The Concept of Cumulative Trauma." *Psychoanalytic Study of the Child* 18 (1963): 286–306.

Kilby, Clyde S. *Tolkien and the Silmarillion*. Wheaton, IL: Harold Shaw, 1976.

Klein, Melanie. *Envy and Gratitude and Other Works*. London: Karnac, 1993.

Kohut, Heinz. *The Restoration of the Self*. Madison, CT: International Univ. Press, 1977.

Kris, E. "The Recovery of Childhood Memories in Psychoanalysis." *Psychoanalytic Study of the Child* 11 (1956): 54–88.

Kristeva, Julia. *Powers of Horror*. New York: Columbia Univ. Press, 1982.

Krystal, Henry. "Trauma and the Stimulus Barrier." *Psychoanalytic Inquiry* 5 (1985): 131–61.

Lacan, Jacques. "The Mirror Stage as Formative of the *I* Function as Revealed in Psychoanalytic Experience." In *Ecrits*, edited by Bruce Fink, 75–81. New York: W. W. Norton, 2006.

Lakowsky, Romuald I. "The Fall and Repentance of Galadriel." *Mythlore* 25, no. 3 (2007): 91–104.

Lasky, Richard, ed. *Symbolization and Desymbolization: Essays in Honor of Norbert Freedman*. New York: Karnac, 2002.

Levy-Warren, M. *The Adolescent Journey*. Northvale, NJ: Aronson, 1996.

Lewis, C. S. *The Pilgrim's Regress*. Grand Rapids, MI: William P. Erdmans, 2014. First published 1933.

———. "Review of *The Hobbit*." *Times Literary Supplement*, Oct. 2, 1937, 714.

Lingiardi, Vittorio, and Nancy McWilliams. *Psychodynamic Diagnostic Manual*. 2nd ed. New York: Guilford, 2017.

Linley, Stephen. "Tolkien and Haggard: Some Thoughts on Galadriel." *Anor* 23 (1991): 11–16.

Lionarons, Joyce T. "Of Spiders and Elves." *Mythlore* 31, no. 3 (2013): 5–13.

Livingston, Michael. "The Shell-Shocked Hobbit: The First World War and Tolkien's Trauma of the Ring." *Mythlore* 25, no. 1 (2006): 77–92.

Loewald, Hans W. "Ego and Reality." In *The Essential Loewald: Collected Papers and Monographs*, edited by Jonathon Lear, 3–20. Hagerstown, MD: Univ. Publishing Group, 2000.

Loftus, Elizabeth. *The Myth of Repressed Memory*. New York: St. Martin's Press, 1994.

MacPherson, W. G., W. P. Herringham, T. R. Elliott, and A. Balfour. *History of the Great War Based on Official Documents—Medical Services—Diseases of the War*. Vol. 1. London: His Majesty's Stationery Office, 1921–23.

Maher, M. W. "A Land without Stain: Medieval Images of Mary and Their Use in the Characterization of Galadriel." In *Tolkien the Medievalist*, edited by Jane Chance, 225–36. London: Routledge, 2003.

Mahler, Margaret S., Fred Pine, and Anni Bergman. *The Psychological Birth of the Human Infant.* New York: Basic Books, 1975.
McDougall, Joyce. *Theaters of the Body.* New York: W. W. Norton, 1989.
McIntosh, Jonathon. *The Flame Imperishable.* Kettering, OH: Angelico Press, 2017.
Merck Manual Professional Version. https://www.merckmanuals.com/professional.
Miller, M. G. "Of Lice and Men: Trench Fever and Trench Life in the AIF." http://www.gwpda.org/medical/liceand.htm.
Moses, Rafael. "Adult Psychic Trauma: The Question of Early Predisposition and Some Detailed Mechanisms." *International Journal of Psychoanalysis* 59 (1978): 353–63.
Nagel, Rainer. "Shelob and Her Kin: The Evolution of Tolkien's Spiders." In *The Mirror Crack'd: Fear and Horror in J. R. R. Tolkien's Major Works,* edited by Lynn Forest-Hill, 81–92. Newcastle upon Tyne: Cambridge Scholars, 2008.
Nagy, Gergely. "The 'Lost' Subject of Middle-earth: The Constitution of the Subject in the Figure of Gollum in *The Lord of the Rings.*" *Tolkien Studies* 3 (2006): 57–79.
Nass, Martin. "The Development of Creative Imagination in Composers." *International Review of Psycho-Analysis* 11 (1984): 481–91.
Novick, Kerry K., and Jack Novick. "The Essence of Masochism." *Psychoanalytic Study of the Child* 42 (1987): 353–84.
Oliner, Marion. "External Reality: The Elusive Dimension of Psychoanalysis." *The Psychoanalytic Quarterly* 65 (1996): 267–300.
———. *Psychic Reality in Context.* London: Karnac, 2012.
Parker, Douglass. "Hwaet We Holbytla . . ." *Hudson Review* 9 (1957): 598–609.
Pearson, Mike Parker, et al. "Craig Rhos-y-felin: A Welsh Bluestone Megalith Quarry for Stonehenge." *Antiquity* 89, no. 348 (Dec. 2015): 1331–52.
Piaget, Jean. *The Psychology of Intelligence.* Totowa, NJ: Littlefield.
Pine, Fred. "Some Refinements of the Separation-Individuation Concept in Light of Research on Infants." *Psychoanalytic Study of the Child* 47 (1992): 103–16.
Rank, Otto. *The Myth of the Birth of the Hero.* Baltimore: Johns Hopkins Univ. Press, 2004. First published 1922.
Rateliff, John D. *The History of The Hobbit.* New York: Harper Collins, 2011.
———. "The Missing Women: Tolkien's Lifelong Support for Women's Higher Education." In Croft and Donovan, *Perilous and Fair,* 13–40.
———. "She and Tolkien." *Mythlore* 8, no. 2 (1981): 6–8.
Reid, Robin. "The History of Scholarship on Female Characters in J. R. R. Tolkien's Legendarium: A Feminist Bibliographic Essay." In Croft and Donovan, *Perilous and Fair,* 13–40.
Renik, Owen. "Typical Examination Dreams, 'Superego Dreams,' and Traumatic Dreams." *Psychoanalytic Quarterly* 50 (1981): 159–89.
Rosegrant, J. "A Comment on '1904: Tolkien, Trauma, and Its Anniversaries.'" *Mythlore* 34 (2016): 167–70.
———. "The Psychoanalytic Play State." *Journal of Clinical Psychoanalysis* 10 (2001): 323–43.
Schutt, Bill. *Cannibalism: A Perfectly Natural History.* Chapel Hill, NC: Algonquin Books, 2017.
Scull, Cristina, and Wayne Hammond. *The J. R. R. Tolkien Companion and Guide: Chronology.* Rev. ed. Boston: Houghton-Mifflin, 2017.

———. *The J. R. R. Tolkien Companion and Guide: Reader's Guide*. Rev. ed. Boston: Houghton Mifflin, 2017.

Sendak, Maurice. *Where the Wild Things Are*. New York: Harper Collins, 2012.

Senior, W. A. "Loss Eternal in J. R. R. Tolkien's Middle-Earth." In *J. R. R. Tolkien and His Literary Resonances: Views of Middle-earth*, edited by George Clark and Daniel Timmons, 173–82. Westport, CT: Greenwood, 2000.

Shengold, Leonard. "The Ring of the Narcissist." *International Journal of Psychoanalysis* 76 (1995): 1205–13.

Shippey, Tom. *J. R. R. Tolkien: Author of the Century*. London: Harper Collins, 2000.

———. *The Road to Middle-Earth*. Boston: Houghton Mifflin, 2003.

Sinex, Margaret. "Wounded by War: Men's Bodies in the Prose Tradition of *The Children of Hurin*." In *Baptism of Fire*, edited by Janet Brennan Croft, 38–59. Altadena, CA: Mythopoeic Press, 2015.

Smol, Anna. "Frodo's Body: Liminality and the Experience of War." In *The Body in Tolkien's Legendarium: Essays on Middle-Earth Corporeality*, edited by C. Vaccaro, 39–63. Jefferson: McFarland, 2013.

Spitz, Rene A. "Hospitalism—An Inquiry into the Genesis of Psychiatric Conditions in Early Childhood." *Psychoanalytic Study of the Child* 1 (1945): 53–74.

Sterba, Editha. "An Important Factor in Eating Disturbances of Childhood." *Psychoanalytic Quarterly* 10 (1941): 365–72.

Stern, Daniel. *The Interpersonal World of the Infant*. New York: Basic Books, 1985.

Stoller, Robert J. "Hostility and Mystery in Perversion." *International Journal of Psychoanalysis* 55 (1974): 425–34.

Sugarman, Alan. "The Use of Play to Promote Insightfulness in the Analysis of Children Suffering from Cumulative Trauma." *Psychoanalytic Quarterly* 77 (2008): 799–833.

Swank, Kris. "Tom Bombadil's Last Song: Tolkien's 'Once upon a Time.'" *Tolkien Studies* 10 (2013): 185–97.

Tatar, Maria. *The Annotated Brothers Grimm*. New York: W. W. Norton, 2004.

———. *Off with Their Heads!* Princeton, NJ: Princeton Univ. Press, 1992.

Thomas, Paul E. "Some of Tolkien's Narrators." In *Tolkien's Legendarium: Essays on the History of Middle-earth*, edited by Verlyn Flieger and Carl F. Hostetter, 161–82. Westport, CT: Greenwood, 2000.

Todorov, Tzvetan. *The Fantastic: A Structural Approach to a Literary Genre*. Ithaca: Cornell Univ. Press, 1975.

Tolkien, Christopher. "Introduction." In J. R. R. Tolkien, *The Hobbit: 75th Anniversary Edition*. Boston: Houghton Mifflin, 2007.

Tolkien, Hilary. *Black & White Ogre Country*. Moreton-in-Marsh: ADC Publications, 2009.

Tolkien, John, and Priscilla Tolkien. *The Tolkien Family Album*. Boston: Houghton-Mifflin, 1992.

Tolkien, J. R. R. *The Adventures of Tom Bombadil*. Edited by Cristina Scull and Wayne Hammond. London: George Allen & Unwin, 2014.

———. *Beowulf: A Translation and Commentary*. Edited by Christopher Tolkien. New York: Houghton Mifflin, 2014.

———. "*Beowulf*: The Monsters and the Critics." In *The Monsters and the Critics and Other Essays*, edited by Christopher Tolkien, 5–48. London: George Allen and Unwin, 1983.

———. *Beren and Lúthien*. Edited by Christopher Tolkien. New York: Houghton-Mifflin, 2017.

———. *The Book of Lost Tales, Part One*. Edited by Christopher Tolkien. New York: Ballantine, 1983.

———. *The Book of Lost Tales, Part Two*. Edited by Christopher Tolkien. New York: Ballantine, 1984.

———. *The Children of Hurin*. Edited by Christopher Tolkien. New York: Houghton Mifflin, 2007.

———. "The Drowning of Anadune." In *Sauron Defeated*, edited by Christopher Tolkien, 329–440. London: Harper Collins, 1993.

———. "The Fall of Numenor." In *The Lost Road and Other Writings*, edited by Christopher Tolkien, 7–38. New York: Ballantine, 1987.

———. *The Hobbit: 50th Anniversary Edition*. New York: Houghton Mifflin, 1966.

———. "Leaf by Niggle." In *The Tolkien Reader*, 100–120. New York: Ballantine, 1966.

———. *The Letters of J. R. R. Tolkien*. Edited by Humphrey Carpenter. New York: Houghton Mifflin, 2000.

———. *The Lord of the Rings*. New York: Houghton Mifflin, 2004.

———. "The Lost Road." In *The Lost Road and Other Writings*, edited by Christopher Tolkien, 39–116. New York: Ballantine, 1987.

———. *Morgoth's Ring*. Edited by Christopher Tolkien. London: Harper Collins, 2002.

———. "The Notion Club Papers." In *Sauron Defeated*, edited by Christopher Tolkien, 143–327. London: HarperCollins, 1993.

———. "On Fairy-Stories." In *The Tolkien Reader*, 33–99. New York: Ballantine, 1966.

———. *The Peoples of Middle-earth*. Edited by Christopher Tolkien. London: Harper Collins, 2002.

———. "The Quest of Erebor." In *Unfinished Tales*, edited by Christopher Tolkien, 321–36. New York: Houghton Mifflin, 1980.

———. *Sauron Defeated*. Edited by Christopher Tolkien. New York: Houghton Mifflin, 1992.

———. *The Silmarillion*. London: George Allen & Unwin, 1977.

———. *Smith of Wootton Major*. London: George Allen & Unwin, 1967.

———. *The Story of Kullervo*. Edited by Verlyn Flieger. Boston: Mariner Books, 2017.

———. *The Treason of Isengard*. Edited by Christopher Tolkien. New York: Houghton Mifflin, 1989.

———. *Unfinished Tales*. Edited by Christopher Tolkien. New York: Houghton Mifflin, 1980.

Trevarthen, Colwyn. "Musicality and the Intrinsic Motive Pulse: Evidence from Human Psychobiology and Infant Communication." *Musicae Scientiae* 3 (1999): 155–215.

Tronick, Ed. *The Neurobehavioral and Social-Emotional Development of Infants and Children*. New York: Norton, 2007.

Weber, Max. "Science as a Vocation." In *The Vocation Lectures*, edited by David Owen and Tracy B. Strong, 1–31. Indianapolis: Hackett, 2004.
———. *The Sociology of Religion*. Boston: Beacon, 1963.
Weinreich, Frank, and Thomas Honegger, eds. *Tolkien and Modernity* 1. Zurich: Walking Tree, 2006.
Winnicott, Donald W. "The Location of Cultural Experience." *International Journal of Psychoanalysis* 48 (1967): 368–72.
———. *Playing and Reality*. London: Tavistock, 1971.
———. "The Theory of the Parent-Infant Relationship." *International Journal of Psychoanalysis* 41 (1960): 585–95.
———. "Transitional Objects and Transitional Phenomena: A Study of the First Not-Me Possession." *International Journal of Psychoanalysis* 34 (1953): 89–97.
Wood, Ralph. *Tolkien among the Moderns*. Notre Dame: Univ. of Notre Dame Press, 2015.
Wulff, Moshe. "Fetishism and Object Choice in Early Childhood." *Psychoanalytic Quarterly* 15 (1946): 450–71.
Zipes, Jack. "Dreams of a Better Bourgeois Life: The Psychosocial Origins of the Grimms' Tales." In *The Brothers Grimm and Folktale*, edited by James M. McGlathery, 205–19. Urbana: Univ. of Illinois Press, 1988.

Index

Aarne-Thompson-Uther system, 34
abjection/the abject, 39–41, 54, 56–58, 61, 65, 122, 148, 152, 156–57; defense against, 56, 66; Frodo and, 148, 155; Gollum and, 55, 61–62, 148
"Adventures of Tom Bombadil, The" (Tolkien), 160–61
Adventures of Tom Bombadil, The (Tolkien), 5, 47, 55, 164
"Akallabêth, The" (Tolkien), 117, 119–20
Alice in Wonderland, 23
Annotated Grimm (Tatar), 33
Aragorn, 5, 86–87, 144
Arda, 113, 115
art/artists, 112–13; creativity as a search for enchantment, 1, 11; inspiration, 123–24; potential space, 115–16; transitional space, 116
Arwen Undómiel, 86, 106
"Athrabeth Finrod ah Andreth" (Tolkien), 168–69
Auden, W. H., 6–8
Aulë, 113–14, 122
aventure, 61–63

Bach, Sheldon, 38–39, 156
Balin, 30, 47, 51–52
Barahir, 146
Bard the Bowman, 46, 48–49
Barliman Butterbur, 4
Barrow-wights, 41, 157, 159
Battle of the Five Armies, 47, 49–50
Battle of the Pelennor Fields, 144
Beorn, 62, 63, 65
Beowulf, 2–3, 6, 62; poet, 3–5; tower in, 3–5
Beren, 14, 29, 72–75, 91, 106, 108, 111, 139–40, 145–46, 149
Bettelheim, Bruno, 43, 97
Bilbo Baggins, 6, 24–25, 44–53, 64–67, 173; Battle of the Five Armies, 47; enchantment, 50; in *The Fellowship of the Ring,* 50; in *The Hobbit,* 24, 30, 44–53, 58–60, 63, 169; return home, 30, 49–50, 61; the Ring and, 61–62, 153; in Rivendell, 50, 108; songs, 10, 108; theft of the Arkenstone, 47, 59; Tookish side, 44–45; transcription of books of Elvish lore, 5
Black Riders, 1–2, 9–10, 106
body orifices, unconscious meanings of, 154–55
Boethian view, 155
"Bombadil Goes Boating" (Tolkien), 160
Boromir, 154, 156
Brandir, 143
Brogan, Hugh, 141
Buffy the Vampire Slayer, 36
Bunting, Nancy, 79, 134, 142

cannibalism: in Greek mythology, 35; intentional, 35; in "The Juniper Tree," 33–42; in "Little Red Riding Hood," 36–37; motivation for, 36–37; orality and, 37; real-world, 35, 36–37; symbolic, 37
Carcharoth, 149
Carpenter, Humphrey, 133, 135

Carter, Angela, 36
Celeborn, 18, 86, 88–90
corpse medicine, 36
Council of Elrond, 24–25, 160
"Crist I," 109
Croft, Janet, 129
Cronus, 35
Culver, Jennifer, 152
Curry, Patrick, 16, 20, 22, 53

Dagnall, Susan, 119
Dahmer, Jeffrey, 35
Dain, 47
Dante, 78
deep time, 91; in "The Juniper Tree," 34; as "Other Time," 34
deferred action, 83
Denethor, 145
disenchantment, 1, 11, 16, 41, 43, 167–68; developmental arc of, 22; in *The Hobbit,* 46–49; in *The Lord of the Rings,* 30; partial, 21; struggle with, 26; Tolkien's tension between enchantment and, 1, 3, 5, 9, 11, 25–26, 174; of the world, 2, 53
Donovan, Leslie, 76
Donner party, 35
"Drowning of Anadüne, The" (Tolkien), 117, 120
Dundes, Alan, 37
dwarves, 48; colors, 65; creation of, 113–14, 122; in *The Hobbit,* 24, 44–45, 46, 47, 58, 59; in *The Silmarillion,* 59, 113–14

Eärendil, 13, 105, 108–11
Eilinel, 146
Elrond, 25, 163
Elves, 5, 10–11, 15–17, 22, 28, 48, 114, 118; creation of the Three Rings of Power, 16; departure of, 18–19, 30; enchantment, loss of, 17; in *The Hobbit,* 45, 47, 50, 59; loremasters, 171; Rivendell, 45, 50; songs, 106–7
enchantment, 5, 10–11, 15–16, 41; creativity as a search for, 1, 4–5, 11; definition of, 8–9, 16, 19–20; developmental arc of, 22; in *The Hobbit,* 22, 44–49; loss and, 15–31, 41–42; magic versus, 9; metaphorical, 20; ordinary, 20, 22; reinstating, 26; retaining a sense of, 21; return from, 30; Tolkien's tension between disenchantment and, 1, 3, 5, 9, 11, 25–26, 174; worldview, 9
"English and Welsh" (Tolkien), 80–81
Ents, 17–18, 123
Éomer, 86
Éowyn, 144–45
Erestor, 160
Erickson, Erik, 127
escapism, 21
eucatastrophe, 83–84

fairy stories, 21; desire in, 22–23; development and maturation in, 43; enchantment in, 30; stepmothers, 97; structure of, 23, 30; transition in, 24; women in, 43
"Fall of Gondolin, The" (Tolkien), 129, 145–46
"Fall of Númenor, The" (Tolkien), 27, 93, 116–17, 119, 126–27; father figures in, 127
"fantastic, the," 40–41
Faramir, 144–45, 153
Fëanor, 124–25
Fellowship of the Ring, The: Bilbo Baggins, 50; Galadriel in, 89
Ferenczi, Sándor, 8
fetish symbols, 151; infantile, 151; the Ring as, 150–63; sexual, 151
Fíli, 47, 58, 65–66
Finduilas, 173
Flieger, Verlyn, 15, 17, 31, 61, 107, 143
Freud, Sigmund, 6–7, 8, 39, 74–75, 83, 96, 174; on anality, 56–57; on creativity, 8; death, 7; on ego, 21; on orality, 37; on play, 8, 23; on the uncanny, 38–39
Frodo, 4–5, 25, 31, 58, 72, 88, 108, 110, 114–15, 121, 129, 146–49, 156, 173; abjection, 148, 155; destruction of the Ring, 11, 17, 30, 106, 153; dreams, 1–3, 5, 9, 84, 104; encounter with Shelob, 85–86, 96–97, 109, 147; encounter with Tom Bombadil, 157–58; first encounter with Ringwraiths, 156–57; Galadriel's Mirror, 98–99, 102, 104–5, 110; Gandalf's death and, 100–101, 103; loss of human connection, 148–49; memories of Galadriel, 85–86; posttraumatic stress disorder, 146–48; return to the Shire, 30; the Ring and, 11, 17, 30, 106, 153, 155, 156–57, 159; sailing with the Elves, 30, 148–49, 158–59; walking songs, 9–11

Galadriel, 18, 50, 75, 77, 85, 88–89, 97, 108, 111, 154, 168; femininity, 86, 91; gaze, 87; loss, 90; masculine qualities of, 88, 89, 91, 96; maternal qualities, 87–89; Mirror, 98–111; phial, 85–86, 88, 96–97, 108–9, 111; rejection of the Ring, 86, 90, 154

Gandalf, 111; death, 99–100, 103; in *The Hobbit*, 24, 30, 44–47, 50–52, 55, 58–61, 63, 169–70; in *The Lord of the Rings*, 24, 87, 100, 145, 147, 156, 158
Garth, John, 121, 135
Geiriadur Prifysgol Cymru, 57
Gilson, Rob, 129–31
Gimli, 63, 86, 89, 100, 102–3
Glaurung, 143–44
Glóin, 63, 66
"Goblin Feet" (Tolkien), 22
Goldberry, 24, 63, 77, 103, 105, 159–61
Gollum, 154; as an abject version of hobbits, 55, 58–59, 61–62, 66–67, 148; feet, 55; in *The Hobbit*, 45, 54, 55, 66–67; in *The Lord of the Rings*, 55, 62, 148; the Ring and, 61–62, 153
Gorlim, 145–46
Greenacre, Phyllis, 151, 162
Grimbeorn, 63
Grimm (Brothers), 32–34, 36, 38, 41, 43
Grownupishness (Tolkien), 63–64
Gwindor, 143, 146

Haggard, H. Rider, 86
Hammond, Wayne, 64, 119, 135, 140, 166
Hannon, P., 15
"Hansel and Gretel," 35, 43
Hargreaves, Dave, 79
Helms, Randel, 6
Hobbit, The (Tolkien), 5, 12, 22, 54–67, 123, 169; Arkenstone, 46–47, 58–59; audience, 52; *aventure* in, 62; Balin, 30, 47, 51–52; Bard the Bowman, 46, 48–49; Battle of the Five Armies, 47, 49–50; Beorn, 62–63; Bilbo Baggins, 24, 30, 44–53, 58–60, 63, 66–67, 169–70; birds in, 46, 48, 59; colors in, 64–65; death in, 17, 47; disenchantment in, 46–49, 52; dwarves in, 24, 44–47, 58–59; Elves, 45, 47, 50, 59; enchantment and loss in, 22, 44–52; first line of, 67–68; "Flies and Spiders," 60; Gandalf, 24, 30, 44–47, 50–52, 55, 58–61, 63, 169–70; Gollum, 45, 54–55, 66–67; holes in, 54, 56, 60, 65–67; Lakemen, 47–48, 59; magic in, 50; Master of Laketown, 44–45, 48–50, 52; publication of, 119; relationships in, 51–52; Riddle-game, 66–67; "Riddles in the Dark," 55, 60, 62; "Roast Mutton," 60; Smaug, 46, 54, 56–61; "There and Back Again," 30; Thorin Oakenshield, 45–50, 58–59, 65; Tolkien's revisions to, 169–70; tone of, 45–46; transition motif in, 24; trolls, 45, 58; "An Unexpected Party," 24, 44
hobbits, 4, 44; description of, 64–65; enchantment and, 44; feet, 55–56; holes, 54, 56, 64–65; symbolism of, 25, 28, 54
Honegger, Thomas, 6
Hooker, Mark, 57

Idril, 146
Ilúvatar, 113–14, 169
Incledon, Marjorie, 139
Inklings, 28, 120
"In Memory of Sigmund Freud" (Auden), 7

"Jack and the Beanstalk," 35, 46
Jackson, Peter, 31, 63
Jung, Carl, 96
"Juniper Tree, The," 32–43; abjection in, 40; bird, 33–34, 36, 42; cannibalism in, 33–42; daughter, 33, 35–39, 42–43; deep time in, 34; father, 33, 35–36, 38, 41–43; mother, 33, 36, 38, 42; murder in, 33, 35–36, 42; My Mother Killed Me, My Father Ate Me classification, 34; son, 33, 35–36, 38–39, 42–43; stepmother, 33, 35–39, 42–43; summary of, 33–34; tone of, 41; the uncanny in, 38–40, 42

Kalevala, 142–43
Kíli, 47, 65–66
Klein, Melanie, 96
"Kortirion among the Leaves" (Tolkien), 29
Kristeva, Julia, 8, 11, 56, 58, 152; on the abject, 39–40, 148
Kullervo, 142–44, 146

Lacan, Jacques, 8, 83; mirroring, 101–3, 110
Lakemen, 47, 48
Lakowski, Romuald, 90
Lamont, Alexandra, 79
Last Alliance, 154
"Leaf by Niggle" (Tolkien), 28
Leaf by Niggle (Tolkien), 164–65
Legolas, 87, 103–6
Letters to Father Christmas (Tolkien), 62
Lewis, C. S., 6, 45, 78, 139; death, 140
Lionarons, Joyce, 86
"Little Red Riding Hood," 36–37
Livingston, Michael, 146–47
Loewald, Hans W., 20–21
"Looney" (Tolkien), 167–68
Lord of the Rings, The (Tolkien), 5, 11, 22, 61, 120–21, 123, 169; appendices, 5, 31, 51, 117; Aragorn, 86–87, 144; audience, 26, 52; Barrow-Downs, 24; Black

Lord of the Rings, The (Tolkien) (cont.) Rider, 106; Boromir, 154, 156; Buckland, 24; cadence of, 18–19; Council of Elrond, 24–25, 160; Dead Marshes, 29, 41, 148; death as a theme of, 17; disenchantment in, 30, 52; Elrond, 25, 163; enchantment in, 15, 16, 22, 24, 52; Fall of Gondolin, 29; Faramir, 144–45, 153; Frodo, 25, 30–31, 58, 72, 86, 88, 96–100, 102, 104–5, 108, 110, 114–15, 121, 146–49, 153, 156–59; Galadriel, 18, 50, 75, 85–90, 96, 105, 108, 168–69; Gandalf, 24, 87, 100, 103, 145, 147, 156, 158; Gimli, 63, 86, 89, 100, 102–3; Glóin, 63, 66; Goldberry, 24, 103, 105, 159–60; Gollum, 55, 62, 148, 154; Hobbiton, 24; Legolas, 87, 103–6; loss as a theme in, 15–17, 22, 90, 99; magic in, 50; Mirrormere, 102–5, 107, 110; mirrors in, 88, 98–111; Nimrodel, 103–6; Old Forest, 24; Old Man Willow, 159; prehistory of, 29; process of creating, 4, 28; publication of, 124, 164, 171; "The Quest of Erebor," 51; return home, 30–31; the Ring, 24–25, 30, 72, 99, 102, 150, 152; Ringwraiths, 106–7, 156–57; Sam, 30–31, 72, 86–87, 96–102, 104–5, 114, 121, 148–49, 154; Sauron, 50, 63, 105–6, 115, 150, 152, 153; "The Shadow of the Past," 24; Shelob, 72, 87, 88, 90–91, 96–97, 109, 147; songs in, 72; stars in, 105–6, 108–9; Tom Bombadil, 24, 63, 103, 157–62; transition motif in, 24; Treebeard, 18, 105, 123; water's symbolism in, 103–4
"Lost Road, The" (Tolkien), 92–93, 117, 120; father-son pairs in, 93–94, 117–18, 119, 127
Lost Tales, 5; Cottage of Lost Play, 22; Elves in, 22; enchantment in, 22; Eriol/Aelfwine, 5, 22; Olórë Mallë/the Path of Dreams, 22
Lothlórien, 5, 88–89
Lúthien, 14, 29, 72–75, 77, 81–82, 91, 106, 108, 111, 139, 145–46, 149

Maeglin, 145–46
Magic versus enchantment, 9, 11
Maher, Michael, 87
Manichean view, 155
marvelous, the, 40–41
Master of Laketown, 44–45, 48–50, 52
McIntosh, Jonathon, 69
Melkor, 69–71, 88, 91, 107, 114–15, 124–25
Merck Manual, 138
Merry, 105, 115, 146–47
Meyers, Stephanie, 36
Mirrormere, 102–5, 107
mirrors, 98–111
Morgan, Francis, 27, 92, 139
Morgoth, 14, 70, 73–74, 81–82, 108, 111, 115, 162–63, 172
Moses, Rafael, 133
mother-child relationships, 68–84; disruption of, 70–71, 82–84, 134; emotional bonding, 70, 81; language and, 81; music and, 74–75, 79–80
"Music of Ainur, The," 69–71, 82
"Mythopoiea" (Tolkien), 121–22

Nagy, Gergely, 148, 153
Nass, Martin, 80
Nazgûl, 156
Nimrodel, 103–6
Níniel/Nienor, 143–44
"Notion Club Papers" (Tolkien), 24, 117, 119–20; Dolbear, 24

Odysseus, 35
Old Man Willow, 9, 159
"Once Upon a Time" (Tolkien), 165–66; color in, 166; lintips, 166; Tom Bombadil, 165–66
"On Fairy-Stories" (Tolkien), 4, 21, 22, 32, 40, 50, 62, 121–22
"On 'The Kalevala' or Land of Heroes" (Tolkien), 81
orcs, 146; creation of, 114–15; symbolism of, 28
"Over Old Hills and Far Away" (Tolkien), 75–76
Oxford English Dictionary, 8–9, 18

Parker, Douglass, 91
Pearl, 18
Perrault, Charles, 36
Persephone, 35
perversion, 151–52, 162–63
Pippin, 87, 105, 115
Playing and Reality (Winnicott), 101, 151
Polyphemus, 35
Procne, 35
"Puss-Cat-Mew," 32

Quenya, 18, 109

rapprochement phase, 57
Rateliff, John, 59, 169–70
reality principle, 102
recovery, 4, 113; definition of, 16

Red Book of Westmarch, 5
Reid, Robin, 76
Return of the King (Tolkien), 164
Rice, Anne, 36
Ring, the/One Ring of Power, 11, 31, 99, 150–63, 172; Bilbo and, 61–62; creation of, 152–54; destruction of, 25, 30, 106, 115, 145–46, 152, 162; discovery of, 62–63; as a fetish symbol, 150–63, 172; Frodo and, 11, 17, 30, 106, 153, 155; Galadriel's rejection of, 86, 90, 154; Gollum and, 61–62; in *The Lord of the Rings*, 24–25, 30, 72, 99, 102, 150, 152; perversion of, 152–53, 156, 162; unconscious meanings of body orifices, 154–55
Ringwraiths, 106, 152, 156–57
Rivendell, 5

sadism, 156
sadomasochism, 152
Sam, 11, 87, 114, 121, 148; on the departure of the Elves, 18–19, 149; encounter with Shelob, 85–86, 96–97; father, 99; Galadriel's Mirror, 98–99, 102, 104–5; Gandalf's death and, 100–101, 103; memories of Galadriel, 85–86, 97; return to the Shire, 30–31, 149; as Ringbearer, 31, 72, 154
Saruman, 15–16, 30; death, 30
Sauron, 50, 63, 99, 106, 111, 115, 117, 146, 150, 152–53, 156, 160, 162; creation of the Ring, 152–54, 172; death, 162; Eye of, 105, 110, 156
Schutt, Bill, 37
Scull, Cristina, 64, 119, 135, 140, 166
"Sea-Bell, The" (Tolkien), 109–11, 147, 167; disenchantment in, 167–68
"Sellic Spell" (Tolkien), 3–4
Sendak, Maurice, 37
"Shadow-Bride" (Tolkien), 94–96
"Shadow Man, The" (Tolkien), 94–96
Sharkey, 17, 77, 147
"She" (Haggard), 86
Shelob, 72, 77, 85–86, 90–91, 96–97, 109, 147; femininity, 86, 91; gaze, 87–88, 96; masculinity, 89, 91, 96; maternal qualities, 87, 91
Shengold, Leonard, 154
Shippey, Tom, 9, 11, 17–18, 25, 153, 155, 167–68
Shire, the, 11; disenchantment of, 30; enchanted nature of, 17; Scouring of, 146–47
Silmarillion, The (Tolkien), 5, 29, 59, 90, 108, 120, 124, 162–64; creation stories/flat-earth cosmology, 107, 113–14, 171–72; music in, 72–75; revisions, 168; stars in, 105; water in, 104
Smaug, 46–49, 54, 56–61
Smith, G. B., 123, 129–31
Smith of Wootton Major (Tolkien), 23, 110–11, 164, 166–67; star in, 110
Smol, Anna, 17, 148
splitting, 96, 152, 154, 156
Sterba, Editha, 151
"Story of Kullervo, The" (Tolkien), 142
Strider, 58, 106

"Tale of Tinúviel," 73–74
Tantalus, 35
Tatar, Maria, 32–33, 37–39, 43
TCBS, 28, 129–31
Ted Sandyman, 19
Tereus, 35
Thingol, 149
Thomas, Paul, 45
Thorin Oakenshield, 45–50, 58–59, 65
Three Rings of Power, 16
Todorov, Tzvetan, 40, 41
Tolkien, Arthur, 27, 97, 126; death, 79, 85, 91–92, 125, 127, 133–34, 173; Tolkien's attempts to memorialize, 96, 108
Tolkien, Christopher, 5, 27, 65, 88–89, 93, 120–21, 139, 164, 171–72
Tolkien, Edith, 27–29, 92, 140, 149; death, 29, 139, 164; illness, 164
Tolkien, Hilary, 27, 79, 134
Tolkien, J. R. R.: Atlantis/wave/sea dream, 5, 26–27, 104, 116–18, 121, 125, 133–34, 144; birth, 27; childhood, 27, 28, 64, 91–92, 125–27, 133–35, 141, 144; colors, use of, 64–65; creative process, 1, 3–5, 11, 28–30, 113, 118–19, 121, 124, 128, 150, 162, 164–72; death, 29; on death of Rob Gilson, 129–31; education, 134; on enchantment, 11, 15–31, 33–34, 68, 112, 174; on escapism, 21, 128; hubris and, 124–26, 128, 167–68, 172; illness, 27–28, 119–21, 134–38, 140–41, 164; isolation, 79; on "The Juniper Tree," 32–35, 38–39, 41, 43; language usage, 17, 80–81; light and dark in work, 40; loss, 15–31, 68, 79, 85, 126, 135, 138, 140–41, 149, 173–74; on love, 78–79, 140, 149, 174; on magic, 9; mother, relationship with, 77–80, 82–84, 91–92, 97, 134, 173; move to Bournemouth, 26; musicality, 79–80, 82; religion, 3, 27, 37, 77, 84, 87, 122–23, 168–69; response to modernization, 2; somatization, 132–33; songs

Tolkien, J. R. R. (cont.)
and music in work, 68–84; subcreation, theory of, 121–22, 124, 167–68; tension between enchantment and disenchantment, 1, 3, 5, 9, 11, 25–26, 174; tower imagery, 2–3; trauma, response to, 134–44, 149; ward of Father Francis Morgan, 27; women characters, 76–77; World War I, 11, 27–30, 121, 129–31, 135–38, 141, 144, 173
Tolkien, Mabel, 27, 68, 76–80, 82, 84, 97, 135; death, 27, 77, 79, 83, 91, 133–34, 139; Tolkien's attempts to memorialize, 96, 108
Tolkien, Michael, 78–79, 121, 139
Tolkien, Priscilla, 62
Tolkien in Oxford, 67
Tom Bombadil, 17, 24, 63, 65, 103, 150–63, 165–66; contrast to the One Ring, 159, 162; nature, 157–58; origin of, 157; power, 159–62; transitionality of, 152, 157–58, 162, 165
transitionality, 21, 40, 163; art and, 116; brief, 23–24; childhood forms of, 21; in infancy, 20, 22; loss of, 164–72; transitional experience, 20–22, 121, 123–24; transitional objects, 20, 22, 51, 112, 150, 152, 162; transitional phenomena, 112, 151; transitional space, 20, 22, 24, 112–13, 115–16, 128, 150, 156
trauma, 116, 121, 132, 136–37; cumulative, 131; desymbolized, 132; response to, 132–33; shock, 131; strain, 131, 134
Treebeard, 18, 105, 123
trench fever, 137–38
Trevarthen, Colwyn, 80
trolls, 45, 58
Tuor, 146
Turgon, 146
Túrin Turambar, 129, 142–44

uncanny, the, 38–42
Undertenishness (Tolkien), 63–64
Ungoliant, 77, 88, 91, 125
Unwin, Rayner, 140–41
Unwin, Stanley, 124
Uses of Enchantment (Bettelheim), 43

Valar, the, 88, 90–91, 107–8, 111, 113, 115, 117–18, 149, 168, 171; cosmic music, 113
vampires, 36
Varda, 107, 110–11
"Voyage of Éarendel the Evening Star" (Tolkien), 109, 123

Weber, Max, 2, 9, 19, 48, 53, 170, 174
Where the Wild Things Are (Sendak), 37
Williams, Charles, 78
Winnicott, D. W., 8, 11, 20; on mirrors, 101, 103, 110; on play, 157; on transitionality, 21, 24, 40, 51, 112, 115–16, 128, 151–52, 157, 162
Wiseman, Christopher, 129–31
Wizard of Oz, The, 23
wonder, imagined, 112–13
World War I, 11, 27–30, 129–31, 135–38, 173; Battle of the Somme, 27, 29
World War II, 121
Wulff, Moshe, 151

Yavanna, 107, 125
"You and Me in the Cottage of Lost Play" (Tolkien), 22

Zeus, 35
Zipes, Jack, 43, 97